Literary Genius

Literary Genius

25 Classic Writers Who Define
English & American Literature

SELECTED & EDITED BY

Joseph Epstein

WITH WOOD ENGRAVINGS BY

Barry Moser

PAUL DRY BOOKS

Philadelphia 2007

Paul Dry Books, Inc.
Philadelphia, Pennsylvania
www.pauldrybooks.com

Copyright © 2007 by Paul Dry Books
All rights reserved

1 3 5 7 9 8 6 4 2
Printed in the United States of America

Library of Congress Cataloging-in-Publication Data

Literary genius : 25 classic writers who define English & American literature /
selected & edited by Joseph Epstein ; with wood engravings by Barry Moser.
p.   cm.
Includes bibliographical references.
ISBN 978-1-58988-039-9 (hardcover : alk. paper) —
ISBN 978-1-58988-035-1 (pbk. : alk. paper)
1. Authors, English—Biography. 2. Authors, American—Biography.
I. Epstein, Joseph, 1937– II. Moser, Barry.
PR105.L56 2007
820.9—dc22
[B]
2007023301

The publisher and the editor wish to thank Garrett Brown, an editor of consummate tact, admirable thoroughness, and high intelligence and solid common sense, for his help throughout the preparation of this book.

Genius, all over the world, stands hand in hand,
and one shock of recognition runs the whole circle round.

Herman Melville,
Hawthorne and His Mosses

TABLE OF CONTENTS

The Style of Genius

BY JOSEPH EPSTEIN

Genius is one of those words upon which the world has agreed to form no clear consensus. But if there is a single modern figure upon whom everyone is ready to confer genius, it is, undoubtedly, Albert Einstein. Since even today too few people understand his scientific contributions, what the rest of us know is one of several photographs of the great man, all featuring the far-away gaze in his eyes, the senior-citizen version of the Harpo Marx hairdo, the utter lack of interest in clothes — the look, taken together, combining the qualities of the visionary and the quite harmless nut.

"He's very scary," said the actress Elaine Stritch, of the musical-theater composer Stephen Sondheim. "I think he's close to a genius, if not a genius, and it's hard to be around people like that. They're mind-boggling, their talent is so explosive and there's a kind of dangerous quietness about them." Stephen Sondheim is not a genius, merely (some *merely*) an admirably talented man, but I hope Miss Stritch's comment makes my point that for most people temperament plays an unduly large role in the estimation of genius.

Genius was long felt to be a gift that, like the magical bow of the mythical figure Philoctetes, carried with it a suppurating and stinking wound. Geniuses used to be thought to suffer deficiencies (Niels Bohr may have been dyslexic), serious physical maladies (Dostoyevsky's epilepsy, Chekhov's tuberculosis), and moral degeneracy (Lord Byron, Charles Baudelaire, please boys, take a bow). Some people even preferred their geniuses stark raving bonkers. As long ago as the first century AD, Seneca wrote, "There is no genius that is not touched by madness." *A Beautiful Mind,* the book and later film made from the life of the mathematician John Forbes Nash, plays nicely into the notion of the mad genius. As long ago as 1869, in his book *Hereditary Genius,* Francis Galton, the English eugenicist, wrote: "If genius means a sense of inspiration, or of rushes of ideas from apparently supernatural sources, or of an inordinate and burning desire to accomplish any particular end, it is perilously near to the voices heard by the insane, to their delirious tendencies, or to their monomanias. It cannot in such cases be a healthy faculty, nor can it be desirable to perpetuate it by inheritance."

To impute madness to genius, or at least to lay claim that madness or physical debility is a serious side effect of genius, is to offer a partial — if wholly unsatisfactory — explanation for the phenomenon, which remains another of those most interesting mysteries of life for which we have no real explanation. Genius, whenever and wherever it pops up, is finally unaccountable, inexplicable. One cannot hope to explain its origins; one cannot plot its course; one must settle for attempting to describe it as it applies itself.

Genius, whenever and wherever it pops up, is finally unaccountable, inexplicable. One cannot hope to explain its origins; one cannot plot its course; one must settle for attempting to describe it as it applies itself.

Others, perhaps out of an unconscious envy, like their geniuses to be lashed to lesser afflictions. "I'm not stupid enough to become what is known as a genius," wrote Théophile Gautier in *Mademoiselle de Maupin.* "Geniuses are very narrow minded." They are often also generally thought to be wildly impractical. Usually they are assumed to be deeply unhappy: the first requisite for a writer is an unhappy childhood, said Ernest Hemingway, who had a miserable one. Sometimes geniuses are considered, outside their work, flat-out stupid. "Picasso seems to me one of those wild, stupid geniuses," notes the diary-keeping narrator of William Boyd's novel *Any Human Heart,* "more Yeats, Strindberg, Rimbaud, Mozart, than Matisse, Brahms, Braque." Yet, when the dust of all these animadversions clears, we are left with this reigning if still unexplained fact about geniuses: they are vastly more intelligent, talented, often deeper than the rest of us.

Perhaps the first distinction that needs to be made in the realm of genius is that between scientific and artistic genius. Scientific genius seems more closely connected to pure intelligence — to intelligence considered as sheer ratiocinative power — than does artistic genius. Scientific genius seems, too, different in kind from artistic genius in requiring the ability to operate at a high level of abstraction, whereas one of the glories of artistic genius is that it may be said to operate at a highest level of particularity. Astonishing intuition, amazing quickness, fantastic grasp of hitherto unrecognized connections, improbable imaginative leaps — all seem part of the mental equipage of the scientific genius, especially those who do modern science.

Geniuses, scientific and artistic, work at the project of discovery. The nature of scientific and artistic discovery is radically different. Scientific discovery is progressive: one discovery generally leads to another; the things to be discovered are really there, already exist, even if not always to the naked eye. Something akin to a corporate effort is entailed in much modern science, so that, hypothetically, a Nobel Prize in chemistry may be awarded in the same year to three scientists, all who worked on the same problem, yet living, respectively, in the United States, Russia, and Japan. The notion of three literary artists working together on a great trilogy or body of plays or works of poetry, though theoretically possible, is nonetheless practically inconceivable.

Because of its progressive and corporate nature, scientific genius lacks the one thing central to artistic genius: the geniuses that science produces are not, in the way that artistic geniuses are, *sui generis*. In the January 2, 1987, issue of the London *Times Literary Supplement,* Lionel Esher, in an article titled "The Plot to Save the Artists," recounts the plan of Lord Esher, his father, hatched on the eve of the Second World War, a plan to save England's important artists from dying in combat in the war then looming over Europe. Consulting men and women with authoritative judgment in the various arts, Lord Esher came up with a list of sixty-one names of writers, visual artists, and composers who were to be drafted into the armed forces but, without their knowledge, kept from the fighting at the front.

The question naturally arose whether other professions ought to be so selected. What about actors, dancers, architects? The poet Geoffrey Grigson suggested extending the plan to cover gifted economists, urban planners, and of course scientists. (Let me remove the suspense from the story by inserting here that the British government, while sympathetic to the intention behind Lord Esher's plan, in the end decreed, "The principle of such a form of protection from the dangers of military service is difficult to accept," and the plan was rejected.) When Lord Esher's committee was sending round to find the names of scientists who might be added to his list of the would-be protected, a group of industrial scientists from Rugby wrote to him to say that saving scientists was nowhere near so important as was the saving of artists. Science, they in effect argued, was somehow larger than scientists, while art was solely, wholly, and purely artists. They wrote:

Perhaps it is scarcely realized how little time science would have lost by the loss of even the greatest scientists. If Newton had never lived, the world would not have had to wait more than one or two years for the law of gravitation and for the calculus. Huygens was hot on the track of the first of Newton's greatest discoveries. Leibniz had independently found the second. If Edison had never lived, Swan would have invented the incandescent lamp, Hughes the microphone, at the same time.

But if Leonardo da Vinci had fallen in the battle of Anghiari, instead of remaining at a safe distance and painting it after the reports of eye-witnesses, the Gioconda would have remained forever unpainted.

If Shakespeare had been sent to fight against the Armada and had added one to the number of glorious but nameless dead, his plays would have been forever unwritten.

The work of a creative artist is individual and unique. His loss is forever irrecoverable. The loss of a scientist — or of an engineer or inventor — is only a loss of time....

In an interesting survey of the history of the idea of genius, "Our Genius Problem," a survey that begins and ends with a consideration of the all-too-loose currency of the word in contemporary usage, Professor Marjorie Garber suggests that genius does not quite exist: not literally, not at least in the way that we have usually construed it. "What all the IQ tests, brain measurements, and supposed telltale pathologies show is that genius in a particular person can't be proved to exist, much less effectively predicted; not that there is no such thing as genius, but, rather, that genius is an assessment or an accolade often retrospectively applied to an individual or an idea — not an identifiable essence."

I, for one, wouldn't argue with Professor Garber's conclusion, and this book, whose subject is genius in literature written in the English language, is devoted to the idea of retrospectively trying to understand what is behind the work of a finite number of English and American writers to whom literary history, if not God or foolproof science, has agreed to assign the label of Genius.

That finite number of geniuses taken up in this book is twenty-five. This number could have been greater or smaller. Yet twenty-five seemed roughly the right number — less would have been too excluding, more would perhaps have opened the gates too widely. The division of literary geniuses yielded fourteen for England, one for Ireland, and ten for America; this, too, seemed appropriate, given the much longer history of England. (No literary figures of the same magnitude writing in English as those chosen for this book have, at least in the judgment of the editor, thus far come from Canada, Australia, New Zealand, India, South Africa, or any other country once part of the British Empire.) Twenty-five literary geniuses we have, then, twenty-one men, four women, all white, none Jews, to get demographics quickly out of the way. Not a very politically correct selection of writers, perhaps, but, let us hope, a literarily impressive and justifiable one.

If Albert Einstein is the unarguable modern scientific genius — his footprints, the theoretical physicist and science-writer Jeremy Bernstein has noted, are all over discoveries in modern physics — surely the indisputable literary genius is William Shakespeare. His genius seems, somehow, enhanced and fortified by our knowing so little about him. So protean is his talent that it is difficult to get anything like a purchase on it, even though no other writer, as John Gross writes in the introduction to his book *After Shakespeare,* "has attracted such widespread and varied comment." My late friend Edward Shils once said to me that we were friends of a kind who could talk about anything but at least we had the good sense not to talk about Shakespeare. His implication here was that, in the face of such genius, what could one say? (In the relatively brief compass of 2,500-odd words, it turns out that Lois Potter has quite a lot of great interest to say by way of locating the genius of Shakespeare.)

Apart from Shakespeare, it may well be that every other name on my list of twenty-five literary geniuses is in the flux of controversy. Is Willa Cather a greater writer than, say, Virginia Woolf? The editor of this book obviously thinks so. Can a critic — Samuel Johnson — really be a genius? Does an essayist and journalist — William Hazlitt — truly qualify? Ought a great historian — Edward Gibbon — to be considered a literary man at all? If my list itself has any tendency, it shows a slight bias against wild geniuses. William Blake failed to make the cut, as did Coleridge and Yeats, Ralph Waldo Emerson and D. H. Lawrence. I wish, alas, there had been room for Wallace Stevens. Oscar Wilde did not make the list for the reason that he himself so accurately described: he put his genius into his life and only his talent into his work.

Normally, I should say that literary genius ought to be prolific, but one of the writers on the list, Mark Twain, wrote only a single splendid book, *Huckleberry Finn,* and even that, as David Carkeet notes in his essay on Twain in this volume, is greatly flawed. James Joyce, as John Gross rightly remarks in his essay, produced a few excellent, one great, and one perhaps mad book, but that one great book, *Ulysses,* is of a magnitude such as to qualify its author as a genius.

My list of literary geniuses, then, is conservative in the sense of being traditional; as a list, it contains, by intention, very few surprises and no shocks whatsoever. What I hope it does is tease out, through the lucubrations of the contributors on the geniuses under consideration in this book, material sufficient to set out an at least incipient theory — perhaps the less grand word "notion" is more in order — for what constitutes literary genius.

That there are no Mozarts in literature, which is to say that there are no prodigies, is borne out by the twenty-five geniuses considered here. The tragical career of John Keats, a meteor so quickly burned out by an hereditary tubercular death, comes closest. But then, on the far side of the prodigy question, one does well to remember that Joseph Conrad did not publish his first novel — in, impressively, his third language — until he was thirty-eight. (It has been argued, too, that no great literary work seems to get done when writers arrive at their eighties.) Unlike much scientific genius, artistic genius tends to be less progressive than random and therefore unpredictable: suddenly, in nineteenth century Russia four great writers of fiction — Tolstoy, Dostoyevsky, Turgenev, Chekhov — arise; a large number of major poets are born between 1880 and 1900, causing W. H. Auden to say that if one is born later than 1900 one may as well forget about becoming a major poet, which may well be so (Auden himself was born in 1907).

Style, it needs to be understood, is never ornamentation or a matter of choice of vocabulary or amusing linguistic tics or mannerisms. Style, in serious writing, is a way of seeing, and literary geniuses, who see things in a vastly different way than the rest of us, usually require a vastly different style.

Social class is not an element taken up by any of the contributors to *Literary Genius,* but it strikes the editor that here, too, genius strikes randomly. In the modern era — from, roughly, the nineteenth century — perhaps only two major literary figures have been born aristocrats: Tolstoy and Lord Byron. Keats, whose parents kept a stable, was rather low-born, and Dickens's father was of course in debtor's prison, though both sons were high-born in natural spirit and largeness of character. Most literary geniuses, then, seem to come of the vast and squishy middle classes, with literature offering them a way to rise above their social origins and perhaps, through the hope of enduring fame, above mortality itself.

The occurrence of genius may be a mystery, but that is no good reason to get mystical about it. Harold Bloom, the most famous literary critic of the day, is very generous in assigning literary genius. "I can identify for myself certain writers of palpable genius now among us," he writes in the introduction to *Genius,* a book composed of his own essays on writers for whom he claims genius: "the Portuguese novelist José Saramago, the Canadian poet Anne Carson, the English poet Geoffrey Hill, and at least a half-dozen North and Latin American novelists and poets (whom I forebear naming)." But he is considerably less generous in dispensing lucidity on what constitutes literary genius. Genius, he instructs, is "clearly both of and above the age." He adds, "Fierce originality is one crucial component of literary genius, but this originality itself is always canonical, in that it recognizes and comes to terms with precursors." Genius also turns out to be "the God within," and genius, "by necessity, invokes the transcendental and the extraordinary, because it is fully conscious of them." He brings in Emerson and Gnosticism, neither of them great flags signifying clarity ahead, and concludes by stating that his rough but effectual test for the literary genius is: "Does she or he augment our consciousness . . . has my awareness been intensified, my consciousness widened and clarified?"

What widens one consciousness and intensifies one's awareness, may, of course, not widen or intensify another consciousness. Or it may not do so to the same consciousness at different times in the life of that consciousness, which is why some writers who swept us away at the age of twenty seem not worth rereading at forty. Nor is Professor Bloom very helpful on the crucial matter of how literary genius operates, which is, inevitably, through style.

Style, it needs to be understood, is never ornamentation or a matter of choice of vocabulary or amusing linguistic tics or mannerisms. Style, in serious writing, is a way of seeing, and literary geniuses, who see things in a vastly different way than the rest of us, usually require a vastly different style. As Edward Gibbon wrote on style (quoted by David Womersley in his essay): "The style of an author should be the image of his mind." Through this distinctive style something like a distinctive philosophy is expressed, though usually not directly. Which is where criticism and plain intelligent

reading enter. Henri Bergson holds that understanding a work or body of art "consists essentially in developing in thought what artists want to suggest emotionally." The style of the literary artist is what allows him powerfully to suggest what he sees.

Literary genius comes in many varieties. Some literary geniuses seem natural (Charles Dickens, Mark Twain), others cultivated (George Eliot, Henry James). Some are prolific (Wordsworth, Whitman), some are more carefully concentrated (Jane Austen, T. S. Eliot). Some literary geniuses are stimulated by the difficult (Alexander Pope, John Milton). Some require absolute originality — entailing the need to invent their own style — to convey their vision (James Joyce, Ernest Hemingway). Some have perfected a form (Pope, the heroic couplet), some have tried to kill off a genre (Joyce, the novel). Not some but all literary geniuses can be read again and again, down through the generations. As Hilary Mantel, in her essay on Jane Austen, writes: "Surely this is the definition of genius in a writer: the capacity to make a text that can give and give, a text that is never fully read, a text that goes on multiplying meanings." Timelessness this is called, and it is another of the hallmarks of literary genius.

But timelessness must be accompanied by a certain grandeur of vision to qualify for genius. Johann Peter Eckermann reports that Goethe did not much like the word "talent," at least when applied to literary creators of large ambition. Speaking with Goethe one evening about Dante, whom Goethe reverenced, Eckermann noticed that Goethe "was not satisfied with the word *talent,* but called him [Dante] a *nature,* as if thus wishing to express something more comprehensive, more full of prescience, of deeper insight, and wider scope." What Goethe called a nature we should call a genius.

Timelessness, grandeur of vision, originality of outlook — all these, in concert and worked at a high power, comprise genius in the writer. This and the ability to make us see constitute literary genius. "My task which I am trying to achieve," wrote Joseph Conrad in the preface to *The Nigger of the 'Narcissus'*, "is by the power of the written word to make you hear, to make you feel — it is above all to make you *see*. That — and no more, and it is everything." Make us see in a way that would never have been possible for us to do on our own: this is what the great artistic geniuses — literary and visual and, in a more complicated way, musical geniuses — finally do.

Another literary genius, Marcel Proust, speaking here as a consumer rather than a creator of great art, wrote: "Only through art can we get outside ourselves and know another's view of the universe which is not the same as ours and see landscapes which would otherwise have remained unknown to us like the landscapes on the moon. Thanks to art, instead of seeing a single world, our own, we see it multiply until we have before us as many worlds as there are original artists — more different from each other than those which revolve in space."

To contribute substantially to this endless project is the payoff, the great point, the task to which all literary geniuses set themselves and for which the non-geniuses among us, which is say everyone else, ought to be everlastingly grateful.

Geoffrey Chaucer

BY TOM SHIPPEY

Chaucer was the best-connected of English poets. His wife's sister, Katherine Swynford, was the long-term acknowledged mistress of John of Gaunt, Duke of Lancaster, Edward III's fourth son. Late in life, after two dynastic marriages, Gaunt scandalized polite society by marrying her. After Gaunt's son by his first wife, Henry Bolingbroke, deposed his cousin Richard to become King Henry IV, Chaucer could say briefly that he was the king's stepmother's brother-in-law. It is unlikely that Henry ever called Chaucer "Uncle Geoffrey," but Chaucer had his place at court. All his life he was on the edge of great events: the Hundred Years War, the Black Death, the Peasants' Revolt, the Merciless Parliament, the deposition and murder of Richard II. One of Katherine's sons by her first husband, Chaucer's nephew, probably organized the murder for his stepbrother.

Almost none of this shows in Chaucer's poetry, but it may account for its air of fascinated yet ironic detachment. Chaucer seems to understand people intimately, from all classes of society and walks of life, yet identifies with none. His works span the range of medieval genres, but he delights in exposing their limitations. His poetry is one of constantly shifting perspectives and unconscious self-betrayal.

His first surviving poem reveals a problem and a characteristic solution. Called *The Book of the Duchess*, its purpose is primarily to praise Gaunt's first wife, Blanche, who died in 1369 of bubonic plague, for her beauty, charm, and good sense. Its secondary purpose is clearly to urge Gaunt to cease mourning and resume normal life — something requiring a great deal of tact under any circumstances and perhaps especially in Chaucer's. Chaucer does it by adopting the pose of an amiable bungler, clumsy and unchallenging, who nevertheless by accident sometimes says the right thing. In a brief prologue he complains of insomnia; then mentions the book he has been reading to get to sleep, the story of a bereaved lover who dies of grief; and then recounts the dream he has after falling asleep, which (as dreams do) seems to mirror what he has been reading. In his dream he follows hunters pursuing a stag or hart, till he loses them but meets a Man in Black, an image of Gaunt himself, who will not say what is troubling him. Slowly the Dreamer draws from him the story of his love-affair, until at last the Man in Black

Chaucer was born in the early 1340s, probably in London, England, and died there on October 25, 1400.

confesses what is the matter: "She ys ded!" The Dreamer says only, "Nay! . . . Is that youre los? Be God, hyt ys routhe!" but as he says, "What a pity!" the horns of the huntsmen blow.

> And with that word *ryght anoon*
> They gan to *strake forth;* al was doon,
> For that tyme, the hert-huntyng.

right away

blow the "return"

The hunt for the hart is over, and so is the hunt for the heart, and possibly (this second pun would work in some forms of Middle English) the hunt for the hurt as well.

The Book of the Duchess is a poem about counseling, and also one about dreams, in which Chaucer took a lifelong interest. Typically, he well understood the developed medieval theory about dreams, but also saw its weakness: It depended on classifying the dream. Some dreams are true visions, some are the result of stress or indigestion, some — the most interesting — conceal messages from the unconscious. To interpret a dream, you have to know which sort it is, but no one ever does! So, in "The Nun's Priest's Tale," Chanticleer the rooster has a true vision of a fox but accepts his wife Pertelote the hen's indigestion explanation, to his own downfall.

Chaucer used his "book and dream" structure to write two more dream-poems, *The Parliament of Fowls* and the unfinished *House of Fame.* Both of them exploit the uncertain way in which dreams reflect preoccupations or anxieties, and both of them leave one puzzled. The first asks the question, "What is love?" Chaucer finds an answer of sorts in a book, but then dreams of a bird-parliament in which the birds all offer different and contradictory opinions. Chaucer wakes from his dream no wiser, com-ically determined to read on till he knows — as if one learned about love from books, as if there were only one answer.

Chaucer's major work is the collection of stories called *The Canterbury Tales.* The frame of this is a pilgrimage. Chaucer joins a company of some twenty-nine pilgrims at Southwark in London, all about to set out for the shrine of St. Thomas à Becket at Canterbury. They agree to tell tales in competition on the way, with a prize for the winner, and Chaucer started twenty-four of these, finishing all but four. One motive may have been to show that he could write anything — epic, romance, fable, saint's life, sermon, moral and immoral stories — for all these and more are represented. Another may have been to give a cross-section of medieval society, from the Knight to the Cook, with strong concentration on the commercial and professional classes, like the Wife of Bath, the Man of Law, and the Physician, and on people of the church, the Prioress, Monk, Friar, Parson, Nun and Nun's Priest, and the disreputable Pardoner and Summoner. A third was to give a comic picture of social conflict, for many of the pilgrims are traditional opposites, or competitors, or enemies, like the Clerk and the Merchant, the Reeve and the Miller, the Friar and the Summoner. A major motive was to tell stories right for the first time. Chaucer enjoyed taking familiar tales and developing them to their ultimate limits.

The "Miller's Tale" thus repeats a widely recorded medieval story about an immoral woman with three lovers, who turn up in sequence. Caught with the first, she hides him in a tub hanging from the ceiling. When the third appears, the second puts his behind out of her window, so that the third and rejected

lover kisses it in the dark. And when the third lover comes back, with a branding-iron, he tries the trick again. The resulting scream of pain and cry for water make the first lover, still in the tub, cut the rope holding him up and crash to the floor. The tale as generally told provokes terribly obvious questions. What is a tub doing hanging from the ceiling? Why in the world would anyone put his behind out of a window? And why *twice?* Chaucer solves all these riddles with perfect skill. It was not the lover but the lady who put her behind out of the window the first time, and she did so because she thought her third admirer was a complete fool. Her lover, who agrees with her, wants to score off him, too, which is why he does it later. The person in the tub is the lady's husband, and he is there because the tale is set in Oxford. The lover is a clever student who lodges with the wife and husband, and to get the ignorant husband out of the way he has persuaded him that Noah's flood is about to come again, so that a tub hanging from the ceiling is the only safe place for him. This also explains perfectly the panicky reaction to a cry of "Water!"

What impresses about this tale, and several others, is its tight construction, careful detail, and — the secret of comedy — its timing. Chaucer can dawdle, as when the angry lover has to get a hot iron quickly, before it cools, from an inquisitive and chatty smith, and he can race:

This carpenter *out of his slomber sterte,*
          started out of slumber
And herde oon crien "water!" as he were *wood,*
          mad
And thoughte, "Allas, now comth *Nowelis flood!*"
          Noah's Flood
He sit hym up *withouten wordes mo,*
          without more words
And with his ax he smoot the corde atwo,
And doun gooth al. . . .

Chaucer has even explained exactly why the carpenter has an axe with him. Nothing is out of place. Yet the tale has severe limitations. Its dominant emotions are lust and triumphant contempt. Anyone who shows finer feeling, like the carpenter's anxious concern for his wife being drowned, is automatically pegged as a fool. Though the tale is set in a university town, in it the only purpose of learning is to deceive your social inferiors. It is dominated not by people but by things — tub, axe, window, iron. Even a medieval "cat-flap" plays its part. To this kind of story the medieval opposite is the romance, highly emotional, even sentimental, strongly aristocratic, giving a major role to the supernatural and magical. The "Miller's Tale" is indeed presented as a contemptuously skeptical response to the "Knight's Tale," which is all those things, but a neater match to the Miller is the "Franklin's Tale."

This, too, is a story of a lady with a husband and a lover, but the characters seem to come from a different world. Fear for her husband's safety causes the lady to make a bargain with her lover: Get rid of the rocks that threaten his ship, I will be yours. He hires a magician to do this seemingly impossible task, and the lady is caught by her promise. She is saved from the consequences of it by the generosity first of her husband, who stands by his own promise never to show jealousy, and then of her lover, who lets her off her bargain. The lover is also released from his payment by the magician, anxious not to be outdone in *gentilesse,* moral nobility. The tale gains an added dimension from being told by the rich but non-noble Franklin, who admires and understands a quality he is not expected to have. But it also contains a strong quasi-Freudian element, in which we can see the wife "projecting" her fear and insecurity on to the black rocks of the Breton coastline, and so creating the threat to her marriage which she fears. Her speech accusing God is a fine example of "good bad poetry," written deliberately to be self-betraying. It is at once passionate and sarcastic, natural and illogical.

Chaucer relies heavily on similar contradictions in his "Knight's Tale," an adaptation of the Italian poet Boccaccio's *Teseida.* (Chaucer knew Italian and traveled twice to Italy on undisclosed royal business.) This contrasts the warm humanity of its mortal characters with the cold harshness of the pagan gods, or planetary deities, who control events. (Chaucer was also an expert astrologer.) Especially striking are the deliberate set-piece descriptions of the violent tournament that is to determine which of her lovers shall win Emily, and of the temples of Diana, Mars, and Venus in which Emily and her rival suitors pray. In the first of these are portrayed not only noble deaths in battle but also murder and the gruesome accidents of the medieval village:

The smylere with the knyf under the cloke;
The *shepne brennynge* with the blake smoke. . . .
      cowshed burning
The sowe *freten* the child right in the cradel;
      devouring
The cook yscalded, for al his longe ladel.

Noght was *foryeten* by the infortune of Marte:
      forgotten
The cartere *overryden* with his carte —
      run over
Under the wheel ful lowe he lay adoun.

In two brilliant speeches Saturn, cruellest of the gods, gives his solution to the gods' dispute over whose prayer shall be answered, which succeeds by ignoring human pain; and Theseus, the senior human, resorts again to "good bad poetry" by papering over what has happened with rhetoric, sensible, fine-sounding, but ever so slightly false.

Self-betrayal is another characteristic Chaucerian theme, shown above all by the long autobiographical prologues of the Pardoner and the Wife of Bath, in which the former explains his routines of salesmanship, and the latter discusses her relationship with men. Both self-portraits gain depth from uncertainty about the speakers' motivation. Selling people religious junk seems to be, for the

Pardoner, a form of sexual therapy. Is he impotent, a eunuch, practising the only kind of seduction he can manage? The Wife of Bath has been a consistent winner in the sex-war she describes with such verve, but seems to realize, in her prologue and the fairy tale she tells, that the odds are now turning against her, for she is growing old. In fairy tale a withered hag can become young and beautiful again: not in real life.

Chaucer's main contribution to the medieval literature of love is his long romance *Troilus and Criseyde,* also based on Boccaccio, which tells the story of a love affair set in Troy during the Trojan War. Troilus wins Criseyde, then loses her as she becomes part of a prisoner-exchange with the besieging Greeks. Their love does not survive separation, as Criseyde gives in to the ruthless sexual predator Diomede. This tale seems to have gotten Chaucer into trouble at the court of King Richard, for in another dream-vision, the Prologue to *The Legend of Good Women,* Chaucer records a kind of trial in which he is charged with misogyny, found guilty despite his protests, and sentenced to write a set of stories about good women as a penance (a penance he never completed). The charge is a superficial one, for while the tale exposes Criseyde's weakness, it also exposes the way in which she is pressurized by Troilus, by Diomede, by the Trojan mob, and most of all by her scheming, cheerful, irresponsible uncle Pandarus.

One of Chaucer's great strokes of "good bad poetry" is the letter which Criseyde sends to Troilus from the Greek camp. It is what would now be called a "Dear John" letter, the first to survive in English. Yet it seems already to have all the familiar excuses and denials: "You're only thinking of yourself. . . . Please don't be angry. . . . I hope we can still be friends. . . . I'm sorry this is so short." Throughout the poem there is no doubt about Criseyde's sincerity. But Chaucer continually queries the value of that sincerity, presenting himself, as the story unfolds, as someone entirely on Criseyde's side, indeed half in love with her himself, but uneasily aware that what people mean and what they do are not the same thing.

As a general rule, one could say that whenever Chaucer uses the word "trewely," there will be some doubt about whatever it is applied to. If his characters say "I am a . . . ," the next thing they say will be a lie. Some of them, like the dishonest Summoner of the "Friar's Tale," lie so much they no longer recognize truth. In that tale the Summoner meets a devil, who tells him exactly what he is and what he aims to do, but the Summoner takes no notice. Another obvious question in a traditional tale: Why not? Chaucer's answer is that the Summoner is in a way an atheist, so used to seeing the Church he serves as a giant financial racket that words like "fiend," or "Hell," or even "truth," literally have no meaning for him left.

Chaucer delights in demonstrating that the meaning of words is determined by their users, of tales by their tellers. He likes to use the same line in different poems, with entirely different meanings in context. His characters, like his poetry, are complex, inscrutable, capable of being read many ways. He is the poet of shifting awarenesses and uncertain boundaries, of mixed motives and mirror images. Chaucer's genius lies above all in his unique ability to combine a clear and penetrating insight into human weaknesses with the warm and wide-ranging sympathy for which he has been famous for six hundred years.

Geoffrey Chaucer

TRANSLATIONS BY TOM SHIPPEY

From The Canterbury Tales, *"Wife of Bath's Prologue,"* lines 469–89

But — Lord Crist! — whan that it remembreth me
Upon my yowthe, and on my jolitee,
It tikleth me aboute myn herte roote....
But age, allas, *that al wole envenyme,*
Hath me biraft my beautee and my pith....
The flour is goon; ther is namoore to telle;
The bren, as I best kan, *now moste I selle;*
But yet to be right myrie wol I fonde.
Now wol I tellen of my fourthe housbonde.

   I seye, *I hadde in herte greet despit*
That he of any oother had delit.
But *he was quit,* by God and by Seint Joce!
I made hym of the same wode a croce;
Nat of my body, in no foul manere,
But certainly, *I made folk swich cheere*
That in his owene grece I made hym frye
For angre, and for verray jalousye.
By God, in erthe I was his purgatorie....

which will poison everything
has taken my beauty and my vigor
the flour is gone
now I have to sell the bran

I felt great anger in my heart
that he had pleasure from any other [woman]
he was paid out
I made him a cross from the same wood

I made such a show to people

····:¦:····

From The Canterbury Tales, *"Nun's Priest's Tale,"* lines 3375–97

This sely wydwe and eek hir doghtres two
Herden thise hennes crie and maken wo,
And *out at dores stirten they anon,*
And *syen* the fox toward the grove gon,
And bar upon his bak the cok away,
And cryden, "Out! Harrow and weylaway!
Ha ha! The fox!" and after hym they ran,
And eek with staves many another man.
Ran Colle oure dogge, and Talbot and Gerland,
And Malkyn, with a dystaf in hir hand;

they rushed out of doors
saw

Ran cow and calf, and *eek the verray hogges,* — *even the hogs as well*
So *fered* for the berkyng of the dogges — *frightened*
And shoutyng of the men and wommen eeke
They ronne *so hem thoughte hir herte breeke.* — *they thought their hearts would break*
They yolleden as feendes doon in helle;
The dokes cryden *as men wolde hem quelle;* — *as if men were going to kill them*
The gees for feere flowen over the trees;
Out of the hyve cam the swarm of bees.
So hydous was the noyse — a, benedicitee! —
Certes, he Jakke Straw and his *meynee* — *followers*
Ne made nevere shoutes half so shrille
Whan that they wolden any Flemyng kille,
As thilke day was maad upon the fox.

····⫶····

Grevous to me, God woot, is youre unreste, — *Your distress grieves me, God knows*
Youre haste, and that the goddes ordinaunce
It semeth nat ye take it for the beste. — *It seems you are not taking the gods' decree for the best*
Nor other thyng nys in youre remembraunce, — *you aren't thinking of anything*
As thynketh me, but only youre plesaunce. — *it seems to me, but your own pleasure*
But *beth nat wroth,* and that I yow biseche; — *don't be angry*
For that I tarie is al for wikked speche....
Come I wole; *but yet in swich disjoynte* — *I am in such a fix just now*
I stonde as now that what yer or what day
That this shal be, that *kan I naught apoynte.* — *I can't say for sure*
But in effect I pray yow, as I may,
Of youre good word and of youre frendship ay;
For trewely, *while that my lif may dure* — *as long as my life lasts*
As for a frend ye may in me assure. — *you can count on me as a friend*

Yet preye ich yow, *on yvel ye ne take* — *don't take it badly*
That it is short which that I to yow write.

From Troilus and Criseyde, *book V, lines 1604–10, 1618–26*

William Shakespeare

BY LOIS POTTER

Near the end of *A Midsummer Night's Dream,* Theseus tries to explain away the story he has heard from the four young people who spent the night in the woods. He attributes it to something that "the lunatic, the lover, and the poet" have in common, the human capacity for creating fantastic characters and situations:

Such tricks hath strong imagination,
That if it would but apprehend some joy,
It comprehends some bringer of that joy;
Or in the night, imagining some fear,
How easy is a bush supposed a bear! (V.i.18–22)

This is one of many passages that have been read as Shakespeare's own view of his work. Should it be? It was written for an actor to speak, and how we feel about Theseus's words depends on how he is played. If he is a wise and genial ruler, we may laugh with him when he reminds us that imagination can fill the night with imaginary beasts. If he is an unimaginative pragmatist, we may side instead with his bride Hippolyta, whose reply shows more willingness to believe that strange things can happen.

At the same time, the lines can legitimately be read as an attempt to describe creativity. Theseus talks of the poet turning "airy nothing" into "a local habitation and a name"; some fifteen years later, Prospero would refer to his own creations as "air." The words "apprehend" and "comprehend" occur at both the beginning and end of the speech. They seem to distinguish between, on the one hand, an intuitive or emotional response and, on the other, our need to make sense of it. In other words (to get back to Theseus's bear), when we experience an emotion we attribute it to a cause, and we tend to imagine that cause in the form of a living being. I believe that Shakespeare himself is someone whom we apprehend rather than comprehend. Although he is most famous for his creation of characters, he himself, the source of these characters, remains a figment of our imaginations, a "bringer of joy," rather than a recognizable personality.

The historical Shakespeare came from a middle-class family in the English Midlands, had a wife and children, made a great deal of money from his career in the theater and the purchase of land, and died at the age of fifty-two. Nothing in that life is incompatible with literary genius; nothing explains it either. We do not

Shakespeare was baptized on April 26, 1564, in Stratford-upon-Avon, England. (The date of his birth is unknown.) He died there on April 23, 1616.

know whether he thought of himself as a genius. What little he says when he is supposed to be speaking in his own person, as in the dedications to his poems or the references in the *Henry V* choruses to "our bending author," is, well, deferential. In Sonnet 29, the speaker says that he has moments of "Desiring this man's art and that man's scope." If this is meant to be autobiographical, it is amazing. Who had more art and scope than William Shakespeare? What did he think he lacked? Perhaps he was uncertain of the status of the commercial drama to which he committed so much of his career. In 1590, probably just as Shakespeare was beginning to become known as a playwright, Edmund Spenser published the first part of *The Faerie Queene,* an intricately structured patriotic, moral, and religious poem, which was at once recognized as the greatest work that England had yet produced. Over the next few years, the relatives of the brilliant Sir Philip Sidney, who died young and received a hero's funeral, published, among many other works, a long and complex prose romance called *The Arcadia.* Shakespeare read both the epic and the novel (and used both in *King Lear*). He must have envied the scope given the authors by their chosen literary forms.

But he achieved a sense of size in his own way, writing unusually long plays and sometimes following the same characters over several dramatizations of English history. In the sequence from *1 Henry IV* to *Henry V,* often

Shakespeare himself is someone whom we apprehend rather than comprehend. Although he is most famous for his creation of characters, he himself, the source of these characters, remains a figment of our imaginations, a "bringer of joy," rather than a recognizable personality.

compared to an epic, the characters range socially from the King of England to the thieves and prostitutes with whom Falstaff, a perpetually impoverished knight, prefers to mingle. In the excerpt quoted here, Falstaff's drunken love-making with the prostitute Doll Tearsheet is overheard by Prince Hal and his friend Poins, disguised as "drawers" (or waiters) in the tavern. The sarcastic comments of the two young men frame, and perhaps intensify, the pathos of Falstaff's recognition of his age and mortality. They see him as a purely comic character; we are shown the despair behind the comedy. Doll's apparent affection for Falstaff, and her attempt to prove it by promising that she will let her looks go while he's away, are touching — yet she probably knows they are being overheard, whereas he does not. Once Hal appears Falstaff hastily disowns her, joking about her "light flesh and corrupt blood," while she retorts with "thou fat fool, I scorn thee." This sparring may be at least partly for the Prince's benefit; it is not necessarily any "truer" than the earlier atmosphere of tenderness. Shakespeare's remarkable fusion of theatrical and poetic skills means that even when he writes, as here, in prose, he still creates a sense of poetry.

Sheer size is a component of Shakespeare's achievement. He wrote all or a good part of thirty-seven plays, at least half of which are still in the regular theatrical repertoire; two narrative poems; 154 sonnets; and other miscellaneous poems

— without counting what were probably a good number of unacknowledged contributions to collaborative plays. Some of his contemporaries also wrote a lot, but no one else combined quantity and quality to anywhere near the same extent. Like Falstaff, he creates an atmosphere of largeness around him. This is not simply because his plays have large casts and sometimes range over wide expanses of space and time. The storm scenes in *King Lear* are immense in scale, though they never show more than four characters on stage, because of the range of mental activity that is being dramatized.

Shakespeare's characters have seemed so real that later authors have written sequels and prequels for the plays in which they appear. Paradoxically, one reason for this reality effect is that his plays are not "well made" in the sense that was given to the phrase in about 1900. Other dramatic characters often seem to be running on a battery that has just enough power to reach the end of the play; Shakespeare's characters seem not to know that their play is going to end in three hours; they make irrelevant jokes; they refer to events in the past; they indulge in moral generalizations. Above all, they are themselves large, examples of "magnanimity" — that greatness of soul that Spenser, in *The Faerie Queene,* described as encompassing all other virtues. One reason why the tragedies are not simply depressing has to do with the scale of what happens. Some of Shakespeare's most memorable passages are those in which characters rise above personal enmity to praise greatness in others. Smallness and cynicism often compete with the sense of greatness for our allegiance. In the extract from *Antony and Cleopatra,* probably the "largest" of all the plays, Caesar and his advisers learn of the death of

Antony, a man who "kissed away" (as one of his followers says) many of his chances in life. Despite the messenger's grand classical style, which is Shakespeare's way of evoking the ancient Roman world, the audience knows that this supposedly loyal servant is lying; for one thing, he has in fact abandoned the dying Antony in order to profit from being the first to report his death. The flatness of some of the language is part of the point: Caesar is stunned by the sense of anticlimax but, as his followers notice, "touched" as well. It may be not only that Antony's fate reminds him of his own mortality, but also that he recognizes the smallness of his own successes beside the gigantic failure that was Antony.

Samuel Johnson said in the eighteenth century that most quotations from Shakespeare give about as much idea of his work as a brick does of the house from which it was taken. Of course, there are famous passages that can be detached from their context — Theseus's speech is one of them — but many of the plays' finest effects occur in scenes like the one between Falstaff and Doll, which starts from what we already know about the characters and then proceeds to surprise us by showing something new; or in the mixture of voices and sound effects that creates the storm inside and outside King Lear; or in the attempts of Maecenas and Agrippa to sum up Antony's status as a tragic hero without even mentioning Cleopatra, whom we cannot forget. The visual is as important as the verbal: Falstaff's fatness and Malvolio's appearance in yellow stockings, in *Twelfth Night*, are infinitely funnier than anyone could imagine merely from reading the plays. Unlike most writers, Shakespeare excels in both comedy and tragedy

and shows the presence of the one in the other. Most Renaissance writing is rich in imagery; Shakespeare develops images or keywords across an entire play, and not only in words. The characters in *A Midsummer Night's Dream* and *The Tempest* not only use the image of dreams to describe what happens to them, they are also said, or perceived, to be asleep at several points in the play. Hamlet talks about acting; we see him act, but we also see actors putting on a play, and at the end he is carried "like a soldier, to the stage," still part of a performance even when dead.

> *Unlike most writers, Shakespeare excels in both comedy and tragedy and shows the presence of the one in the other. Most Renaissance writing is rich in imagery; Shakespeare develops images or keywords across an entire play, and not only in words.*

Shakespeare was initially most famous for writing about love. He sometimes does it poetically, as when Juliet tells Romeo,

It was the nightingale and not the lark
That pierced the fearful hollow of thine ear.
Nightly she sings on yon pomegranate tree;
Believe me, love, it was the nightingale.

The meaning ("we still have time before morning") is only a part of the lines. They sound like an unrhymed quatrain in a sonnet, with the beginning and ending of the passage echoing each other, just as, throughout the scene, the words "stay" and "be gone," "night" and "day," create the effect of music. It is hardly surprising that so many composers have turned this passage into a love duet. The boy who originally played Juliet hardly needed to act when he had words like this to speak. The part of Rosalind, on the other hand, is obviously designed for a boy with comic gifts, but he needs also to make the audience think of him as a disguised woman rather than the boy that the woman is pretending to be; prose speeches like the third excerpt, below, allow him to show off rapid diction, talent for mimicry, and a light touch with double meanings; at the same time — a fact that helps the modern actress play the part — their effect is greater if we do not forget that Rosalind is deeply in love with the man to whom she utters these male clichés about women.

Though his plots and characters have made the plays popular in many languages, Shakespeare's reputation owes something to the dominance of the English language in the twentieth and twenty-first centuries, and the fact that the ability to understand Shakespeare has become the ultimate test of the ability to use that language. Some of his language is immensely difficult, either because he is deploying parts of speech in unusual ways (for instance, turning nouns into verbs) or because he is depicting minds on the edge of incoherence. (An example of both at once is the jealous Leontes's strangulated "Inch-thick, knee-deep, o'er head and ears a fork'd one!" [*The Winter's Tale*, I.ii.186].) His most memorable lines, however, are often simple and repetitive: "Romeo, Romeo, wherefore art thou Romeo?," "To be or not to be," Lear's "Never, never, never, never, never," and (in a play peculiarly obsessed with doubleness) the witches'

"Double, double, toil and trouble," Macbeth's "If it were done when 'tis done," and "Tomorrow, and tomorrow, and tomorrow." It is the repetitions in the comic scenes that guide us through the now obsolete wordplay: "Follow me this jest now," says Mercutio, "till thou hast worn out thy pump, that when the single sole of it is worn, the jest may remain, after the wearing, soly singular" (*Romeo and Juliet,* II.iv.61–4). Romeo does follow, and even caps, the jest, which puns on the sole of a shoe (pump) and sole meaning "only." The audience probably does not follow but enjoys the scene anyway because it *sounds* funny. On the other hand, in the quoted passage from *The Winter's Tale,* any listener can take pleasure in the many levels of absurdity inherent in the constant repetition of "gentleman" and "gentleman born." The clown's typically inaccurate use of language makes him speak the truth when he explains that the shepherd's relation to the newly identified princess Perdita has suddenly made them "preposterous." The thief Autolycus enjoys feeling intellectually superior to them, but their simplicity does not prevent them from seeing through him, and the old shepherd finally demonstrates his own greatness of soul, as he persuades his son to forgive Autolycus because "we must be gentle, now we are gentlemen."

Does one have to be magnanimous to depict magnanimity? We would like to think so, but, then, what about the depiction of prejudice, misogyny, hatred, and despair? As an actor, Shakespeare imagined, perhaps even performed, these qualities as he wrote, but always in the voices of imaginary characters, not his own. Bernard Shaw said, not as a compliment, that the dramatist had "much to show but little to teach," but to show so much is in fact to teach. From the beginning, Shakespeare's words were felt to be applicable to more than their immediate context. Lovers are said to have quoted his love scenes, *Julius Caesar* and *Henry V* became models of oratory, and, ironically, many moral statements, including those spoken by such villains as Iago, were treated as authoritative lessons on life. As with Theseus's speech, words can be true in a larger sense than their speaker could possibly realize. If asked to say what genius is, many people simply point to Shakespeare's writings. This is because, in the popular imagination, he has become not only *a* genius but Genius itself, the standard by which other writers are measured.

William Shakespeare

From 2 Henry IV,
act 2, scene 4

Falstaff. Thou dost give me flattering busses.

Doll Tearsheet. By my troth, I kiss thee with a most constant heart.

Fal. I am old, I am old.

Doll. I love thee better than I love e'er a scurvy young boy of them all.

Fal. What stuff wilt have a kirtle of? I shall receive money a-Thursday, shalt have a cap tomorrow. A merry song! Come, it grows late, we'll to bed. Thou't forget me when I am gone.

Doll. By my troth, thou't set me a-weeping and thou sayst so. Prove that ever I dress myself handsome till thy return, — Well, hearken a' th' end.

Fal. Some sack, Francis.

Prince, Poins. Anon, anon, sir.

Fal. Ha! A bastard son of the King's? And art not thou Poins his brother?

Prince. Why, thou globe of sinful continents, what a life dost thou lead!

Fal. A better than thou — I am a gentleman, thou art a drawer.

····:·····

From
Antony and
Cleopatra,
act 5, scene 1

Caesar. The breaking of so great a thing should make
A greater crack. The round world
Should have shook lions into civil streets
And citizens to their dens. The death of Antony
Is not a single doom; in the name lay
A moiety of the world.

Dercetas.   He is dead, Caesar,
Not by a public minister of justice,
Nor by a hired knife, but that self hand
Which writ his honour in the acts it did
Hath, with the courage which the heart did lend it,
Splitted the heart. This is his sword;
I robbed his wound of it. Behold it stained
With his most noble blood.

Caes.   Look you, sad friends.
The gods rebuke me, but it is tidings
To wash the eyes of kings.

Agrippa.   And strange it is
That nature must compel us to lament
Our most persisted deeds.

Maecenas.   His taints and honours
Waged equal with him.
Agr.   A rarer spirit never
Did steer humanity; but you gods will give us
Some faults to make us men. Caesar is touched.
Maec. When such a spacious mirror's set before him,
He needs must see himself.

····:│:····

Rosalind. Now tell me how long you would have her, after you have possessed her?
Orlando. For ever, and a day.
Ros. Say a day, without the ever. No, no, Orlando, men are April when they woo, December when they wed. Maids are May when they are maids, but the sky changes when they are wives. I will be more jealous of thee than a Barbary cock-pigeon over his hen, more clamorous than a parrot against rain, more new-fangled than an ape, more giddy in my desires than a monkey. I will weep for nothing, like Diana in the fountain, and I will do that when you are disposed to be merry. I will laugh like a hyen, and that when thou art inclined to sleep.
Orl. But will my Rosalind do so?
Ros. By my life, she will do as I do.

From As You Like It, *act 4, scene 1*

····:│:····

Clown. You are well met, sir. You denied to fight with me this other day, because I was no gentleman born. See you these clothes? say you see them not and think me still no gentleman born: you were best say these robes are not gentlemen born: give me the lie; do; and try whether I am not now a gentleman born.
Autolycus. I know you are now, sir, a gentleman born.
Clown. Ay, and have been so any time these four hours.
Shepherd. And so have I, boy.
Clown. So you have: but I was a gentleman born before my father; for the king's son took me by the hand, and called me brother; and then the two kings called my father brother; and then the prince, my brother, and the princess, my sister, called my father father; and so we wept; and there was the first gentleman-like tears that ever we shed.
Shepherd. We may live, son, to shed many more.
Clown. Ay; or else 'twere hard luck, being in so preposterous estate as we are.

From The Winter's Tale, *act 5, scene 2*

25

John Milton

BY REYNOLDS PRICE

There are two minimal constituents of literary genius. The first is a probably innate power for the manipulation of word, phrase, and rhythm toward a sizable and comprehensible end — ends that are large enough to prove significant in more than one culture. The second is a fertility of mind and language that results in a large body of enduringly magnetic and

challenging work. It has been widely accepted since the early eighteenth century — well before the depredations of modern critical theory — that no other writer of poetry in the English language approaches the genius of Shakespeare or Milton.

John Milton was born in 1608, in the heart of London, to a prosperous scrivener, a type of paralegal. Shakespeare had eight years yet to live; and though the two men never met, it is a fact that Milton, at the age of about twenty-two, wrote a not especially distinguished poem "To Shakespeare," which appeared as a prologue in the Second Folio of Shakespeare's plays. That so far inexplicable opportunity for such a young man may have been a component in Milton's increasing conviction that he was ordained by God to be a writer of what he considered the highest kind, an epic poet. Other crucial components of that conviction seem to have been the encouragement of his father (an excellent composer of music), the guidance

of a Puritan private tutor, rigorous training under excellent masters in the neighborhood's St. Paul's School, and the beginnings of a life-long addiction to voracious reading in Hebrew, Greek, Latin, Italian, and English.

Milton was born on December 9, 1608, in London, England. He died there on November 8, 1674.

The most powerful early component of his genius became visible in December 1629. While on the winter vacation from his studies at Cambridge, he wrote his initial indispensable poem, an ode "On the Morning of Christ's Nativity." It was, almost certainly, the result — only two weeks after his twenty-first birthday — of his eagerness to exhibit a first fruit of the high calling he sensed within himself. And in the free-wheeling rhetorical rapture which pours out memorable phrases in joyous profusion, in its complex musical urgency, and its unquestioned Christian sense of God's immanence in nature, the ode continues to be the supreme Christmas poem in the English language.

Interestingly, it comes to us accompanied by a simultaneous verse letter to Milton's best friend, Charles Diodati, the son of an Anglo-Italian family of important physicians and theologians. In the letter, his "Elegia Sexta" (for the friends communicated in Latin), Milton implies that, through stringent personal control, he can hope to fulfill the epic destiny he feels growing in him. In the recent shadow of his Nativity Ode, he hopes to become a poet who — to translate his Latin literally — "breathes out Jove." That early, then, he hoped to be a transmitter of the mind and will of God, however often his transmission might be distorted by the unavoidably human nature possessed by any poet.

Through the next decade, and during a leisurely postgraduate period of study that his father generously funded, Milton wrote a handful of poems that are still beloved — among them, "L'Allegro," "Il Penseroso," and "At a Solemn Music." He also rose to the unexpected challenge of a commissioned and deliciously comic masque, later called *Comus*. But he reached the age of twenty-nine with no further large delivery on his promise to surpass his youthful lyricism and move on to full identity as the poet-priest whom English poetry had yet to provide its readers. Then only a few months before his departure to continental Europe for the last phase of his formal education, he learned of the accidental drowning of a college friend. A small memorial volume was planned, and the invitation to contribute pressed from Milton the substantial pastoral elegy "Lycidas."

No other English poem of middle length has been more continuously admired by poets — Tennyson called it "the greatest touchstone of poetic appreciation in the English language" — and no other funeral elegy has been more

mercilessly, and oddly, examined for the degree of personal grief involved. Since the would-be withering comments of Samuel Johnson in the eighteenth century, it has grown increasingly automatic to say that "Lycidas" laments the passing of Milton's own disappointing youth and expresses his own dread of an early death before he has fulfilled his own ambitious destiny.

A long familiarity with the poem — and frequent recitation of its 193 lines — have convinced me that such an unprecedented outpouring of verbal and emotional mastery is strongly suggestive of a genuine involvement in the sadness of a particular younger friend's death. Even Shakespeare offers no such sustained and memorable stretch of human sympathy. And for more than three centuries of readers, "Lycidas" has worked phenomenally well as a condensation and verbal display of human grief in the face of untimely death, the cutting off of a young man's promise, and of the surviving poet's confidence in a blessed afterlife for a soul as deserving as his friend's (and, he hopes, his own).

When Milton returned from the rich pleasures of more than a year in France, Switzerland, and Italy, England had launched itself on the terrible civil war that would result in the beheading of God's anointed king, Charles I, and enduring changes in the power of Parliament and the theology and hierarchy of the established Church of England. As soon as he was home, Milton undertook his first job (a private school for boys) and wrote a single startlingly intense, though cumbersome, Latin elegy for his friend Diodati, who had died while Milton was on the continent. But for the next thirty years, he completed no serious long poem.

In London, he had quickly flung himself into the furious pamphleteering wars of debate that surrounded the actual fields of battle and gave Milton a ready outlet for his passionate convictions in the matter of religious and personal freedom. At the start, he felt urgently required to throw his huge gifts and energies into transforming the life of his country in whatever ways came readily to hand in such critical times. (More than once, he proudly signed himself "John Milton, Englishman.") One of his essays — "Areopagitica," a defense of the freedom of individual expression — has remained a classic of eloquence and argument. Another — "The Doctrine and Discipline of Divorce," a direct result of the flight of his first wife only a few weeks after their wedding — is a pioneering exploration of the absolute necessity of physical, intellectual, and spiritual compatibility in marriage and the desirability of divorce if any of those components was lacking. (At the time, divorce was available only in the case of adultery by one of the partners.) A briefer essay, "Of Education," offers a cheerfully daunting glimpse of one genius's plan for expanding the minds of young men destined to lead a newly righteous country, one that rewarded all its citizens.

In 1649 — as a bloody and bloodthirsty veteran of those intellectual wars, one who had specifically defended the right of Parliament to execute its king — Milton was appointed Secretary of Foreign Tongues to the Council of State, which would guide Britain through the revolutionary but increasingly disillusioning decade before the monarchy was restored with the return of Charles II from continental exile. In that exhausting trek of clerical work and sometimes scurrilous prose defenses of his party, a poet as lavishly endowed as Milton wrote only a slim handful of fine personal and political sonnets and a few unmemorable translations of Hebrew psalms.

The same years saw him afflicted by mounting sadness — the death of his returned first wife and his only son and the inexorable decay of his eyesight. When total blindness overcame him in his mid-forties, his governmental position became untenable, and he retired to his small house with the second of three wives and his three daughters. Deserts of empty time lay before him, time in which to consider what must have seemed his disgraceful private and public failures — failures with which his numerous enemies would never cease to taunt him. From those years, the famous sonnet on his blindness is one of the most devastating of all documents arising from near-despair.

Not only had his fervent hopes for a government to accomplish the will of God collided with an inescapable awareness that he had lent his skills to a lost and corrupt cause, he was likewise compelled to admit to himself that the hopes of his youth to be God's great English poet were unfulfilled and might well be dead in the hands of a blind man in late middle age. Yet somehow he rose from the ashes of his own combustion. (He would have said that he revived and succeeded at the will of God.) He managed to write a few more political tracts, a few lesser prose works, and an elaborate theological exposition, *De Doctrina Christiana,* composed apparently to prepare a background for his epic. Then, in a final decade, he astonished the small world of contemporary poetry readers — and vindicated himself in the eyes of his enemies — with *Paradise Lost,* the only successful, full-scale European epic since Virgil. Then he wrote a briefer epic, *Paradise*

Regained, and a verse tragedy on the ancient Greek model, *Samson Agonistes.*

Paradise Lost is, of course, his prime accomplishment. At its beginning, he invokes the Holy Spirit:

What in me is dark
Illumine, what is low raise and support;
That to the height of this great Argument
I may assert Eternal Providence,
And justify the ways of God to men.

It's seldom noticed that Milton begs to *assert* Eternal Providence, not prove it (even he would have known it was not provable), and the word *justify* had multiple meanings for him, as the succeeding 10,000 lines of heroic verse demonstrate. His great question — perhaps one of only two or three ultimate questions — is how did evil enter a creation that both Christianity and Judaism claim was created good? To the account of the fall of Adam and Eve as related in the Hebrew Book of Genesis, he added his own rich variant of an early Judeo-Christian myth of the expulsion of rebel angels from heaven. And as his enormous narrative grew — with its unfolding cast of intricately detailed characters (a man, a woman, two of the three persons of the Holy Trinity, and numerous good and evil angels) — his project of assertion and justification grew, far more interestingly and darkly than even he may have foreseen.

What led him of course, other than the Spirit, was his own gift for language and music, a gift that had miraculously survived his years in the dirty mills of politics and special pleading. And it had not merely survived the long ordeal, it had learned a great deal from those years — primarily how to speak memorably and as clearly as the complexity of a given moment permitted, while allowing the words and rhythm within his looping baroque sentences to become his chief tools for exploring the minutest concealed implications of the simplest or grandest gestures of his extraordinarily credible characters. Every philosophical, theological, moral, and dramatic nuance is laid bare and probed till it holds no remaining secret.

So credible are Milton's characters — even his menacing God the Father — that they lead him to ask, and almost always answer unnervingly, questions so shocking that it took nearly three centuries of close reading before his readers were free enough of orthodox Christian assumptions to comprehend the magnificence of the boldness of his explorations. Not only *Is God just?* but *Could Adam and Eve ever not have disobeyed the declared will of God and thus permitted the entry of evil into Paradise and the remainder of the planet? Wasn't the entire apparatus of God's warnings of Satan's forthcoming assault so flawed and so alluring to Satan's cause that our first parents really had no chance of not succumbing to fatal disobedience? Aren't God and His angelic messengers essentially lying when they assure Adam and Eve that their own will is, to paraphrase Milton, "sufficient to stand yet free to fall"? Isn't our mother Eve clearly a far superior creature — intellectually and spiritually — to our father Adam, who stands convicted of the worst male faults: uncontrolled libido, deplorable self-pity, and an emotionally violent mistreatment of his wife?* Finally, few readers have noted the radical core of Milton's theology. All things, including evil, derive directly from God the Creator because — as God makes clear in Book VII: 162–173 — all things are literally made from His own substance, a physical nature from which He withholds only a single quality, His "goodness." One valid reading of the evidence laid down so unflinchingly by Milton can easily find God the poem's villain — unavoidable, yes, but God all the same, just as Job's God is horrific but inescapable.

After the publication of *Paradise Lost* in 1667, Milton lived for another seven years, years that saw his genius amply acknowledged by the small audience of his time and place. The two final poems further consolidate his claim on both intellectual and verbal supremacy. In the dry and chaste rhetoric of *Paradise Regained,* he studies further, and profoundly, contradictory aspects of the nature of human will as displayed in Satan's temptation of Jesus of Nazareth, a man whom Milton did not believe to be the earthly equivalent of God. The will of this Jesus proves exemplary, nonetheless, more than a match for Satan's.

In his tragedy, *Samson Agonistes,* Milton rouses himself for one last verbal invention — a massively effective (sometimes heroic verse, sometimes free verse) means of illuminating characters as different as Samson, the blunderbuss judge of Israel; an ambivalent chorus of Samson's fellow tribesmen who call themselves his "friends" but prove more nearly his enemies; his uncomprehending father; his still-tempting Philistine wife, who surrendered him to her own countrymen for blinding and enslavement; and the Philistines' own boisterous giant, who challenges Samson to the final contest that leads to his suicidal death and paradoxical triumph in his enemies' arena on their heathen god's feast day. In the end, Samson's will has been entirely commandeered by the God of Israel's will.

When Milton died in 1674, just short of the age of sixty-six, this man — who had begun his adult life with such an outrageous announcement of prophetic destiny, who had detoured his best gifts for twenty years through the bloody exchanges of a civil war and its grim aftermath, who had endured unusual domestic trials and finally been totally blinded — could reflect on an ultimate triumph unlike any other in literature.

Not only is he, with Homer, one of the world's two broadest-gauged epic poets (and no distinguished epic has yet succeeded him), his three long poems constitute the most relentless and profound examination in Western letters — an examination in endlessly memorable and often surprisingly tender words — of the mysteries that endure, tease, and torment us still. *Who made us? How? Why? Why is suffering, to the point of tragedy, the fate of most human lives? What do I do in the face of personal defeat? Can I truly choose to perform even the least of my actions with any degree of freedom? How must I treat my kin, friends, and enemies? How must I approach and adore my Creator? What if I refuse?* Even an unbeliever has much to learn from his daring portrayals of creaturely nature.

Whether or not John Milton succeeded in transmitting the voice of God, whether he justified the ways of God to humankind, he lodged himself where he longed to be — as a spur in the depths of our minds, a balm to our souls, a companionable hand in our solitary journey.

John Milton

From "Lycidas,"
lines 1–49

In this monody the author bewails a learned friend,
unfortunately drowned in his passage from Chester
on the Irish Seas, 1637, and by occasion fortells the ruin
of our corrupted clergy, then in their height.

Yet once more, O ye laurels, and once more
Ye myrtles brown, with ivy never sere,
I come to pluck your berries harsh and crude,
And with forced fingers rude,
Shatter your leaves before the mellowing year.
Bitter constraint, and sad occasion dear,
Compels me to disturb your season due;
For Lycidas is dead, dead ere his prime,
Young Lycidas, and hath not left his peer.
Who would not sing for Lycidas? He knew
Himself to sing, and build the lofty rhyme.
He must not float upon his watery bier
Unwept, and welter to the parching wind,
Without the meed of some melodious tear.
  Begin then, sisters of the sacred well,
That from beneath the seat of Jove doth spring,
Begin, and somewhat loudly sweep the string.
Hence with denial vain, and coy excuse;
So may some gentle Muse
With lucky words favor my destined urn,
And as he passes turn,
And bid fair peace be to my sable shroud.
For we were nursed upon the selfsame hill,
Fed the same flock, by fountain, shade, and rill.
  Together both, ere the high lawns appeared
Under the opening eyelids of the morn,
We drove afield, and both together heard
What time the grayfly winds her sultry horn,

34

Battening our flocks with the fresh dews of night,
Oft till the star that rose at evening bright
Toward heaven's descent had sloped his westering wheel.
Meanwhile the rural ditties were not mute,
Tempered to th' oaten flute,
Rough satyrs danced, and fauns with cloven heel
From the glad sound would not be absent long,
And old Damoetas loved to hear our song.

But O the heavy change, now thou art gone,
Now thou art gone, and never must return!
Thee, shepherd, thee the woods and desert caves,
With wild thyme and the gadding vine o'ergrown,
And all their echoes mourn.
The willows and the hazel copses green
Shall now no more be seen,
Fanning their joyous leaves to thy soft lays.
As killing as the canker to the rose,
Or taint-worm to the weanling herds that graze,
Or frost to flowers that their gay wardrobe wear
When first the white-thorn blows;
Such, Lycidas, thy loss to the shepherd's ear.

····⋮····

Th' infernal serpent; he it was, whose guile,
Stirred up with envy and revenge, deceived
The mother of mankind, what time his pride
Had cast him out from Heaven, with all his host
Of rebel angels, by whose aid aspiring
To set himself in glory above his peers,
He trusted to have equaled the Most High,
If he opposed; and with ambitious aim
Against the throne and monarchy of God
Raised impious war in Heaven and battle proud,
With vain attempt. Him the Almighty Power
Hurled headlong flaming from th' ethereal sky
With hideous ruin and combustion down

From Paradise
Lost, *book 1,*
lines 34–49

35

From "On the Morning of Christ's Nativity," lines 1–28

To bottomless perdition, there to dwell
In adamantine chains and penal fire,
Who durst defy th' Omnipotent to arms.

····:·····

1

This is the month, and this the happy morn
Wherein the son of Heaven's eternal King,
Of wedded maid and virgin mother born,
Our great redemption from above did bring;
For so the holy sages once did sing,
    That he our deadly forfeit should release,
And with his Father work us a perpetual peace.

2

That glorious form, that light unsufferable,
And that far-beaming blaze of majesty
Wherewith he wont at Heaven's high council-table
To sit the midst of Trinal Unity,
He laid aside; and here with us to be,
    Forsook the courts of everlasting day,
And chose with us a darksome house of mortal clay.

3

Say, heavenly Muse, shall not thy sacred vein
Afford a present to the infant God?
Hast thou no verse, no hymn, or solemn strain,
To welcome him to this his new abode,
Now while the heaven by the sun's team untrod
    Hath took no print of the approaching light,
And all the spangled host keep watch in squadrons bright?

4

See how from far upon the eastern road
The star-led wizards haste with odors sweet:
O run, prevent them with thy humble ode,
And lay it lowly at his blessed feet;

Have thou the honor first thy Lord to greet,
    And join thy voice unto the angel choir,
From out his secret altar touched with hallowed fire.

····⁛····

When I consider how my light is spent,
    Ere half my days, in this dark world and wide,
    And that one talent which is death to hide,
    Lodged with me useless, though my soul more bent
To serve therewith my Maker, and present
    My true account, lest he returning chide;
    "Doth God exact day-labor, light denied?"
    I fondly ask; but Patience to prevent
That murmur, soon replies, "God doth not need
    Either man's work or his own gifts; who best
    Bear his mild yoke, they serve him best. His state
Is kingly. Thousands at his bidding speed
    And post o'er land and ocean without rest:
    They also serve who only stand and wait."

"When I Consider How My Light Is Spent"

Alexander Pope

BY ANTHONY HECHT

The work of any artist or poet is bound to reflect something of the period in which it is composed, and there's a modern tendency to dismiss Alexander Pope's poetry as conventional and as formulaic as the gardens of André Le Nôtre. This would be a mistake for several reasons. But it may also be confidently asserted that gifted persons of all periods whatever find themselves negotiating between two absolutely contradictory impulses: to pursue and exploit, on one hand, all their natural propensities, gifts, and talents, and, on the other, to choose, in W. B. Yeats's words, "whatever task's most difficult / Among tasks not impossible" — in other words, to rise to extreme challenges they set or find before themselves, both technical and moral. We can see both of these tendencies at work in Pope. He tells us that he "lisp'd in numbers," and we have from his hand a superb poem of great imaginative maturity composed before he was twelve. He taught himself to write "by copying from printed books," and not from English alone: "In a few years I had dipped into a great number of English, French, Italian, Latin, and Greek poets. This I did without any design but that of pleasing myself, and got the languages by hunting after the stories in the several poets I read."

On the other hand, he suffered handicaps that made Lord Byron's clubfoot look like a trifle. He was, to begin with, a Catholic in a land where that faith was severely penalized by heavy taxes that eventually forced the poet's father to give up his home at Binfield, near Windsor Forest. The distrust and contempt in which Catholics were held was lasting and pervasive and afflicted the poet his life long. To this we must add that he was probably never free from physical pain from childhood on, having at first to fit himself into rough canvas bodices, "being scarce able to hold himself erect till they were laced," owing to the ravages of the tubercle bacillus in his bones, which allowed him to achieve his full height of only four and a half feet. In his forties and early fifties he was unable to dress himself or get into bed without help; "nor could not stand upright till a kind of stays, made of stiff liner, were laced on him, one of his sides being contracted almost to the backbone." In his fifties "his body had required the support of 'an iron case.' So a friend testified, (who saw his warped and shriveled figure lifted out

Pope was born on May 21, 1688, in London, England. He died in Twickenham, England, on May 30, 1744.

39

of it after he was dead) . . . 'like a man whom you hang in chains.'" His enemies, who were many, and for whom his Catholic faith was enough justification, did not scruple to abuse him for his deformity. Said the critic John Dennis, "As there is no Creature so venomous, there is nothing so stupid and impotent as a hunchback'd Toad." And the bookseller Edmund Curll: "There is no one Disease but what all the rest of Men are subject to; whereas the Deformity of this Libeller, is Visible, Present, Lasting, Unalterable, and Peculiar to himself. 'Tis the mark of God and Nature upon him, to give us warning that we should hold no Society with him, as a Creature not of our Original, nor of our Species."

In addition to Pope's religion and his deformity, contemporaries despised him because of his extraordinary financial success, attained chiefly through his translation of Homer. In *The Pleasures of the Imagination,* a survey of the English eighteenth century, John Brewer writes in regard to the monetary value of selected copyrights of the time: "In 1716 . . . the copyright of Pope's *Works* was valued at an astonishing £4,400, Shakespeare at £1,800, and Addison and Steele's *Spectator* as a part-book at £1,300." With his earnings he bought a modest estate at Twickenham, which remained his home until his death in 1744.

Consider the following as the work of an eleven-year-old.

ODE ON SOLITUDE

Happy the man whose wish and care
A few paternal acres bound,
Content to breathe his native air,
In his own ground.

Whose herds with milk, whose fields with bread,
Whose flocks supply him with attire,

Whose trees in summer yield him shade,
In winter fire.

Blest, who can unconcern'dly find
Hours, days, and years slide soft away,
In health of body, peace of mind,
Quiet by day,

Sound sleep at night; study and ease,
Together mixt; sweet recreation,
And Innocence, which most does please
With meditation.

Thus let me live, unseen, unknown.
Thus unlamented let me die,
Steal from the world, and not a stone
Tell where I lie.

Such cheerful resignation on the part of a boy, such stoic fortitude, is quite remarkable even when we suppose he has appropriated consecrated pastoral themes and attitudes. Yet to have written out verses as serene as these must have meant to come face to face with the austerity and anonymity they envision, an anonymity plainly at odds with poetic ambition and hope of reputation. The brief phrase about "health of body" must have come with special meaning to one who by age fifteen was agonized by such constant pain that he told a friend he had "resolved to give way to his distemper, and sat down calmly, in full expectation of death."

In his splendid biography of Pope, Maynard Mack makes these penetrating comments on the poet's extraordinary poem *Eloisa to Abelard,* which was sent to Lady Mary Wortley Montagu in Constantinople, who was the covert object of Pope's deep feelings. The story of the famous medieval lovers, Mack writes,

offered latent possibilities of emotional identification with both lovers. In Abelard, he might, if he chose, sense one kind of actuation of his own situation, both as it was and as he might wish it to be. Though there is no evidence whatever that Pope was sexually crippled, he had been penalized from boyhood by a dwarfish stature and deformity that seemed capable of bringing about similar frustrations so far as normal relations with women were concerned and were just as certain to last his lifetime. . . . On the other hand (going back to Pope's source), Abelard was deeply loved despite all. Hence at least in Pope's fantasy, he could be an emblem of hope. Had not a letter from him precipitated Eloisa's outpouring of passion? What if a letter of his own — to Lady Mary, say — should prove a comparable invitation?

A love that can never be physically consummated takes on a nobility of a special and almost religious kind, committed to anguish and transcendence.

Pope's brilliant, light-hearted mock-epic, *The Rape of the Lock,* is virtually impossible suitably to illustrate by small extracts, since much of its ingenuity consists in the sustained employment of parallels to the epics of John Milton, Virgil, and Homer, but ludicrously applied to a small social contretemps. We need care no more about Arabella Fermor and Lord Petre (the persons on whom the poem is based) than about John Dennis or Edmund Curll or any of the named targets of *The Dunciad.* In the following lines, Belinda, the heroine, just before waking, experiences a dream of sublime fatuity and self-flattery, in which she finds herself the center of terrestrial adoration (in the shape of a handsome courtier dressed as for the monarch's birthday) and the celestial focus of the vast hosts of spiritual creatures.

A Youth more glitt'ring than a Birth-night Beau,
(That ev'n in Slumber caus'd her Cheek to glow)
Seem'd to her Ear his winning Lips to lay,
And thus in Whispers said, or seem'd to say,
    "Fairest of Mortals, thou distinguish'd Care
Of thousand bright Inhabitants of Air!

If e'er one Vision touch'd thy infant Thought,
Of all the Nurse and all the Priest have taught,
Of airy Elves by Moonlight Shadows seen,
The silver Token, and the circled Green,
Or Virgins visited by Angel-Pow'rs,
With Golden Crowns and Wreaths of Heav'nly Flow'rs,
Hear and believe! thy own Importance know,
Nor bound thy narrow Views to things below.
Some secret Truths, from Learned Pride conceal'd,
To Maids alone and Children are reveal'd:
What tho' no credit doubting Wits may give?
The Fair and Innocent shall still believe.
Know then, unnumber'd Spirits round thee fly,
The light Militia of the lower sky.

An alert reader might hear an echo of Milton's "Millions of spiritual creatures walk the earth / Unseen, both when we wake and when we sleep" (*Paradise Lost,* 4. 677–78), but a student of Freud might detect something about human egotism operating in the realm of the unconscious, not excluding the self-congratulation of the untutored as being certifiably the moral superiors of the educated. To be sure, this is a biblical as well as a pastoral commonplace. But the more we see of Belinda, the more she seems like Marie-Antoinette masquerading as a milkmaid, and the notion of her "simplicity," even in the dreamworld, equally suspect and self-promoting. As the poem progresses, mockery is directed at the moral codes of the day. Pope is amusing throughout and sometimes downright funny. In fact, no sooner has Belinda's delightful dream ended than she awakens to perform the first religious act of the day, which is self-adoration, cunningly likened to the preparatory arming of an epic hero.

    And now, unveil'd, the Toilet stands display'd,
Each Silver vase in mystic Order laid.
First, rob'd in White, the Nymph intent adores,
With Head uncover'd, the Cosmetic Pow'rs.
A heavenly image in the Glass appears,

To that she bends, to that her Eyes she rears;
Th' inferior Priestess, at her Altar's side,
Trembling begins the sacred Rites of Pride.
Unnumber'd Treasures ope at once, and here
The various Off'rings of the World appear;
From each she nicely culls with curious Toil,
And decks the Goddess with the glitt'ring Spoil.
This casket India's glowing Gems unlocks,
And all Arabia breathes from yonder Box.
The Tortoise here and Elephant unite,
Transform'd to Combs, the speckled, and the white.
Here Files of Pins extend their shining Rows,
Puffs, Powders, Patches, Bibles, Billet-doux.
Now awful Beauty puts on all its Arms;
The Fair each moment rises in her Charms,
Repairs her Smiles, awakens ev'ry Grace,
And calls forth all the wonders of her Face;
Sees by Degrees a purer Blush arise,
And keener Lightnings quicken in her eyes.

One is reluctant to belabor with detailed commentary the complexly poised wit of these lines, but I will permit myself two slight observations. When the passage begins Belinda is a votary, and her maid the "inferior Priestess," who will assist in her "devotions." Before the passage is done, Belinda has transformed herself into the "Goddess" she adores. And her

blush, in the penultimate line quoted, is "purer" than even the dream that "caus'd her Cheek to glow" in the lines quoted earlier, because it is, ironically, altogether artificial, thus unprompted by personal feelings.

In the early drafts of *The Waste Land,* T. S. Eliot had at one time included a section in heroic couplets, deliberately imitative of Pope, about "white-armed Fresca," which Ezra Pound persuaded him to delete. In his 1928 Introduction to Pound's *Selected Poems,* Eliot recalls, "Pound once induced me to destroy what I thought was an excellent set of couplets; for, said he, 'Pope has done this so well that you cannot do it better; and if you mean this as a burlesque, you had better suppress it, for you cannot parody Pope unless you can write better verse than Pope — and you can't.'"

In "Epistle IV: To Richard Boyle, Earl of Burlington," Pope writes a poem that, though again in his favored couplets, resembles in its substance, and in some of its ideas, Andrew Marvell's "Upon Appleton House," which is also in couplets, but in tetrameter lines divided into eight-line stanzas. Both poems recommend a scrupulous, moral judiciousness as regards to architectural planning and the laying out of grounds and gardens. Both warn against the vulgarity of ostentation. In all things *taste* must govern, and taste is a form of judiciousness.

> You show us, Rome was glorious, not profuse,
> And pompous buildings once were things of Use.
> Yet shall (my Lord) your just, your noble rules
> Fill half the land with Imitating Fools;
> Who random drawings from your sheets shall take,
> And from one beauty many blunders make;
>
> . . . .
>
> At Timon's Villa let us pass a day,
> Where all cry out, "What sums are thrown away!"
> So proud, so grand, of that stupendous air,
> Soft and Agreeable come never there.
> Greatness, with Timon, dwells in such a draught
> As brings all Brobdignag before your thought.
> To compass this, his building is a Town,
> His pond an Ocean, his parterre a Down:
> Who but must laugh, the Master when he sees,
> A puny insect, shiv'ring at a breeze!
> Lo, what huge heaps of littleness around!
> The whole, a labor'd Quarry above ground.
> Two Cupids squirt before: a Lake behind
> Improves the keenness of the Northern wind.
> His Gardens next your admiration call,
> On ev'ry side you look behold a Wall!
> No pleasing intricacies intervene,
> No artful wildness to perplex the scene;
> Grove nods at grove, each Alley has a brother,
> And half the platform just reflects the other.
> The suff'ring eye inverted Nature sees,
> Trees cut to Statues, Statues thick as trees,
> With here a Fountain, never to be play'd,
> And there a Summer-house, that knows no shade;
> Here Amphitrite sails thro' myrtle bow'rs;
> There Gladiators fight, or die, in flow'rs;
> Unwater'd see the drooping sea-horse mourn,
> And swallows roost in Nilus' dusty Urn.

The Dunciad (1728), together with *The New Dunciad* (1742), is a monumental undertaking that, though it takes fatal aim at particular targets who had abused or harmed Pope, enlarges to epic dimensions that encompass coruscating views of the politics of the day, of society at large, and of religion, as well as other general topics. It was eventually accompanied by a huge critical apparatus of notes, as rich in wit and acidulous comment as the text itself, all of it by the poet, and a kind of precursor of the still more celebrated notes to Eliot's *The Waste Land.* Certainly anyone who is not a victim of Pope's wrath will be suitably grateful; it can also be said that when personal venom rises to epic proportions it ceases to be purely personal and becomes a universe of comic rage, in which the comic predominates.

Finally, by way of preface to his satires, there is Pope's splendid "Epistle to Dr. Arbuthnot," a verse dialogue of great freedom and invention, bracingly harsh in its contempt, learned as always in its allusions, but at moments deeply touching in its modest glimpse of something deeply vulnerable about the poet himself.

> Why did I write? what sin to me unknown
> Dipt me in Ink, my Parents', or my own?
> As yet a Child, nor yet the Fool of Fame,
> I lisp'd in Numbers, for the Numbers came.
> I left no Calling for this idle trade,
> No Duty broke, no Father disobey'd.
> The Muse but serv'd to ease some Friend, not Wife,
> To help me thro' this long Disease, my Life,
> To second, ARBUTHNOT! thy Art and Care,
> And teach, the Being you preserv'd, to bear.

It would be hard to deny that Pope's poetry does not enjoy a large reading audience today, even among the tiny readership that takes poetry seriously. Introducing his selection of Augustan poetry, Paul Fussell, Jr., comments, "Even when this poetry has not been specifically dismissed on charges of artifice and conventionality, it has been benignly neglected in favor of the sort which seems to reflect back onto us those extreme emotional states made peculiar to our own modern history — strain, personal and collective guilt, hysteria, madness." The inexorable chimings of rhyme at the fixed and inviolable intervals of ten syllables seems limited and predictable when contrasted with the prosodic and rhyming freedoms enjoyed by, say, John Donne, George Herbert, William Wordsworth, and John Keats. Yet one has only to hear G. F. Handel's eloquent setting of these lines from "Summer" from Pope's *Pastorals:*

Where-e'er you walk, cool Gales shall fan the Glade,
Trees, where you sit, shall crowd into a shade,

Where-e'er you tred, the blushing Flow'rs shall rise,
And all things flourish where you turn your Eyes

to feel that the composer has found in these words an expression of love which he has beautifully emancipated from any possibility of prediction and to which he has added his own reverence and admiration. As for the conventions of regular form, W. H. Auden has wisely observed, "continuous practice in the same form trains [the poet's] mind to think easily and naturally in it and makes him sensitive to the subtlest variations of which it is capable." To go on to hone that form to the power of perfection, as Alexander Pope did the heroic couplet, required the quality known as genius.

Alexander Pope

But you who seek to give and merit fame,
And justly bear a critic's noble name,
Be sure your self and your own reach to know,
How far your genius, taste, and learning go;
Launch not beyond your depth, but be discreet,
And mark that point where sense and dullness meet.

One science only will one genius fit;
So vast is art, so narrow human wit.
Not only bounded to peculiar arts,
But oft in those confined to single parts.
Like kings we lose the conquests gain'd before,
By vain ambition still to make them more:
Each might his sev'ral province well command,
Wou'd all but stoop to what they understand.
First follow Nature, and your judgment frame
By her just standard, which is still the same,
Unerring Nature, still divinely bright,
One clear, unchang'd, and universal light,
Life, force, and beauty, must to all impart,
At once the source, and end, and test of art.
Art from that fund each just supply provides,
Works without show, and without pomp presides.

. . . .

Those rules of old discover'd, not devis'd,
Are Nature still, but Nature methodized;
Nature, like liberty, is but restrained
By the same laws which first herself ordain'd.

From An Essay
on Criticism,
part 1, lines 46–91

45

Samuel Johnson

BY DAVID BROMWICH

How the eighteenth century prized its nicknames. Matthew Lewis was called Monk Lewis after his Gothic bestseller *The Monk.* The landscape improver Lancelot Brown turned into Capability Brown when he did fine work on a big scale. And in a life that knew no sweeter sound than the clash of arms over a doubtful fact or a twisted syllogism, Samuel Johnson was thought of naturally as Dr. Johnson. His fame rests on an intellectual honor that he defended without intermission — a restless search for wisdom in the traditions of learning, a decent humility in the conduct of life toward the generous and the good.

Dr. Johnson was a large man, grotesque from scrofula that had left his face pockmarked, with an involuntary flinch and gesticulation that punctuated his talk. He was haunted in private by a nameless dread, as his written prayers show, and by the conviction of his weakness and indolence. He seems to have been at once the loneliest and the most gregarious of writers. He loved to talk, and he talked for victory. "There is no arguing with Johnson," said his friend Oliver Goldsmith, "for when his pistol misses fire, he knocks you down with the butt end of it." An orthodox Christian in an age of reason, he was himself a believer in reason, progress, and science, and kept a chemical apparatus in his rooms. Charity was a rooted principle of his nature. When he discovered a prostitute once, collapsed in exhaustion in the street at night, he carried her on his back to a safe lodging. Johnson seems to have lived two lives. To his generation, he was a literary dictator, the first and last authority on the history and the proper fame of words. Yet the hero of Boswell's *Life of Johnson* is an amiable holder-forth, bluff, downright, and clubbable.

Was he Dr. Johnson even as a child? His writings exhibit a born learner and teacher, one who, steeped in doctrine, has perfected the conversible art of making himself understood. High regard for his readers is the other side of his self-respect. He was the first writer in Europe to achieve worldly distinction without title or patronage; the first large talent to treat writing as a profession demanding the continuous use of brains and nerves. His saying, "No one but a blockhead ever wrote, except for money," is easily misunderstood, and comes chiefly from the pride of being able to earn a living: not to

Johnson was born on September 18, 1709, in Lichfield, Staffordshire, England. He died in London on December 13, 1784.

write for money means to write for favor. This pride was indeed inseparable from Johnson's idea of the profession of writer. Anything that an author writes, the author alone should get credit for; and for shoddiness in the result, he alone is to blame and is answerable. Johnson had been promised a notable patron for his *Dictionary of the English Language,* but Lord Chesterfield's interest grew slack while the dictionary was maturing; and when Chesterfield tried, rather late, to felicitate Johnson on his success, he received a letter of rebuke that has since become a declaration of independence for authors everywhere. "Is not," wrote Johnson, "a patron, my Lord, one who looks with unconcern on a man struggling for life in the water, and, when he has reached ground, encumbers him with help?"

He showed great impartiality of assault toward any author whose cheat or swindle or obsequiousness marred the dignity of his calling. James Macpherson tapped a vein of eighteenth-century primitivism with his supposed translation of the Highland epic *Poems of Ossian.* Johnson found internal and circumstantial evidence for supposing the work a forgery. When Macpherson threatened him, Johnson replied in another letter: "You want me to retract. What shall I retract? I thought your book an imposture from the beginning. I think it upon surer reasons an imposture still. I shall not desist from detecting what I think a cheat from any fear of the menaces of a ruffian." A resolve to sift the genuine from the spuri-

He was the first writer in Europe to achieve worldly distinction without title or patronage; the first large talent to treat writing as a profession demanding the continuous use of brains and nerves.

ous was a maxim, too, that guided his *Dictionary of the English Language.* Johnson disapproved of the verb *to banter* ("a barbarous word, without etymology") both for what it meant and for the people who would use it. Yet the credo of the *Dictionary,* propounded in its preface, is the reverse of mandarin: "I am not yet so lost in lexicography, as to forget *that words are the daughters of earth, and that things are the sons of heaven.*" Johnson was unusually sensitive to the way that words, themselves sprung out of earlier words, may give their own peculiar coloring to things — the way, as he puts it, "the metaphorical will become the current sense." This will be found true (to borrow two later examples) regarding clichés like *trial balloon* and *quagmire,* which we may use without forming an image of the upper air or a mire; but it also makes sense of the general application of such Latin words as "inundate" or "domesticate," which have strayed from their literal senses to enrich the common idiom.

When Johnson advised his disciple Boswell to "clear your *mind* of cant," he did not mean to quell the background noise of standard usage. Rather, he was alluding to the human propensity to speak and think in formulae that make a habit of falsehood. "When a butcher tells you that his *heart bleeds for his country,* he has, in fact, no uneasy feeling." Again, "You tell a man, 'I am sorry you had such bad weather the last day of your journey, and were so much wet.' You don't care six-pence whether he was wet or dry." You say the canting words, and continue with your business. It is a harmless convention of society to speak such phrases, but you must never permit your mind to think them. Even as you sign a letter, "I am your humble servant," always remember that you are not humble and are not a servant.

Johnson has two styles — three if one counts his conversation. He comments sensibly and without pomp on the imputed madness of the poet Christopher Smart that had led to his confinement: "His infirmities were not noxious to society. He insisted on people praying with him; and I'd as lief pray with Kit Smart as any one else. Another charge was, that he did not love clean linen; and I have no passion for it." And on the poetry of Thomas Gray: "He was dull in a new way, and that made many people think him GREAT." The natural rapidity and bluntness of his speech came late into Johnson's writing. By contrast, the Latinate style that pervades the *Rambler* and *Rasselas* is marked by a gravity whose base note is the chiming of grammatical balance and antithesis. "Marriage has many pains, but celibacy has no pleasures." "If you are pleased by prognosticks of good, you will be terrified likewise with tokens of evil." "We are all prompted by the same motives, all deceived by the same fallacies, all animated by hope, obstructed by danger, entangled by desire, and seduced by pleasure." This early style was finely adapted to a view of the world in which every light is edged with shadow, every hope counteracted by fear, a sense of the moral order that admits of rewards but not of luck that lasts. The essays of the *Rambler* have a melancholy assurance that suggests a wide reserve of power even in resignation. When harnessed to a narrative, this style can rise to an unforgettable resonance, its

premonitions borrowing now the sweep of conclusions. So the *Life of Richard Savage,* a memoir of a friend of Johnson's youth, gathers up all its weight to declare near the start: "Born with a legal claim to honor and to riches, he was in two months illegitimated by the parliament, and disowned by his mother, doomed to poverty and obscurity, and launched upon the ocean of life, only that he might be swallowed by its quicksands or dashed upon its rocks." We feel the booming of the pipes of an organ on which these chords are to be only occasionally touched.

The later prose of the *Journey to the Western Islands of Scotland* and the *Lives of the Poets* is a more portable instrument. The antithetical manner can still be put to appropriate use, as in the judgment of Pope's ambition: "He seems to have wanted neither diligence nor success in attracting the notice of the great." Yet Johnson now is able, by the force of implied metaphor, to transfer intuitions at a jump from a narrow to a wider field of fact. So we are told of John Milton that his eyes "are said never to have been bright; but, if he was a dexterous fencer, they must have been once quick." Such descriptions were for Johnson part of the duty of biography, and splinters of detail about posture or physiognomy may turn up almost anywhere in one of his *Lives*. He always begins with a proper narrative of a life, sometimes evoking the texture of the poetry through the echoes, quotations, and allusions that his own writing absorbs. Criticism of the work is normally offered near the end and preserves a tincture of the person's assignable motives and peculiar traits. In this double rendering of lives and works, a poem for Johnson never dwindles to a symptom of weakness or of all-too-human passion. He can align himself with the sentiments of the common reader (a phrase he invented) or condole with the first-time reader of a difficult poem — saying, for example, of *Paradise Lost* that "None ever wished it longer than it is." But he always ends with a considered judgment of his own.

The "Life of Milton" is the most acute, searching, and profound of all Johnson's writings. It is also one of the most powerful acts of appreciation in the history of criticism, alert to the subtlest implications of the poetry, sharing something of the mental energy in which *Paradise Lost* excels. Thus with great precision Johnson remarks how, by "comparing the shield of Satan to the orb of the Moon," Milton "crowds the imagination with the discovery of the telescope and all the wonders which the telescope discovers." The complex figure of the shield and the moon, as Johnson makes us see, brings to mind an adventurous image of the poet Milton and the scientist Galileo, explorers of parts of the universe hidden from the bodily eye. The "Life of Milton" ends with the most stirring compliment that one writer has ever paid to another. For Milton was Johnson's opposite in every countable way: a revolutionist, a puritan, self-isolated and arrogant in his solitude. Yet Johnson more than pardons him: "He was naturally a thinker for himself, confident of his own abilities and disdainful of help or hindrance. . . . His great works were performed under discountenance and in blindness, but difficulties vanished at his touch; he was born for whatever is arduous; and his work is not the greatest of heroic poems, only because it is not the first."

The preface to *The Plays of William Shakespeare* aims at and achieves a more imper-sonal homage. This essay in criticism was written not only to introduce Johnson's edition of Shakespeare's plays, but to declare that Shakespeare had attained the status of a classic. What is a classic? A work or body of works that has "pleased many and pleased long" because it affords "just representations of general nature." Johnson praises most of all in Shakespeare an unfeigned naturalness in the use of words, a perpetual animation by which "the dialogue is level with life." A host of neo-classical critics had objected to the lack of decorum in Shakespeare's histories and tragedies, as in the portrayal (in *Coriolanus*) of the buffoonery of the Roman senator Menenius. Johnson replies that such a pretension of delicacy is hackneyed. Shakespeare "knew that Rome, like every other city, had men of all dispositions; and wanting a buffoon, he went into the senate-house for that which the senate-house would certainly have afforded him." Of Shakespeare's violation of the dramatic unities of time and place, Johnson offers here a far more sustained defense. Unity of action is all-important in drama, as Aristotle's *Poetics* had shown, but later critics, with a servile literalism, required that plots be confined to one place and the duration of performance be kept equal to the duration of the action. With a masterly irony, Johnson turns these expectations against themselves: "The objection arising from the impossibility of passing the first hour at Alexandria and the next at Rome supposes that when the play opens the spectator really imagines himself at Alexandria and believes that his walk to the theater has been a voyage to Egypt, and that he lives in the days of Antony and Cleopatra. Surely he that imagines this may imagine more." This exuberance of wit enlarges the prospects of life by grasping the purpose of the conventions of art. Rarely can it be said that a single argument has exploded an aesthetic fallacy, but Johnson's attack did in fact decisively weaken the faith in the neoclassical unities. It was a generous exertion of understanding in the cause of imagination.

Johnson wrote from a reverence for experience, which he prized above art. His criticism is remarkable — in a way unmatched by any writer before or since — for a stubborn distrust of artifice. He despised all pastoral, which he ridiculed wherever the chance arose, not stinting the ultimate test in a dry disparagement of Milton's pastoral elegy "Lycidas," a poem that combines sincere emotion with the luxury of fiction in a manner that Johnson finds "easy, vulgar, and therefore disgusting." He scorns erudition when it does not add to the possible store of available experience. "Life," he says in the *Rambler,* "is surely given us for higher purposes than to gather what our ancestors have wisely thrown away, and to learn what is of no value, but because it has been forgotten." Similarly all readers are too apt to believe what they read, including opinions they would never credit without the signature that gains them a hearing. Even in a polite and learned age, a writer may "let loose his invention, and heat his mind with incredibilities," and enjoy success as a maker of books "without knowledge of nature, or acquaintance with life."

A critic with so pronounced a piety toward nature and experience might be expected to value history and biography over poetry and drama. Yet Johnson kept up a rueful sympathy with "that hunger of imagination which preys incessantly upon life." He would have readers cherish the knowledge they gain from fiction, while knowing that it is fiction. This requires, in turn, an awareness of the distance that separates works of art from reality — a distance liable to contract under the pressure of depicted actions that are possible and deeply disturbing. More than most readers, Johnson was a prey to violent imaginings. When he encountered a scene in a work of art (however exalted) that conveyed a sudden excess of violence, he felt that a trespass had been committed beyond his powers of assimilation. He concurred with the approval given in the eighteenth century to the happy ending of *King Lear* that had been introduced during the Restoration. "And," he says in his notes on the play, "if my sensations could add anything to the general suffrage, I might relate, I was many years ago so shocked by Cordelia's death that I know not whether I ever endured to read again the last scenes of the play till I undertook to revise them as an editor." We commonly distrust a story that we think too good to be true. Johnson warns against the fascination of a story so painful it can only be believed at a cost to feelings of humanity.

The writing he cares for, Johnson tells us in *The Vanity of Human Wishes,* comes out of observation tempered by fellow-feeling. So the genuine writer must

Remark each anxious toil, each eager strife,
And watch the busy scenes of crowded life;
Then say how hope and fear, desire and hate,
O'erspread with snares the clouded maze of fate.

It seemed to Johnson a natural necessity of human beings to seek a reflected glory in things associated with themselves. All of his writings, from the verse satire *The Vanity of Human Wishes* to the oriental tale *Rasselas* to the private letters and prayers, are a summons to fight against this vanity, which, Johnson asserts, is natural, is human, and is everywhere to be resisted. It becomes so constant a theme with him that a tactical reminder may crop up in the middle of advice about prose. "Read over your compositions, and whenever you meet with a passage which you think is particularly fine, strike it out." And yet he knows that illusions give to life a clothing of belief, without which desire and exertion are unimaginable; and when the illusions comfort, and do not foster a selfish greed of aggrandizement, they are not to be tampered with.

In his tour of the Western islands, Johnson encountered the venerable minister of Col, and he later wrote of their meeting: "I honored his orthodoxy, and did not much censure his asperity. A man who has settled his opinions, does not love to have the tranquility of his conviction disturbed; and at seventy-seven, it is time to be in earnest." Johnson did not always treat himself with the same tenderness. "For many reasons," he remarks in the *Rambler,* "a man writes much better than he lives." Though true in general, the axiom is not true of him. Johnson wrote as he lived.

Samuel Johnson

From the Life of
Jonathan Swift

The person of Swift had not many recommendations. He had a kind of muddy complexion, which, though he washed himself with oriental scrupulosity, did not look clear. He had a countenance sour and severe, which he seldom softened by any appearance of gaiety. He stubbornly resisted any tendency to laughter.

To his domestics he was naturally rough; and a man of rigorous temper, with that vigilance of minute attention which his works discover, must have been a master that few could bear. That he was disposed to do his servants good on important occasions is no great mitigation; benefaction can be but rare, and tyrannic peevishness is perpetual. He did not spare the servants of others. Once, when he dined alone with the Earl of Orrery, he said, of one that waited in the room, "That man, since we sat to the table, committed fifteen faults." What the faults were Lord Orrery, from whom I heard the story, had not been attentive enough to discover. My number may perhaps not be exact.

In his economy he practiced a peculiar and offensive parsimony, without disguise or apology. The practice of saving being once necessary, became habitual, and grew first ridiculous, and at last detestable. But his avarice, though it might exclude pleasure, was never suffered to encroach upon his virtue. He was frugal by inclination, but liberal by principle; and if the purpose to which he destined his little accumulations be remembered, with his distribution of occasional charity, it will perhaps appear that he only liked one mode of expense better than another, and saved merely that he might have something to give. He did not grow rich by injuring his successors, but left both Laracor and the Deanery more valuable than he found them.

With all this talk of his covetousness and generosity, it should be remembered that he was never rich. The revenue of his Deanery was not much more than seven hundred a year. His beneficence was not graced with tenderness or civility; he relieved without pity, and assisted without kindness; so that those who were fed by him could hardly love him. He made a rule to himself to give but one piece at a time, and therefore always stored his pocket with coins of different value. Whatever he did, he seemed willing to do in a manner peculiar to himself, without sufficiently considering that singularity, as it implies a contempt of the general practice, is a kind of defiance which justly provokes the hostility of ridicule; he, therefore, who indulges peculiar habits is worse than others, if he be not better.

·····:¦:·····

One of his favorite topics is contempt of his own poetry. For this, if it had been real, he would deserve no commendation, and in this he certainly was not sincere; for his high value of himself was sufficiently observed, and of what could he be proud but of his poetry? He writes, he says, when "he just has nothing else to do"; yet Swift complains that he was never at leisure for conversation because he "had always some poetical scheme in his head." It was punctually required that his writing box should be set upon his bed before he rose; and Lord Oxford's domestic related that, in the dreadful winter of forty, she was called from her bed by him four times in one night to supply him with paper, lest he should lose a thought.

He pretends insensibility to censure and criticism, though it was observed by all who knew him that every pamphlet disturbed his quiet, and that his extreme irritability laid him open to perpetual vexation; but he wished to despise his critics, and therefore hoped that he did despise them.

As he happened to live in two reigns when the Court paid little attention to poetry he nursed in his mind a foolish disesteem of kings, and proclaims that "he never sees Courts." Yet a little regard shown him by the Prince of Wales melted his obduracy, and he had not much to say when he was asked by his Royal Highness "how he could love a Prince while he disliked Kings?"

He very frequently professes contempt of the world, and represents himself as looking on mankind, sometimes with gay indifference, as on emmets of a hillock below his serious attention, and sometimes with gloomy indignation, as on monsters more worthy of hatred than of pity. These were dispositions apparently counterfeited. How could he despise those whom he lived by pleasing, and on whose approbation his esteem of himself was superstructed? Why should he hate those to whose favor he owed his honor and his ease? Of things that terminate in human life the world is the proper judge: to despise its sentence, if it were possible, is not just; and if it were just is not possible. . . .

Of his intellectual character the constituent and fundamental principle was good sense, a prompt and intuitive perception of consonance and propriety.

He saw immediately, of his own conceptions, what was to be chosen, and what to be rejected; and, in the works of others, what was to be shunned, and what was to be copied.

But good sense alone is a sedate and quiescent quality, which manages its possessions well, but does not increase them; it collects few materials for its own operations, and preserves safety, but never gains supremacy. Pope had likewise genius; a mind active, ambitious, and adventurous, always investigating, always aspiring; in its widest searches still longing to go forward, in its highest flights still wishing to be higher; always imagining something greater than it knows, always endeavoring more than it can do.

To assist these powers he is said to have had great strength and exactness of memory. That which he had heard or read was not easily lost; and he had before him not only what his own meditation suggested, but what he had found in other writers that might be accommodated to his present purpose.

These benefits of nature he improved by incessant and unwearied diligence; he had recourse to every source of intelligence, and lost no opportunity of information; he consulted the living as well as the dead; he read his compositions to his friends, and was never content with mediocrity when excellence could be attained. He considered poetry as the business of his life, and, however he might seem to lament his occupation, he followed it with constancy: to make verses was his first labor, and to mend them was his last.

····:····

In the character of his "Elegy" I rejoice to concur with the common reader; for by the common sense of readers uncorrupted with literary prejudices, after all the refinements of subtlety and the dogmatism of learning, must be finally decided all claim to poetical honors. The "Churchyard" abounds with images which find a mirror in every mind, and with sentiments to which every bosom returns an echo. The four stanzas beginning "Yet even these bones" are to me original: I have never seen the notions in any other place; yet he that reads them here persuades himself that he has always felt them. Had Gray written often thus, it had been vain to blame, and useless to praise him.

From the Life of
Thomas Gray

Edward Gibbon

BY DAVID WOMERSLEY

On February 18, 1776, Horace Walpole wrote to William Mason with the latest literary news from London: "Lo, there is just appeared a truly classic work.... This book is Mr. Gibbon's *The History of the Decline and Fall of the Roman Empire.* He is son of a late foolish alderman, is a member of Parliament, and called a whimsical one because he votes as variously as his opinion leads him.... I know him a little, never suspected the extent of his talents, for he is perfectly modest ... but I intend to know him a great deal more."

This is a cruelly abbreviated, although not actually misleading, account of Gibbon's life until the publication in 1776 of the first volume of the work that would establish his literary reputation, *The History of the Decline and Fall of the Roman Empire.* Born in 1737 into a gentry family of slowly subsiding affluence, Gibbon was educated at Westminster and Oxford, but was forced to leave the university after an impulsive conversion to Roman Catholicism in 1753. An enforced residence of nearly five years with a Calvinist pastor in Lausanne rectified Gibbon's religious opinions, and on his return to England in 1758 he divided his time between London and the main family estate in Hampshire, with a precious interval of European travel between January 1763 and June 1765. He entered the House of Commons in 1774, thanks to the interest of a kinsman, and published *opuscula* in 1761 and 1770. So, as Walpole implied in his letter to Mason, there was nothing in Gibbon's earlier existence which hinted that he would suddenly blaze forth as one of the few truly great historians of western civilization. Yet, as we shall see, unexpectedness was not just a characteristic of Gibbon's achievement: it was also its essence.

For instance, had any historian before Gibbon expended literary talent of this quality on a minor North African playboy?

His manners [those of the Younger Gordian] were less pure, but his character was equally amiable with that of his father. Twenty-two acknowledged concubines, and a library of sixty-two thousand volumes, attested the variety of his inclinations; and from the productions which he left behind him, it appears that the former as well as the latter were designed for use rather than for ostentation.

It is a passage meant to be read and then re-read, for the final clause, having detonated

Gibbon was born on May 8, 1737, in Putney, Surrey, England. He died in London on January 16, 1794.

the joke, sends the reader back to the beginning to see quite how such a subtly indecent rabbit has been pulled out of the unlikely hat of the provincial politics of late antiquity. Once the passage has been re-read in the light of knowledge of where it ends up, it is clear that Gibbon's careful choice of language is accompanied by a lubricious whisper almost from the outset. "Amiable" announces that Gordian had a gentle and pleasing quality of heart, but because of its etymology it also introduces a hint of love, which ripens with alarming speed into libertinism under the warming influence of our knowledge that the son's manners were "less pure" than those of his father. "*Equally* amiable with that of his father": but not therefore or necessarily *identically* so. The spread of meaning in "amiable" (a word capable of spanning the poles of innocence and experience) allows the very different behavior of the continent father and the promiscuous son to shelter behind a common adjective. As we move onward, "acknowledged" raises the possibility of still further *un*acknowledged concubines, while "the variety of his inclinations" urbanely captures that ethical sophistication which can see both literary and sexual hunger as enthusiasms equally appropriate for a polite and well-bred man. The equivocation between sex and letters is prolonged by "productions," which covers both books and children, and is then given a final, energetic, twist by the concluding words: "… it appears that the former as well as the latter were designed for use rather than for ostentation." That books should be for use rather than for ostentation seems right. Earlier in the century had not Pope satirized those who displayed books rather than studying their contents?

In Books, not Authors, curious is my Lord;
To all their dated Backs he turns you round,
These Aldus printed, those Du Suëil has bound.
Lo, some are Vellom, and the rest as good
For all his Lordship knows, but they are Wood.
(Alexander Pope, "Epistle to Burlington," ll.134–38)

If utility is a good principle to follow when we are thinking about books, then why not when we are thinking about women? Such is the unsettling question Gibbon mischievously and implicitly poses. Like the best wit, this writing does not simply collude with its readers. Gibbon initially creates a mood of accommodating and unthreatening amusement ("we are all men of the world"), only in the end to make his reader glimpse the brutal premise sheltering within that cultivated worldliness. It is a startling thought, which edges with shadow the passage's urbane comedy.

The virtues of this style were not confined to the coining of aphorisms and the venting of a mild prurience. It leant itself equally to the encapsulation of penetrating insights into the dynamics of human progress:

The value of money has been settled by general consent to express our wants and our property; as letters were invented to express our ideas; and both these institutions, by giving a more active energy to the powers and passions of human nature, have contributed to multiply the objects they were designed to represent.

The perception of unexpected congruity and the elegantly compressed rendition of that perception, are qualities of style common to both the incidental remark on Gordian, and this more substantial historical insight into the affinities between currency and language. The example of Gibbon's prose obliges us to think of the historian's style, not as a mere vehicle for historical understanding, but as itself a — perhaps even, ultimately, *the* — means whereby the finest shades of historical understanding are first grasped and then placed before a readership.

"The style of an author should be the image of his mind." After the successful completion of *The Decline and Fall,* and while composing *Memoirs of My Life* in the early 1790s, Gibbon's experience as an author prompted him to place style at the very center of things. As befits a comment on style, it is in itself a stylish remark, and (as is again often the case with stylishness) on inspection, it turns out to be a measured adjustment of something pre-existing. The great eighteenth-century French naturalist Georges-Louis Leclerc, comte de Buffon — whom Gibbon had met in Paris in 1777, whose works he owned, and whom he quotes with approval in both *The Decline and Fall* and *Memoirs of My Life* — had also linked style and personality in a dictum which it is easy to imagine stirring within Gibbon's memory when he cast his own sense of the relation between life and writing into words: "Le style, c'est l'homme même." Gibbon shackled the sweep of Buffon's aphorism in two ways. In the first place, he made the linkage between style and author less automatic, less a question of identity and more a matter of process or aspiration: "*should be* the image . . ." Gibbon knew that style might lapse into insignificance — that one could not simply count on language taking the impress of thought. Secondly, whereas Buffon expansively bestowed on style the power to capture nothing less than "l'homme même," Gibbon confined its powers to the figuring of "mind." (In an earlier draft of his autobiography, Gibbon had been closer to Buffon when he wrote that "style is the image of character,

and the habits of correct writing may produce, without labour or design, the appearances of art and study.") Nevertheless, and even when the aphorism is so restricted, quite how style might be an image of mind is not made absolutely clear. And in fact over the length of *The Decline and Fall* Gibbon moved between two different ways in which style might be an image of mind: first, as the crystallization of a quality of intellection or outlook; secondly, as the intimate trace of that process of thought whereby the historian's mind digests and gives shape to the mere material of information.

In his *Memoirs* Gibbon went on to take us into his confidence over how the style of *The Decline and Fall* was forged: "the choice and command of language is the fruit of exercise; many experiments were made before I could hit the middle tone between a dull Chronicle and a Rhetorical declamation; three times did I compose the first chapter, and twice the second and third, before I was tolerably satisfied with their effect." Two emphases here are crucial. First, that the mastery of style is the consequence of repeated labor. It is a principle illustrated, happily enough, by the example from *The Decline and Fall* with which we began, and which in the first and second editions of the history had read, "both the one and the other were designed for use rather than for ostentation." In the third edition, Gibbon's fastidious ear rejected that awkward cluster of five monosyllables.

The second important emphasis is that the historical style is a hybrid, pitched halfway between the blankness of chronicle and the vapidity of declamation. Gibbon suspended his prose between the poles of mere material and mere stylishness, because historical style is produced by the interaction of material and

treatment. Style marks the point where the historian meets his subject. As a young man of twenty-five, Gibbon seems to have understood that this is what style in history had to be, since he deplored the absence of it even in the most glamorous literary figure of his age: "when he [Voltaire] treats of a distant period, he is not a man to turn over musty monkish writers to instruct himself. He follows some compilation, varnishes it over with the magick of his style, and produces a most agreable, superficial, inacu-rate [sic] performance." Style as varnish, as an alluring coating designed to conceal the deficiencies of what lies beneath: this, Gibbon already knew in 1762, was not the model to follow. As a historian, it was his great achievement to immerse himself in "musty monkish writers" and yet to present the fruits of that immersion in prose untainted by the mustiness of its sources. No other English historian before Gibbon would have been prepared to lavish on so trivial a figure as the Younger

Gordian a series of remarks as well-turned as those that launched this essay. Despite lending itself to being misread as mere witticism, that passage in fact shows Gibbon doing something properly historiographical: retrieving an historical character, and embalming it in language.

Gibbon had not always possessed even competence in English. Following his conversion to Catholicism in March 1753, he had been sent to Lausanne by his exasperated and enraged father to recover good sense and true religion at the hands of a Calvinist minister, Daniel Pavilliard. The expedient was a great success, as Gibbon would eventually acknowledge: "Such as I am, in Genius or learning or manners, I owe my creation to Lausanne: it was in that school, that the statue was discovered in the block of marble; and my own religious folly, my father's blind resolution, produced the effects of the most deliberate wisdom." But the price of this rescue from the shipwreck of his adolescence, the toll exacted by the discovery of the statue within the block, was paradoxically a loss of identity. After five years in the Pays de Vaud, Gibbon was more at ease in French than in his native language. As a result, he "had ceased to be an Englishman." On his return home in 1758, that estrangement from his native language was repaired by a course of well-chosen reading:

The favourite companions of my leisure were our English writers since the Revolution; they breathe the spirit of reason and liberty, and they most seasonably contributed to restore the purity of my own language, which had been corrupted by the use of a foreign Idiom. By the judicious advice of Mr. Mallet, I was directed to the writings of Swift and Addison: wit and simplicity are their common attributes; but the style of Swift is supported by manly original vigour; that of Addison is adorned by the female graces of elegance and mildness....

Swift and Addison: one Tory, the other Whig; one an embittered exile from the sources of power and influence, the other a worldly success; one manly, the other female; one vigorous, the other mild. Yet we can see their joint influence in the passage on the Younger Gordian. The extended equivocation between passions and productivity both literary and sexual is an instance of Addison's definition of "true wit" as "a Resemblance and Congruity of Ideas ... that gives *Delight* and *Surprize* to the Reader" (*Spectator,* no. 62). The final turn to unsettle the reader recalls the vigor of Swift's style, which so often involves just such a repudiation of any alliance between author and readership. Furthermore, the epicene style that Swift and Addison might produce together looks forward to the hybridity that eventually satisfied the mature Gibbon. And to discover that genealogy in Gibbon's style also encourages us to see how stylistic impurity might be the signature of intellectual independence. It might signal to its readership a freedom from merely partisan attachments.

Gibbon's own judgment on how his command of style changed over the years of composition of the three installments of *The Decline and Fall* (1776, 1781, and 1788) tells of a development that got slightly out of hand: "The style of the first Volume is, in my opinion, somewhat crude and elaborate; in the second and third it is ripened into ease, correctness, and numbers; but in the three last I may have been seduced by the facility of my pen." "Crude and elaborate" is surely an overly harsh evaluation of the style of the first volume, although in the trace of inflexible and self-conscious mannerism in that style we can perhaps see what Gibbon is driving at. The characteristic irony of Gibbon's early style is attractive to us, not only because of the humor that it delivers, but because of the reassurance it provides. It is the prose of a man secure in the possession of his own principles of judgment, and sufficiently confident to feel no need to broadcast them. However, this security might shade into a historiographic weakness. Do we not want our historians to be sensitive to the past they describe, and might not a condition of that sympathetic description be the possibility of laying aside, even if only temporarily and as an heuristic strategy, the historian's own principles and standards of judgment?

If so, then we might look with more indulgence than did Gibbon on the consequences of the "facility" of the pen that overtook his style in the final installment of *The Decline and Fall*. Here, for instance, is Gibbon's account of how Greek learning came to Italy. It is therefore an account of how a vital link in the chain of literary transmission from antiquity to the modern world came to be forged — vital to, amongst other things, the subsequent possibility of writing *The Decline and Fall* itself:

... the restoration of the Greek letters in Italy was prosecuted by a series of emigrants, who were destitute of fortune, and endowed with learning, or at least with language. From the terror or oppression of the Turkish arms, the natives of Thessalonica and Constantinople escaped to a land of freedom, curiosity, and wealth. ... In the shipwreck of the Byzantine libraries, each fugitive seized a fragment of treasure, a copy of some author, who, without his industry, might have perished: the transcripts were multiplied by an assiduous, and sometimes an elegant pen; and the text was corrected and explained by their own comments, or those of the older scholiasts.

This is a less showy, more diffuse, style than that in which Gibbon had celebrated the various inclinations of the Younger Gordian. Yet it has its own strengths and achievements. The word "industry," for instance, seems an odd one to apply to what was surely a hurried act of seizure. However, that word gently reminds us that it was the commercial energies of Byzantium — for which that civilization was routinely castigated by many of Gibbon's less imaginative and subtle contemporaries — that ensured the survival into the modern world of the literature of ancient Greece.

Gibbon's genius as a historian and as a writer was connected with his eventual readiness to go outside the palisade of irony and to lay aside the bejeweled style with which his irony had become associated. He entered into the fullest possession of his literary character when he no longer resisted the seductive lure of the strange, the surprising, the paradoxical — and the pen.

Edward Gibbon

On his return from the East to Rome, Philip, desirous of obliterating the memory of his crimes, and of captivating the affections of the people, solemnised the secular games with infinite pomp and magnificence. Since their institution or revival by Augustus, they had been celebrated by Claudius, by Domitian, and by Severus, and were now renewed the fifth time, on the accomplishment of the full period of a thousand years from the foundation of Rome. Every circumstance of the secular games was skilfully adapted to inspire the superstitious mind with deep and solemn reverence. The long interval between them exceeded the term of human life; and as none of the spectators had already seen them, none could flatter themselves with the expectation of beholding them a second time. The mystic sacrifices were performed, during three nights, on the banks of the Tiber; and the Campus Martius resounded with music and dances, and was illuminated with innumerable lamps and torches. . . . The magnificence of Philip's shows and entertainments dazzled the eyes of the multitude. The devout were employed in the rites of superstition, whilst the reflecting few revolved in their anxious minds the past history and the future fate of the empire.

Since Romulus, with a small band of shepherds and outlaws, fortified himself on the hills near the Tiber, ten centuries had already elapsed. During the first four ages, the Romans, in the laborious school of poverty, had acquired the virtues of war and government: by the vigorous exertion of those virtues, and by the assistance of fortune, they had obtained, in the course of the three succeeding centuries, an absolute empire over many countries of Europe, Asia, and Africa. The last three hundred years had been consumed in apparent prosperity and internal decline. The nation of soldiers, magistrates, and legislators, who composed the thirty-five tribes of the Roman people, was dissolved into the common mass of mankind, and confounded with the millions of servile provincials, who had received the name, without adopting the spirit, of Romans. A mercenary army, levied amongst the subjects and barbarians of

From The Decline and Fall of the Roman Empire, *chapter* 7

the frontier, was the only order of men who preserved and abused their independence. By their tumultuary election, a Syrian, a Goth, or an Arab, was exalted to the throne of Rome, and invested with despotic power over the conquests and over the country of the Scipios.

The limits of the Roman empire still extended from the Western Ocean to the Tigris, and from Mount Atlas to the Rhine and the Danube. To the undiscerning eye of the vulgar, Philip appeared a monarch no less powerful than Hadrian or Augustus had formerly been. The form was still the same, but the animating health and vigour were fled. The industry of the people was discouraged and exhausted by a long series of oppression. The discipline of the legions, which alone, after the extinction of every other virtue, had propped the greatness of the state, was corrupted by the ambition, or relaxed by the weakness, of the emperors. The strength of the frontiers, which had always consisted in arms rather than in fortifications, was insensibly undermined; and the fairest provinces were left exposed to the rapaciousness or ambition of the barbarians, who soon discovered the decline of the Roman empire.

····:|:····

From The Decline and Fall of the Roman Empire, *chapter 71*

But the clouds of barbarism were gradually dispelled; and the peaceful authority of Martin the Fifth and his successors restored the ornaments of the city as well as the order of the ecclesiastical state. The improvements of Rome, since the fifteenth century, have not been the spontaneous produce of freedom and industry. The first and most natural root of a great city is the labour and populousness of the adjacent country, which supplies the materials of subsistence, of manufactures, and of foreign trade. But the greater part of the Campagna of Rome is reduced to a dreary and desolate wilderness: the overgrown estates of the princes and the clergy are cultivated by the lazy hands of indigent and hopeless vassals; and the scanty harvests are confined or exported for the benefit of a monopoly. A second and more artificial cause of the growth of a metropolis, is the residence of a monarch, the expense of a luxurious court, and the tributes of dependent provinces. Those provinces and tributes had been lost in the fall of the empire; and if some streams of the silver of Peru and the gold of Brazil have been attracted by the Vatican, the revenues of the cardinals, the fees of office, the oblations of pilgrims and clients, and the remnant of ecclesiastical taxes, afford a poor and precarious supply, which maintains however the idleness of the court and city. The population of Rome, far below the measure of the great capitals of Europe, does not exceed one hundred and seventy thousand inhabitants; and within the spacious enclosure of the walls, the largest portion of the seven hills is overspread with vineyards and ruins. . . . The map, the description, the monuments of ancient Rome, have been elucidated by the diligence of the antiquarian and the student; and the footsteps of heroes, the relics, not of superstition, but of empire, are devoutly visited by a new race of pilgrims from the remote, and once savage, countries of the North.

Of these pilgrims, and of every reader, the attention will be excited by an history of the decline and fall of the Roman empire; the greatest, perhaps, and most awful scene in the history of mankind. The various causes and progressive effects are connected with many of the events most interesting in human annals: the artful policy of the Caesars, who long maintained the name and image of a free republic; the disorders of military despotism; the rise, establishment, and sects of Christianity; the foundation of Constantinople; the division of the monarchy; the invasion and settlements of the barbarians of Germany and Scythia; the institutions of the civil law; the character and religion of Mahomet; the temporal sovereignty of the popes; the restoration and decay of the Western empire of Charlemagne; the crusades of the Latins in the East; the conquests of the Saracens and Turks; the ruin of the Greek empire; the state and revolutions of Rome in the middle age. The historian may applaud the importance and variety of his subject; but, while he is conscious of his own imperfections, he must often accuse the deficiency of his materials. It was among the ruins of the Capitol that I first conceived the idea of a work which has amused and exercised near twenty years of my life, and which, however inadequate to my own wishes, I finally deliver to the curiosity and candour of the public.

William Wordsworth

BY DAN JACOBSON

Readers of Wordsworth's work are likely to think of him first as a nature poet, or a narrative poet, or a philosophical and reflective poet, or a poet of rural life. Many admirers value him also as a lyricist and sonneteer, or even as a political and patriotic poet. Obviously these categories are not exclusive of one another; some of his poems can be classified in several at once,

or can be moved from one to another with repeated readings. Early in his career he also was considered to be a strikingly "egotistical" and self-absorbed poet — the first of these adjectives being used about him most famously, though by no means uniquely, by the young John Keats. (In a letter to Richard Woodhouse, Keats distinguished between his own character as a poet — "unpoetical" he called it — and the "wordsworthian or egotistical sublime.") Surprisingly, perhaps, Wordsworth himself came close to acknowledging in a letter to a friend that something of this sort could justly be said about him. Referring to the epically long, unfinished autobiographical poem that became known after his death as *The Prelude*, he wrote that it was "unparalleled in literary history that a man should talk so much about himself," which suggests not only a degree of self-knowledge but some self-satisfaction, too.

As a quality of mind and character his "egotism" actually lies at the heart of much of

his greatest verse, as I hope to show shortly. I want, however, to add here one more descriptive term to those mentioned earlier. It is a word that I do not recall seeing used about Wordsworth's verse elsewhere and one for which I have not found a plausible alternative. I want to suggest that Wordsworth was also a peculiarly *physiological* poet. By this I mean that his sensibility was peculiarly alert to those physical processes that precede all thinking and without which thinking cannot take place. He is the poet of the autonomic nervous system: the spinal cord, the digestive tract, the circulation of the blood, the conditioned reflex. It follows that he is also a poet who celebrates our capacity to take notice of things without any consciousness that we are doing so and to retain them in the memory without our knowing that they await us there. At one point in *The Prelude* he writes that his "theme has been / What passed within me," as if his "me," his conscious, reflective self, is not the initiator of the activities he has been writing

Wordsworth was born on April 7, 1770, in Cockermouth, Cumberland, England. He died in Rydal Mount, Westmorland, England, on April 23, 1850.

about but rather the site or vessel within which they take place. In the same passage he says that his "theme" is "far hidden from the reach of words" — which implies that he has to do more than find some approximate, verbal mode of representing what is going on within him. Rather, he goes on to say, his task is to "make / *Breathings* for incommunicable powers" (my emphasis).

The use of the word "breathings" at that point is typical of the language — part metaphorical, part literal — that Wordsworth uses when referring to and exploring these subliminal areas of experience. Breathing is an activity we ordinarily perform without noticing what we are doing, though any interruption of it will remind us sharply that our lives depend on it. The same is true of "drinking," a word that Wordsworth uses in a variety of contexts and that he applies not just to the slaking of thirst but to the inducing of such states as pleasure, calm, "visionary power." "Feeding" and "flowing" also recur (the latter used to evoke, among other things, both the movement and the "suspension" of blood in the veins). "Trance" or "trances" recur, too, figuring in each case not as a doorway to the supernatural but, on the contrary, as a description of moods of heightened receptivity to "the very world which is the world / Of all of us." This is a poet who listens not only to his own voice but more significantly to the "internal echo of the imperfect sound" — the suggestion here plainly being that the inaudible, internal voice is the more "perfect" of the two. Like his own Cumberland Beggar ("seeing still / And never

He is also a poet who celebrates our capacity to take notice of things without any consciousness that we are doing so and to retain them in the memory without our knowing that they await us there.

knowing that he sees"), or the suckling infant at the breast "*drinking* passion from his mother's eye" (my emphasis), he is in some ways most open to whatever is around him when his attention appears to be in abeyance.

In fact, in book 1 of *The Prelude,* he describes how he arrives at the subject of his greatest poem inadvertently, in the midst of chiding himself for having got nowhere with the ambitions to write an epic poem that have beguiled him for so many years, and for thus failing to live up to the promise and happiness of his childhood. A single disappointed yet ecstatic recollection of that time of his life ("Was it for this / That one, the fairest of all rivers . . . / . . . sent a voice / That flowed along my dreams?") is followed rapidly by a succession of other such memories — all of them bringing him to realize that the epic theme he has been searching for will never be that of the founding of a nation or empire, to which traditional epics have been devoted, but to the story of his own *Bildung* ("the growth of a poet's mind"). Thereafter "the road lies plain" before him.

William Hazlitt, who had been among the first to take note of the "egotism" of Wordsworth, both as a personality and as a poet, wrote admiringly of him that he was someone who "contemplates the passions and habits of man not in their extremes but in the first elements." To schematize Wordsworth's mode of contemplating and employing in his verse those "first elements" is to falsify it; nevertheless it is useful to think of him making articulate three

distinct levels of human awareness. The most basic is Hazlitt's "first elements," which are the same for all men and women, though they manifest themselves differently within each individual. Since they are beyond "the reach of words," they cannot be articulated by direct assault; such elements can be brought into the light of day only through the creation of particular poetic and narrative contexts for them — which means in effect the depicting of places, incidents, emotions, persons (the poet himself among them, often enough), and what Wordsworth characteristically calls "the fluxes and refluxes of the mind." It is in the creation of contexts like these that all the resources of language have to come into play: metaphor, rhythm, rhyme (in some cases), and the many varieties of poetic form not least among them. The overall effect is to interfuse the first level of experience with the second and thus to communicate what would otherwise remain incommunicable. Once that has been done, Wordsworth often feels himself compelled to continue this process of moral hydraulics by drawing his verse toward a third,

yet "higher" level of meaning; and it is here that he not infrequently topples over into didacticism, into trying to present a considered, established, and universally applicable worldview. In his anxiety to "rectify men's feelings" (as he wrote in another letter), he comes uncomfortably close to formulating rules for living, an ambition directly at odds with the passion and tentativeness that mark his writing about and within the first two levels.

These considerations are closely related to Wordsworth's preoccupation with boundaries and margins of all kinds, a feature of his verse on which several critics have commented. Knowing from experience (sometimes almost to the point of despair) just how fixed and unyielding boundaries can appear to be, he knows also that the more closely any boundary is looked at the more fluid and deceptive it can either promise or threaten to become. (As the philosopher Ludwig Wittgenstein put it: "In order to set a boundary to thought, one has to think on both sides of the boundary.") He sees such boundaries and their literally infinite number of possible crossing-points wherever he turns his gaze. Many of them lie of course within himself: between sleep and wakefulness; memory and forgetfulness; compassion and indifference; energy and sloth; thought, emotion, and whatever is below them both; the past as it was when it was present and as it now exists in his memory; the unimaginable future in which what he has now forgotten will return to haunt him.

And outside himself? There too countless distinctions are to be made and unmade. Between himself and all other humans, for example. Between all humans as a class and other speechless forms of existence — some seemingly insentient (trees, rocks, lesser celandines), others unmistakably sentient (dogs, sheep, birds). Between all that lives and dies and that which has never been alive. Between his own singular species, which is conscious of its mortality, and the innumerable creatures that are spared that fate. Hence, on this last point, the fascination that outcast figures like tramps, discharged soldiers, "old men travelling," leech-gatherers and other such folk have for him. About Wordsworth's attitude to these people there is nothing Oxfam-like: he cannot take his eyes off them, he wants them to remain just as they are, and he finds various specious excuses why busybodies and do-gooders should leave them alone in their uncomplaining weakness and incomprehension, so that he can continue to marvel at their tottering, hovering existence between the two incommensurate worlds they simultaneously appear to inhabit.

It is in responding to Wordworth's treatment of topics like these that one can most clearly discern how "positive" an element in his verse that famous egotism of his can be.

What relation, he seems constantly to be asking himself, do these lakes and mountains, these trees and monuments of the past, have with *me* — and I with them? Am I not in danger of being crushed by them? By their ignorance of and indifference to me? How can I be so aware of them, so exhilarated and frightened by their variety and solidity, their change and durability, while they, who have such an effect on me, do not even know that I exist? Am I nothing to them, then? If so, why am I so drawn to them, why does their presence or the mere thought of them affect me so greatly? Why don't they respond in kind? Don't they owe me something — an acknowledgment at least, even perhaps a little gratitude? How is it that natural phenomena sometimes appear to have so vivid a life — when clouds move together in the sky or water is ruffled or trees sway or, perhaps most compellingly of all, when they stand motionless, as if in tranquil self-contemplation, and yet also remain mute, incomprehending and incomprehensible, forever beyond my reach? Or does the truth of the matter not lie the other way around: is it not they who would forever remain "in disconnection dead and spiritless" were I not here to wonder at them? In which case it is they who depend on me to give them life and awareness, to speak to them and speak *for* them? More than that, surely I am not deceiving myself at those dizzying moments when I feel that I can take them into myself and transform them, make them me? I eat them, drink them, breathe them; they flow within me; they hear with my ears and see with my eyes; I reflect them as a lake reflects all that is above and around it, myself included, and like a lake I have depth enough within me to receive and contain all that is present to me.

If all this is so — the hidden "argument" of his verse seems to continue — and if I use to the utmost the capacities I have had the good fortune to be endowed with, then in speaking for myself I do so not only for the inanimate and speechless world around me, but also for all other men and women who are not endowed as I am and to whom I am therefore indispensable. For it is precisely through the capacities which mark me out as exceptional, different from them, a true poet, that they will be able to discover everything that makes me representative of them (of them as they should be, anyway). If I manage that, I will truly have proved myself equal in stature to the epic heroes of the past, those whose lives inspired millions to follow them and in so doing enabled the populace at large to see a reflection of itself (again!) in its heroes' lives and achievements.

It may seem anticlimatic (though I doubt that Wordsworth would have thought it so) to add that though he wrote some rhyming poems that will be read as long as English poetry is read by anybody — lyrics like the Lucy poems, narrative poems like "Resolution and Independence," sonnets like "Upon Westminster Bridge" and "Surprised by Joy" — he is in my view at his greatest in his blank verse. (That is, in his own highly distinctive development of the traditional unrhymed iambic pentameter that, via Milton and various minor eighteenth-century pastoralists, came to him from the Elizabethan and Jacobean dramatists.) I am thinking here of *The Prelude,* above all, but also of tales like "Michael" or the story of Margaret from another long unfinished poem, *The Recluse,* as well as of vignettes like "Old Man Travelling," "The Old Cumberland Beggar," and poems of recollection and reaffirmation like "Tintern Abbey."

It seems that the essentially frame-like nature of rhyme, its manner of continually creating expectations and then fulfilling them at appropriate moments, would have cut across the expression of some of Wordworth's deepest gifts and compulsions as a poet. Rhyme is a source of strength and aesthetic pleasure for poet and reader alike, but not if the poet seeks constantly to both establish and dissolve the contours of his own selfhood at its deepest levels. Not if he moves by a continual probing forward into the dark, with all the caution of a speleologist who never knows when he might suddenly find himself hanging over vertiginous space. Not if his "labour," as he himself writes, in a passage that is not merely "physiological" in its reach, but positively uterine, is to trace "the stream / From darkness, and the very place of birth / In its blind cavern, whence is faintly heard / The sound of waters" — and to follow it "to light / And open day."

William Wordsworth

*"Old Man
Travelling"*

    The little hedge-row birds,
That peck along the road, regard him not.
He travels on, and in his face, his step,
His gait, is one expression; every limb,
His look and bending figure, all bespeak
A man who does not move with pain, but moves
With thought — He is insensibly subdued
To settled quiet: he is one by whom
All effort seems forgotten, one to whom
Long patience has such mild composure given,
That patience now doth seem a thing, of which
He hath no need. He is by nature led
To peace so perfect, that the young behold
With envy, what the old man hardly feels.
— I asked him whither he was bound, and what
The object of his journey; he replied
'Sir! I am going many miles to take
A last leave of my son, a mariner,
Who from a sea-fight has been brought to Falmouth,
And there is dying in a hospital.'

····:····

*The Prelude,
book 1
(1850 version)*

    One summer evening (led by her) I found
A little boat tied to a willow tree
Within a rocky cave, its usual home.
Straight I unloosed her chain, and stepping in
Pushed from the shore. It was an act of stealth
And troubled pleasure, nor without the voice
Of mountain-echoes did my boat move on;
Leaving behind her still, on either side,
Small circles glittering idly in the moon,
Until they melted all into one track

Of sparkling light. But now, like one who rows,
Proud of his skill, to reach a chosen point
With an unswerving line, I fixed my view
Upon the summit of a craggy ridge,
The horizon's utmost boundary, for above
Was nothing but the stars and the grey sky.
She was an elfin pinnace; lustily
I dipped my oars into the silent lake,
And, as I rose upon the stroke, my boat
Went heaving through the water like a swan;
When, from behind that craggy steep till then
The horizon's bound, a huge peak, black and huge,
As if with voluntary power instinct
Upreared its head. I struck and struck again,
And growing still in stature the grim shape
Towered up between me and the stars, and still,
For so it seemed, with purpose of its own
And measured motion like a living thing,
Strode after me. With trembling oars I turned,
And through the silent water stole my way
Back to the covert of the willow tree;
There in her mooring-place I left my bark, —
And through the meadows homeward went, in grave
And serious mood; but after I had seen
That spectacle, for many days, my brain
Worked with a dim and undetermined sense
Of unknown modes of being; o'er my thoughts
There hung a darkness, call it solitude
Or blank desertion. No familiar shapes
Remained, no pleasant images of trees,
Of sea or sky, no colours of green fields;
But huge and mighty forms, that do not live
Like living men, moved slowly through the mind
By day, and were a trouble to my dreams.

Jane Austen

BY HILARY MANTEL

This is England still: occluded sun, dappled fields, hedgerow and shady copse, swollen, sullen raindrops sizzling on summer lawns; this is England and someone owns it. No inch of the countryside lies uncontested. Conservationists plead for it, developers bribe for it. As you cross the border from Surrey into Hampshire, a signboard reads, "Jane Austen's county."

So she is patroness of these lush, promising acres? She had no money to spare, and she was economical with words. She was a spare woman in every sense: no one married her, and she grew lean, and died at forty-two. "The poor young woman," the neighbors called her, as they saw her drag herself around the garden. She's the patroness of those people who stand in corners, who lean against the wall and watch; of those artists who are frugal with their effects. Every joke she makes is a struggle toward seriousness, toward consequence. She wanted to count in the world. She might not object to her name on the sign; might not mind it at all.

In 1809 Jane Austen went to live with her mother and sister in a former bailiff's cottage in the village of Chawton. Despite the literary pilgrims, and the tea-shop industry they have spawned, Chawton is quieter these days. In Jane's time the main road from London ran through the village. When carriages passed at night the cottage-dwellers were shaken in their beds. Occupants of slower conveyances would stare into the house. Just before Jane moved in, the big roadside window was blocked in an attempt to secure privacy. Wide, blank, still unfaded, the brickwork almost invites graffiti. But who would write on Jane Austen's house? We write on her person, of course, and all over her text. Posterity has tugged every draft from under her shrinking fingers. It has written on her body, grinding her skeleton with critical teeth: it has teased out the fiber of the paper between her lines.

Everything should be against her: her short life, the smallness of her oeuvre, the restrictions of her viewpoint. Above all, her fans have given her a bad name: her fans with their faint praise settling like dust on fine china, their camp *petit-point* sensibilities, their retreat into a dimity Neverland where only hearts bleed. Her work has bred, as writing of genius does, whole libraries of imitation: puppets instead of people, *pro forma* plots without ingenuity, dogged

Austen was born on December 16, 1775, in Steventon, Hampshire, England. She died in Winchester, Hampshire, on July 18, 1817.

narratives of wish-fulfillment without the spice of her malice and wit. There is the *ersatz* Jane and there is Jane on the page, acid, crisp, and smart: Jane more short than sweet, with her spiteful eye, her cutting economy of phrase, her gravity concealed by grace.

What keeps her readers constantly attentive is that we can't agree on an interpretation of her novels, or settle them in our mind. Every time you read her, the story seems to be slightly different; you notice a different emphasis, a nuance that had escaped you. Surely this is the definition of genius in a writer: the capacity to make a text that can give and give, a text that is never fully read, a text that goes on multiplying meanings.

In 1814, three years before she died, she described the limits she had chosen for herself: "Three or four families in a country village is the very thing to work upon." She meant, of course, three or four families of country gentry, with their relatives, connections, and visitors and the many interactions and cross-connections between them. Often she takes her characters out of their country setting and sends them to Portsmouth or London or Bath. The single plot is this: a young woman must marry. Who will she marry? Will she make a good choice? She having chosen, will the man comply?

Yet her six major novels are very different from each other. *Northanger Abbey* is an exuberant satire on writers, readers, and their expectations; indeed, a joke about expectations in general. *Sense and Sensibility* is dark, almost a tragedy. Two girls must marry; Elinor is injured

Surely this is the definition of genius in a writer: the capacity to make a text that can give and give, a text that is never fully read, a text that goes on multiplying meanings.

despite her moral poise and discernment, but her sister Marianne, vulnerable and generous-hearted, suffers far more deeply and seriously than we think this sardonic author will permit. *Pride and Prejudice* is a romance, a high comedy with an underlying note of panic; the dark spiders of ruin and social disgrace scurry across the threads of the narrative. *Mansfield Park* is a problem novel, with its plaintive, unlikeable heroine and its anti-heroine who makes the kind of bad-taste jokes that Jane herself liked to make. *Emma* is a complex farce that subverts sexual stereotypes. It offers an excruciatingly class-conscious and wrong-headed heroine, who appears to be in love with another girl when the story begins. Emma is passionately feminine, and yet she is very bad at what women are supposed to do best — understanding herself and understanding other people. Tact and psychological acuity belong to Mr. Knightly, the father-figure she will marry in the hope of learning from him. Jane's last completed novel, *Persuasion*, is a hushed and autumnal story, with a happy ending fished from the depths for an isolated, strong-minded heroine who had despaired of romance.

Yet *Sanditon,* incomplete at Jane's death, is anything but elegiac; it is a lively, liberal comedy set in a village that is being developed into a health resort and seems startlingly modern both in its preoccupations and the dash and attack of its prose. It is astonishing, people say, that England was at war for most of Austen's lifetime, yet she seldom seems to mention it. But why would she? She wrote for her contem-

poraries, and they knew the facts. It's easy to form a mistaken picture of a whole nation in arms, with only the authoress wilfully shutting her ears to the martial clamor. But consider, how warlike is Mr. Woodhouse? What knightly deeds does Mr. Knightly do? What Austen gives us is a fair picture of an uninvaded island going about its business. After the battle of Albuera in 1811, she wrote to her sister Cassandra, "How horrible it is to have so many people killed! — And what a blessing that one cares for none of them!" She was willing to state what others only think.

Plenty of people were ready to tell her how she should write, to suggest how she could become trite or pious. They wanted sensational incidents, heroines who were pure, obedient yet incredibly unlucky; they wanted her to draw morals and punish the wicked. Instead, she presented them with portraits of foolish fathers, mercenary mamas, feather-headed gold-diggers and doltish gents living on their expectations. Even her heroes and heroines are often not quite what the term should encompass. "Pictures of perfection," she wrote, "make me sick and

wicked." She's subversive of the notion of heroism, in either sex. To see the expectations she inherited, the form and typology she had to subvert, you must look at her early work, wildly parodic and satirical.

As a girl of fourteen, she writes sentences that have the reassuring cadence of her mature self. Only their conclusion startles the reader. Says one character of another, in *Jack and Alice*, "She has many rare and charming qualities, but sobriety is not one of them." *Jack and Alice* takes place in a village called Pammydiddle. Despite the limitation of the locality, one of the women characters is poisoned, one is hanged, and another enters a harem. All female hearts are engaged by one Charles Adams, "an amiable, accomplished and bewitching young man," she says. So far so good with the Austen sentence; then she carelessly adds that he was "of so dazzling a beauty that none but eagles could look him in the face." In Jane's later novels, impetuous girls run out of doors and turn their ankles. In *Jack and Alice*, Charles has a female stalker who treks toward him from wildest Wales and, when in sight of his mansion, is caught in a steel man-trap and breaks a leg.

These early works mocked all the tropes and familiar devices of romance: love at first sight, elopement, mysterious foundlings. They were whimsical stories, but they were ruthless. Application to craft drove whimsy on, until the faun developed muscles like a workhorse and was able to pull the weight of a whole novel. The workhorse became a racehorse; Austen whisks her characters from scene to scene with a comic ferocity, unsparing as they weaken and falter. They are frequently blinkered, clueless about their own feelings, self-deceivers, and the reader watches, half-laughing and half-appalled, as they learn to win or lose. Among writers who specialize in social embarrassment, Austen is the sniggering princess; but the comedy's edge is sharp. An inch beyond the whip-flick of embarrassment lies the terminal cut of social ruin.

If Jane Austen disappointed her contemporaries by not writing sermons and posterity by not describing battles, what is to be said for her? She exercised the liberty of choosing her subject matter — the most basic right that genius demands. When the Prince Regent's librarian wrote to her to suggest she write a romance about the princely house of Coburg, she brushed the suggestion politely aside. There were enough chroniclers of public affairs, she may have felt, and what one could say about public affairs, in an era of censorship, was limited anyway. Working as she did, she was subject only to self-censorship. It was time for someone to write, without constraint, about the constraints of private lives and about the constraints of women's lives in particular: to redefine private life and make it into art.

If the reality of men's lives was hidden from women, so the reality of women's lives was hidden from men. Jane cast a cold eye on the rituals of courtship. The circumspect heart should not pledge itself much above or below its own income group; the clever woman should pretend to need instruction from a man. Says Lady Susan, in the early novel named after her:

> ...to be mistress of French, Italian, German, Music, Singing, Drawing etc. will gain a woman some applause, but will not add one lover to her list.

Jane Austen's novels, as everyone has observed, end at the church door: with the wedding, not the marriage. Jane's private observation did not. She looked about her and saw what marriage meant. "Poor animal," she wrote of a woman too often pregnant, "she will be worn out before she is thirty." Love within a marriage might compensate for what marriage demanded of women — the cyclical facing-down of the risk and pain of childbirth — but the ideal matches Jane sets up for her characters are outnumbered in her fiction by those that are botched together in bad circumstances, contracted in haste, and repented at leisure or simply arranged by cold and grand family interests. Marriage could be a brutal bargain, but what was the alternative? "Single women have a dreadful propensity for being poor," Jane remarked. The unwed became social nullities and, as they grew older, burdens. Says Lydia in *Pride and Prejudice,* "Jane will be quite an old maid soon, I declare! She is almost three and twenty. Lord, how ashamed I should be of not being married before three and twenty."

Lydia chatters; so do other people, opening our ears to machinations previously veiled in the decent obscurity and reticence of English family life. We hear the father-daughter wheedles and manipulations, observe the brute pressure — think of Mrs. Bennet — of feminine ignorance and stupidity; we dwell with tensions, strains, pressures that have not been described before. What is peculiar to Austen's genius is the collusion she enforces on us, the intimacy with her characters; so although her stories are very much of their time and place, they seem to be telling us something tough, enduring, and valuable about how power is negotiated, exercised, yielded. In Austen's books, history is not written by the winners, and society is not described by its overlords. Anne Elliot in *Persuasion* tells us, "Men have had every advantage of us in telling their own story. . . . The pen has been in their hands."

For what have women had to tell? In her essay "Women and Fiction," Virginia Woolf wrote:

Often nothing tangible remains of a woman's day. The food that has been cooked is eaten; the children that have been nursed have gone out into the world. Where does the accent fall? What is the salient point for the novelist to seize upon? It is difficult to say. Her life has an anonymous character which is baffling and puzzling in the extreme.

To the food eaten, to children nursed, one might add the words spoken, for so much of her talk has a phatic, futile quality — "don't do that, dear, put that down" — and so much of it consists of the relayed words of others, as if women were only a series of echo chambers: "So she said to me. . . ." Austen moves freely through what Woolf called the "dark country" of feminine interaction. She knows how to signpost us, how to alert us to the point of change. She is expert at directing our attention. If you call a hero George Knightly, you

are in effect naming him after England's patron saint, George in his glittering armour, whose mission is to save maidens from dragons. He is not likely to fall off his horse. If you call him D'Arcy, you can see the arch of the nostril and the supercilious lift of the brow. This is the easy bit, Jane is saying, I've done that for you. We all know what a painted hero is like. Look over here instead, at what is going on in the corner of the room.

There, two silly girls are whispering on a sofa, or two old women are conspiring. A deck of cards is shuffled; a bored gentleman from town turns over some prints with an enigmatic air. A girl galumphs to the piano and hammers out her party piece: "You have delighted us long enough." Glances are exchanged, glances of flickering, uncertain significance. Married men share gnomic comments about "politics, inclosing land and breaking horses." Two women, stifled and desperate for movement, take a turn about the room, arms linked in a stiff amity. The party breaks up: "The sooner every party breaks up the better." It is one of a string of evenings, all similar — perhaps a little variation in the company, the music. Neighbors visit when the moon is full, to light the road home. Sometimes there is dancing. But nothing *happens*.

Yet in that room something is being negotiated, patiently, exquisitely. It is the English game; it is exactly like the game of cricket, so slow and baffling till you know how to watch it. When nothing seems to be happening, everything is happening. The weather is deteriorating, the pitch is breaking up, one of the players is losing his nerve: his nerve, or hers. Out of this passivity comes activity. Out of what seems mere reactivity, something amazing unfolds. A game is won or lost, at some

moment indiscernible to many spectators. Tacitly, without immediate declaration, a match is made. And the onlookers — men, mostly — stare around in astonishment and ask, "How did that happen?"

These matches, these marriages are not only the hoped-for foundation of private happiness; they are business transactions. It is really surprising that Jane Austen's books are as much about love as about money. She is more likely to introduce you to a family by telling you about their legal affairs than by telling you directly what they hope or fear. She trusts you to tune in to the brute economic facts and understand that what they need is security and what they fear is penury. *Sense and Sensibility* could just as well be called Probate and Probity, and *Pride and Prejudice,* Entails and Entitlement; if, like Mrs. Bennet, the reader does not understand what an entail is, she will soon catch on when

the beneficiary turns up, Mr. Collins smirking fatly on the doorstep and demanding a daughter as the price of forbearing to turn the family into the road.

No one who read it closely was ever comforted by an Austen novel. Jane offers examined lives, placed within a society she has scrutinized. Her project might be called "against illusion." It is to look at the world squarely, knowing that altering it is, essentially, outside your powers. Is the project of scrutiny worthwhile in itself? You could take this lesson from her life and work: grit your teeth and believe that it is. In one of her two attested portraits, she wears what may be an incipient smile: a mere, ambiguous flicker. In the other, she turns her back to the viewer.

It is only genius that can say, make of me what you like.

Jane Austen

He took out his watch: "How long do you think we have been running it from Tetbury, Miss Morland?"

"I do not know the distance." Her brother told her that it was twenty-three miles.

"*Three*-and-twenty!" cried Thorpe; "five-and-twenty if it is an inch." Morland remonstrated, pleaded the authority of road-books, innkeepers, and milestones; but his friend disregarded them all; he had a surer test of distance. "I know it must be five-and-twenty," said he, "by the time we have been doing it. It is now half after one; we drove out of the inn-yard at Tetbury as the town-clock struck eleven; and I defy any man in England to make my horse go less than ten miles an hour in harness; that makes it exactly twenty-five.... Three hours and a half indeed coming only three-and-twenty miles! Look at that creature, and suppose it possible if you can."

"He *does* look very hot to be sure."

"Hot! he had not turned a hair till we came to Walcot Church ... tie his legs and he will get on. What do you think of my gig, Miss Morland? a neat one, is not it? Well-hung; town built; I have not had it a month.... Curricle-hung you see; seat, trunk, sword-case, splashing-board, lamps, silver moulding, all you see complete; the iron-work as good as new, or better."

····:¦····

He was giving orders for a toothpick-case for himself, and till its size, shape, and ornaments were determined, all of which, after examining and debating for a quarter of an hour over every toothpick-case in the shop, were finally arranged by his own inventive fancy, he had no leisure to bestow any other attention on the two ladies, than what was comprised in three or four very broad stares; a kind of notice which served to imprint on Elinor the remembrance of a person and face, of strong, natural, sterling insignificance, though adorned in the first style of fashion....

From Northanger Abbey, *chapter 7*

From Sense and Sensibility, *chapter 33*

At last the affair was decided. The ivory, the gold, and the pearls all received their appointment, and the gentleman having named the last day on which his existence could be continued without the possession of the toothpick-case, drew on his gloves with leisurely care, and bestowing another glance on the Miss Dashwoods, but such a one as seemed rather to demand than express admiration, walked off. . . .

····⋮····

From Pride and Prejudice, *chapter 19*

"My reasons for marrying are, first, that I think it a right thing for every clergyman in easy circumstances (like myself) to set the example of matrimony in his parish. Secondly, that I am convinced it will add very greatly to my happiness; and thirdly — which perhaps I ought to have mentioned earlier, that it is the particular advice and recommendation of the very noble lady whom I have the honour of calling patroness. Twice has she condescended to give me her opinion (unasked too!) on this subject. . . . 'Mr Collins, you must marry. A clergyman like you must marry. — Chuse properly, chuse a gentlewoman for *my* sake, and for your *own*, let her be an active, useful sort of person, not brought up high, but able to make a small income go a good way. This is my advice.'"

····⋮····

From Emma, *chapter 3*

Such another small basin of thin gruel as his own, was all that he could, with thorough self-approbation, recommend, though he might constrain himself, while the ladies were comfortably clearing the nicer things, to say:

"Mrs Bates, let me propose your venturing on one of these eggs. An egg, boiled very soft, is not unwholesome. Serle understands boiling an egg better that any body. I would not recommend an egg boiled by any body else — but you need not be afraid — they are very small, you see — one of our small eggs will not hurt you. Miss Bates, let Emma help you to a *little* bit of tart — a *very* little bit. Ours are all apple tarts. You need not be afraid of unwholesome preserves here. I do not advise the custard. Mrs Goddard, what say you to *half* a glass of wine? A *small* half glass — put into a tumbler of water? I do not think it could disagree with you."

····⋮····

"I am doatingly fond of music — passionately fond. . . . I assure you it has been the greatest satisfaction, comfort, and delight to me, to hear what a musical society I am got into. I absolutely cannot do without music. It is a necessary of life to me; and having always been used to a very musical society, both at Maple Grove and in Bath, it would have been a most serious sacrifice. I honestly said as much to Mr E. when he was speaking of my future home, and expressing his fears lest the retirement of it should be disagreeable; and the inferiority of the house too — knowing what I had been accustomed to — of course he was not wholly without apprehension. When he was speaking of it in that way, I honestly said that *the world* I could give up — parties, balls, plays — for I had no fear of retirement. Blessed with so many resources within myself, the world was not necessary to *me.* . . . And as to smaller-sized rooms than I had been used to, I really could not give it a thought. I hoped I was perfectly equal to any sacrifice of that description. Certainly I had been accustomed to every luxury at Maple Grove; but I did assure him that two carriages were not necessary to my happiness, nor were spacious apartments. 'But,' said I, 'to be quite honest, I do not think I can live without something of a musical society. I condition for nothing else; but without music, life would be a blank to me.' "

From Emma, *chapter 32*

····::····

Early in her career, the heroine must meet with the hero: all perfection of course, and only prevented from paying his addresses to her by some excess of refinement. Wherever she goes someone falls in love with her, and she receives repeated offers of marriage, which she refers wholly to her father, exceedingly angry that *he* should not be the first applied to. Often carried away by the anti-hero, but rescued either by her father or the hero. Often reduced to support herself and her father by her talents, and work for her bread; continually cheated and defrauded of her hire, and now and then starved to death.

"Plan of a novel according to hints from various quarters," quoted in James Austen-Leigh, Memoir of Jane Austen, *1870.*

William Hazlitt

~~~~~~~~~~~~~~~~~~~~~~∞∞∞∞∞∞∞~~~~~~~~~~~~~~~~~~~~~~

BY FREDERIC RAPHAEL

William Hazlitt gave much thought to genius and was not reluctant to recognize it in the writers, actors, and artists of his and earlier times, but he was not himself a manifest instance: he produced no single masterpiece, nor did he impress his contemporaries with startling innovations or dazzling fame. In the age of Wordsworth, Coleridge, Shelley, Keats, and Byron and

of Charles Lamb and Walter Scott (whose novels he assessed with admiring severity), he was hardly the brightest star. Nothing ever made him instantly famous as *Childe Harold's Pilgrimage* did the precocious Byron. Already heir to a substantial estate, Byron was to have money pressed upon him by his publisher; Hazlitt was merely pressed for money.

Hazlitt's reputation, like his precarious living, was accumulated in petty increments. His essays and occasional prose amounted, in his surviving son's loving edition of them, to some thirteen volumes, but he was usually paid by the piece, like any Grub-street hack. His books — mostly reprints of essays and lectures — were never bestsellers. The quality of his work might be a function of his genius; its quantity was the fruit of penury: "It may be indelicate," he wrote, "but I am forced to write an article every week." On other occasions, he made a virtue of necessity: "The more we do, the more we *can* do. . . . I do not conceive rapidity of execution

necessarily implies slovenliness or crudeness . . . it is often productive both of sharpness and freedom." Love of liberty was "stronger than his allegiance to any friend or benefactor," the mark of the true critic.

In *The Spectator,* Addison and Steele had made the causerie into a genteel hobby, but if Hazlitt had a grand predecessor, it was Michel de Montaigne, who made an art of the essay (not without a *clin d'oeil* at Marcus Tullius Cicero). The Frenchman's diversity was similarly replete with humane observation and truffled with evidence of wide reading. Both men took part in contemporary life (Montaigne as counsellor to the *parlement* of Bordeaux, Hazlitt as critic and lecturer), but both inherited a slightly alienated posture toward it: Montaigne's mother was a converted Spanish Jewess, Hazlitt's father an outspoken Unitarian minister.

Hazlitt made a virtue of what he called "intellectual bias": less a matter of glorifying one's prejudices than of a frank declaration of, as they

Hazlitt was born on April 10, 1778, in Maidstone, Kent, England. He died in London on September 18, 1830.

87

now say, where he is coming from. "The mind," he observed, "contrives to lay hold of those circumstances and motives which suit its own bias and confirm its natural disposition." A critic should have *character,* not merely reflect the temper and taste of the times or seek to conform to the views of his readers. "Genius is ... exclusive and self-willed, quaint and peculiar ... it excels in some one pursuit by being blind to all excellence but its own."

In criticism, this definition required that judgments have the nuance that comes from *personality,* not from the application of some adopted measure. Never academic, Hazlitt's opinions were marked by what he called "gusto," unquenchable zeal for the imaginative expression of nature in art: before becoming a journalist, he had hoped to be a painter. He dared to say, on one occasion, that he thought for a while that he might "accomplish what Rembrandt or Titian did, but not what Raphael did." Failing to make a success, he abandoned the brush for the pen. To earn a growing family its bread, "I was called upon to do a number of things all at once. I was in the middle of a stream, and must sink or swim." He observed in later life, "There are two things that an Englishman understands, hard words and hard blows." Life dealt him his share of the latter, and he was not slow to deliver the former.

The Englishness of Hazlitt, who was born in Maidstone, Kent, in April 1778, was varied by a childhood spent first in Ireland, where his father found a precarious living (and no little antagonism), and then in New England. Despite his willingness to remain in the New World (where he strongly supported the new republic), William Hazlitt senior was obliged, for financial motives, to return, alone, to England

to seek another preaching post, after which his family would follow him. His son's earliest extant writing is a letter from Dorchester, Massachusetts, on November 12, 1786:

My dear Papa,
    I shall never forget that we came to America.... I think for my part that it would have been a great deal better if the white people had not found it out. Let the [Indians] have it to themselves, for it was made for them.

The eight-year-old's bold opinions probably echoed rather than challenged his father's. In adolescence, however, filial geniality was displaced by sullen and unsociable dissidence. As a young man, Hazlitt became irretrievably disposed to quarrel with those close to him, including seniors such as Coleridge and Wordsworth, who had shown him much favor. Reflecting in 1827, he wrote, "I set out in life with the French revolution and that event had considerable influence on my early feelings.... Youth was then doubly such. It was the dawn of a new era, a new impulse had been given to men's minds."

The reference to Wordsworth's "Bliss was it in that dawn to be alive, / But to be young was very heaven" is obvious. As a twenty-year-old, Hazlitt said, he wept when he had to criticize Wordsworth's *The Excursion.* Later, however, he was thoroughly disillusioned by the poet's reactionary attitudes, as he was by the sententiousness of Coleridge, whom he had also venerated. He ascribed their perversions of genius, with much exactness, to egotism: Wordsworth, in particular, preferred to be taken for a great man rather than leave his greatness implicit in the work, a fault from which Shakespeare (of whom Hazlitt remarked that he "is enough for us") was manifestly exempt.

"The Lakers'" sense of betrayal encouraged them to spread word of the young Hazlitt's indecorous conduct when on a pilgrimage to the northwest. If Hazlitt's sexual impulses were not as reckless, nor as richly funded, as Byron's, he, too, could be a man of "tumultuous passions." Exasperation with a local tease led Hazlitt, so Wordsworth and his friends alleged, to throw up her skirts and spank the girl's behind. Narrowly escaping outraged peasant retribution, he scampered back to London, pursued by embarrassing rumors about his sadistic appetites.

As his own guileless *Liber Amoris* was later to detail, Hazlitt remained prone to undignified crushes on young girls. The book is a candid and self-mocking confession of a middle-aged passion for Sarah Walker, the nineteen-year-old daughter of his then landlady. The dialogue is shamelessly accurate, not least in recording the girl's open admiration for another lodger's "seven inches." This brand of candor might make a modern bestseller, but it appalled Victorian readers, who evicted Hazlitt from the canon. Robert Louis Stevenson, however, recanted from his earlier prudishness and conceded "none of us can write like Hazlitt."

Hazlitt's first marriage had ended in divorce, his second — not to the venal girl whose charms made a fool of him, but to a widow with the means, if not the patience, to support him — would soon flounder. An inept and perhaps uncaring husband, he was a loving father: mourning his beloved first son, Hazlitt kept a locket of the boy's hair always with him.

Even as a critic, tears came easily, especially in the theater, but when delivering a verdict he was inflected neither by sentiment nor by affinity. Politically, he and Byron were close to two of a kind, but he could savage the latter's verses even when composed in an encomium on a common idol. "If my lord Byron will do these things, he must take the consequences: the acts of Napoleon Bonaparte are subjects of *history,* not for the disparagement of the Muse." Hazlitt's last — some might say *only* — major literary undertaking was a biography of Bonaparte that was remarkable more for its bulk — some of it "borrowed" wholesale from other sources — than for its success with the public or with posterity. If in little else, Hazlitt would have seconded Byron's regret at the fall of his "little pagod."

Throughout his life, Hazlitt, like Iago, was "nothing if not critical." He was sceptical of flights of the imagination that lost contact with, and respect for, mundane truth: "Genius," he observed in "Madame Pasta and Mademoiselle Mars," "is the power which equalises or identifies the imagination with the reality or with nature." If he never had a critical scheme, there was obdurate consistency in Hazlitt's aversion from impractical conceits. His lifelong radicalism had no strict doctrine. While he sustained his youthful sympathy with the French Revolution, he also regarded Edmund Burke — its most eloquent opponent — as a model writer of English prose.

Hazlitt's curious confidence, his opposition to cant, and his advocacy of robust self-expression were functions of the England that had triumphed in the Napoleonic wars and whose world hegemony was in its prime. He did not have to applaud the empire in order to derive the benefit of the assurance that, over two centuries, gave English writing its assumption of cultural mission and priority. Hazlitt rode a great wave of confidence that armed

Whigs no less than Tories with pens rendered mightier by Wellington's sword. However heartlessly he was lampooned, Castlereagh's diplomacy lent his critics the assumptions of dominance that gave English writing its fine swagger.

Although Hazlitt admired lofty diction, and deplored Wordsworth's rejection of poetic fancy in favor of common speech, he held that great art had to be rooted in observation. Protagonists were the more interesting for their human frailties: "Shakespeare," he observed, "does not set his heroes in the stocks of virtue." By the same token, in *On Paradox and Common-place,* he spelled out his reservations about his contemporary Percy Bysshe Shelley:

The author of the Prometheus Bound . . . has a fire in his eye, a fever in his blood, a maggot in his brain, a hectic flutter in his speech which mark out the philosophic fanatic. . . . He is clogged by no dull system of realities, no earth-bound feelings, no rooted prejudices, by nothing that belongs to the mighty trunk and hard husk of nature and habit, but is drawn up by irresistible levity to the regions of mere speculation and fancy. . . . Bubbles are to him the only realities. . . though a man in knowledge, he is a child in feeling. . . . He strives to overturn all established creeds and systems: but this is in him an effect of constitution. He runs before the most extravagant opinions, but this is because he is held back by none of the mechanical checks of sympathy and habit.

Although Shelley was a fellow radical, Hazlitt had the cruel integrity never to temper his bias; he was willing to incur ostracism rather than applaud a false note. The true critic must play the willing pariah. Hazlitt's lonely tactlessness afforded him a warrant to ironize on the opportunism of others:

An author now-a-days, to succeed, must be something more than an author — a nobleman, or rich plebeian:

the simply literary character is not enough. . . . It is name, it is wealth, it is title and influence that mollifies the tender-hearted Cerberus of Grub-street malice; secondly, by holding out the prospect of a dinner or a vacant office to successful sycophancy. This is the reason why a certain magazine praises Percy Bysshe Shelley and vilifies 'Johnny Keats'; they know very well that they cannot ruin the one in fortune as in fame, but they may ruin the other in both, deprive him of a livelihood together with his good name, send him to Coventry, and into the Rules of a prison; and this is a double incitement to the exercise of their laudable and legitimate vocation.

This is our man in the blithe flow of his raillery: at once acute and flamboyant, effusive and spontaneous, without program but always principled. He sided with Keats both for the sake of fair play and from a sense of social similarity: neither man had any birthright but his genius. Keats, who attended and admired Hazlitt's lectures, appreciated his champion, of whom he wrote: ". . . he thinks himself not estimated by ten People in the world — I wishe he knew he is."

Hazlitt's definition of genius as being in touch with "nature" accorded sweetly with his own practice of descanting, often in swaggering sentences and flights of prosaic fancy, on the basis of observed instances. Despite his excursions into metaphysics, he was rooted in the empiricism that anchored English philosophy in what could be known through the senses. He took a serious view of his philosophical ideas, which had something in common with those of his German contemporary Johann Gottlieb Fichte. Hazlitt contrived a synthesis of the mind's innate creativity (Fichte's "will") with its duty to shape a coherent vision of reality. He would have been mortified, and with some justice, to find that Bertrand Russell devoted a whole chapter, in his *History of West-ern Philosophy,* to Byron, but did not accord Hazlitt so much as a footnote.

Hazlitt's true genius was never blanched with abstraction; his prose and his temper were of an order unthinkable before the Age of Journalism. "Many of these articles," he con-ceded, when prefacing a collection of his pieces, "are unavoidably written over night, just as the paper is going to press, without correction or previous preparation . . . what is struck off at a blow, is in many respects better than what is produced on reflection, and at several heats." A century or so later, Karl Kraus would offer sour endorsement, when he wrote, "A journal-ist is someone who, given time, writes worse."

"At several heats" is sweetly to the point: the critic who wonders whether his opinions should be modified to suit the fashion, or dressed to seem more stylish than his first impression, sacrifices integrity to parade. Hazlitt's incautiousness was his private flaw and his literary merit: he might be hurt by being "sent to Coventry," but he excoriated the coer-cive pressure of what we call political correct-ness: ". . . when the community take the power into their own hands and there is but one body of opinion, and one voice to express it, there can be no *reaction* against it, and to remonstrate or resist, is not only a public outrage, but sounds like a personal insult to every individual in the community. It is by differing from the com-pany you become a *black sheep in the flock.* There is no excuse or mercy for it."

Writing in his mid-forties, Hazlitt himself acknowledged that much he did was written on the run. He affected typically mordant modesty about its value: ". . . if what I wrote at present is worth nothing, at least it costs me

nothing. But it cost me a good deal twenty years ago. I have added little to my stock since then, and take little from it. I 'unfold the book and volume of the brain', and transcribe the char-acters I see there as mechanically as anyone might copy the letters of a sampler."

He might not have welcomed another's rel-egation of his talents in the same terms, but he was as much a stranger to vanity as an example of pride. He never put on airs: he confessed frankly in a lecture on comedy that — although obliged to cite them — he knew little of Aristophanes or Lucian. If conspicu-ous in print, he was unassuming in company. His friend Peter Patmore said of him, "He tried *not* to shine, but, on the contrary, to be and to seem not a whit superior to those about him."

The abiding merit of a critic is to pay close attention. When, in October 1813, Hazlitt became the drama critic of the *Morning Chronicle* instead of Leigh Hunt (who had been imprisoned for attacking the Prince Regent), he found his vocation in a medium hitherto as fugitive as the performances it described. Today, we are spoilt for recordings of star performers (we can replay DVDs till we weary of the best performance), but Hazlitt's words are the only record of the great age of English acting. When he saw a fault, he nailed it sweetly, as when he said of Kemble that his supercilious airs when playing Coriolanus "remind one of the unaccountable abstracted air, the contracted brows and suspended chin, of a man who is just going to sneeze." Is that not, as Byron would have said, *"the thing"*?

On his debut, the actor Junius Brutus Booth is reproached for "borrowing Kean's coat and feathers . . . if he wishes to gain a permanent reputation, he must come forward in his own person. . . . The imitation of original genius is the *forlorn hope* of candidates for fame. . . . The secrets of Art may be said to have a common or *pass* key to unlock them; the secrets of Nature have but one master-key — the heart."

Hazlitt's greatest regret was that he never saw Garrick ("Mrs. Siddons," he would say, "was the only person who ever embodied our idea of high tragedy"), but his word-pictures make Edmund Kean flash before us again in all his electric brilliance. No fan could have been more devoted to the great actor than Hazlitt, but the critic's mirror catches not only Kean's genius but also his mistakes. Hazlitt was emphatic in finding fault with productions that, by wilful distortions, "improve" the work and words of genius. Of Kean's misguided King Lear, he remarks, "We do not admire these cross-readings. . . . They may be very well when the actor's ingenuity, however paradoxical, is more amusing than the author's sense, but it is not so in this case." He deplored over-inventive staging and unnaturally protracted pauses. We can imagine how he would have derided today's cult of attention-seeking directors.

The theater was not merely a place of entertainment for Hazlitt; it was a laboratory of the emotions and a demonstration of what great actors (and playwrights) made of them: ". . . the stage is a test and school of humanity. We do not much like persons who do not like plays; and

for this reason, that we imagine they cannot much like themselves or anyone else." Kenneth Tynan, a modern theatrical wit and *provocateur,* was the direct (and perhaps conscious) inheritor of Hazlitt's mantle when he said that he could never love anyone who did not love John Osborne's *Look Back in Anger.*

Hazlitt was the most human and the least pretentious of great critics. He once said that he had "a much greater ambition to be the best racket-player than the best prose writer of the age." When he "flubbed a shot," he shouted in despair, "Sheer incapacity, by God!" and would literally dash his head against the wall. Balked in his ambition to be a great painter or a rackets champion, he realized his genius in journalism. His victims may have thought him malicious, but his greatest quality was accurate enthusiasm. Byron advised a friend who was about to write a favorable review, "Don't just praise him, praise him *well!*" In criticism at least, Hazlitt excelled in both backhand and forehand. "What a fine thing it is to be an author," he once observed, albeit ironically, "and dream of immortality, and sleep o'nights!"

Hazlitt died of cancer of the stomach in 1830 at the age of fifty-two, but his unlikely dream of enduring fame was realized. He gave journalism a good name and made the ephemeral into a lasting monument. Posterity has rightly said of William Hazlitt what Robert Schumann said of Chopin, "Hats off, gentlemen: a genius!"

William Hazlitt

Coming forward and seating himself on the ground in his white dress and tightened turban, the chief of the Indian Jugglers begins with tossing up two brass balls, which is what any of us could do, and concludes with keeping up four at the same time, which is what none of us could do to save our lives.... Man, thou art a wonderful animal, and thy ways past finding out! Thou canst do strange things, but thou turnest them to little account! — To conceive of this effort of extraordinary dexterity distracts the imagination and makes admiration breathless.... There is something in all this which he who does not admire may be quite sure he never really admired any thing in the whole course of his life. It is skill surmounting difficulty, and beauty triumphing over skill.... The hearing a speech in Parliament, drawled or stammered out by the Honourable Member or the Noble Lord, the ringing the changes on their common-places, which any one could repeat after them as well as they, stirs me not a jot, shakes not my good opinion of myself: but the seeing the Indian Juggler does. It makes me ashamed of myself. I ask what there is that I can do as well as this! Nothing. What have I been doing all my life? Have I been idle, or have I nothing to shew for all my labour and pains? Or have I passed my time in pouring words like water into empty sieves, rolling a stone up a hill and then down again, trying to prove an argument in the teeth of facts, and looking for causes in the dark, and not finding them? Is there no one thing in which I can challenge competition, that I can bring as an instance of exact perfection, in which others cannot find a flaw? The utmost I can pretend to is to write a description of what this fellow can do. I can write a book: so can many others who have not even learned to spell. What abortions are these Essays! What errors, what ill-pieced transitions, what crooked reasons, what lame conclusions! How little is made out, and that little how ill! Yet they are the best I can do.

From "The Indian Jugglers"

93

John Keats

BY EAVAN BOLAND

"I think I shall be among the English Poets after my death." So wrote John Keats to his brother in the Autumn of 1818. It was an extraordinary claim for a twenty-three-year-old, whose first book of poems had been savagely dismissed, whose financial circumstances were hopeless, and who was only three years from his own death. Yet, in time, the claim would come to fit

the circumstance. No poet in history has had a more extraordinary path from start to finish than John Keats. Time has borne him out: his poems are central to our literature.

At the time of his birth in London in 1795 such an outcome would have seemed impossible. The son of a livery stable keeper, his childhood was full of uncertainty. His parents were not without means, but illness, misfortune, and naïve handling of money meant they only scratched the surface of stability and respectability. Keats's boyhood was shadowed by their deaths. In 1804 his father was killed in a fall from a horse. In 1810 his mother died at the age of thirty-four. "It runs in my head," he said a few years later, "that we shall all die young."

Chestnut-haired, short in stature (he was just five feet tall), quick-tempered, articulate, and generous, Keats was a mixture of the best characteristics of his afflicted parents. But his youth ended forever in 1810 when, at the age of fifteen, he began his medical apprenticeship.

The work did not suit him. He did not like the duties of an apothecary nor the science — such as it was — of dressing wounds. What suited him was to read voraciously, to dream of greatness, and even to imagine a place for himself in the fast-moving literature of the time.

A young man without means could be forgiven for dreaming. England in 1800 was a country of eight million. The age of empire was beginning. There was a broad, eager, and well-connected reading public, particularly in London. Poetry was popular and even profitable. Byron's *Corsair* sold 10,000 copies on the day of its publication. Walter Scott's *Lay of the Last Minstrel* sold 44,000 copies in 1805. It was not out of the question that Keats might make his way by talent alone.

In March 1817 his first book, *Poems,* was published by C. and J. Ollier. In 1818 Taylor and Hessey brought out his long poem *Endymion.* Both were the outcome of an accelerated process of reading, of writing, of acid-etching poetic

Keats was born on October 31, 1795, in London, England. He died in Rome on February 23, 1821.

95

example into his own style. *Endymion* was a poem of 4,000 lines, finished in 1818. Its rhymed couplets, detailing the love of a goddess for a shepherd, seem a world away from the England of Keats's moment. But the opening is celebrated and memorable:

A thing of beauty is a joy for ever:
Its loveliness increases; it will never
Pass into nothingness; but still will keep
A bower quiet for us, and a sleep
Full of sweet dreams, and health, and quiet breathing.

Keats's early work has had harsh critics. "It may be said that the merit of his work at twenty-five was hardly by comparison more wonderful than its demerit at twenty-two," remarked Swinburne. Nevertheless, these poems already displayed a signature gift, his ability to combine the music of ideas with an exact and sweet-natured evocation of the real world, as in this passage from "Sleep and Poetry":

Stop and consider! life is but a day;
A fragile dewdrop on its perilous way
From a tree's summit; a poor Indian's sleep
While his boat hastens to the monstrous steep
Of Montmorenci. Why so sad a moan?
Life is the rose's hope while yet unblown;
The reading of an ever-changing tale;
The light uplifting of a maiden's veil;
A pigeon tumbling in clear summer air;
A laughing schoolboy, without grief or care,
Riding the springy branches of an elm.

His first book contains one of the finest lyrics he ever wrote, the extraordinary sonnet on Chapman's Homer:

Much have I travell'd in the realms of gold,
    And many goodly states and kingdoms seen;
    Round many western islands have I been
Which bards in fealty to Apollo hold.

Oft of one wide expanse had I been told
    That deep-brow'd Homer ruled as his demesne;
    Yet did I never breathe its pure serene
Till I heard Chapman speak out loud and bold:
Then felt I like some watcher of the skies
    When a new planet swims into his ken;
Or like stout Cortez when with eagle eyes
    He star'd at the Pacific — and all his men
Look'd at each other with a wild surmise —
    Silent, upon a peak in Darien.

This sonnet was written when Keats was twenty-one. We have a front-row glimpse of its composition from an account left by his friend Charles Cowden Clarke. He describes himself and Keats leaning over Chapman's translation of Homer, wondering at it together:

A beautiful copy of the folio edition of Chapman's translation of Homer had been lent me. . . . When I came down to breakfast the next morning, I found upon my table a letter with no other enclosure than his famous sonnet, "On First Looking into Chapman's Homer." We had parted, as I have already said, at day-spring, yet he contrived that I should receive the poem from a distance of, may be, two miles by ten o'clock.

Clarke's account is important. It hints at the great, secondary adventure of Keats's writing life. Vivid, argumentative, often lonely and without resources, his friends were vital to him. As he gathered them to him, he began to weave an extraordinary epistolary web around them. Between the years of 1816 until a week before his death he wrote letters almost incessantly. They were far more than ordinary commentaries. They became, to borrow a phrase from Yeats, "the fiery shorthand" of his brief and fiercely imagined life. When he fell in love with Fanny Brawne in 1818, they became love letters as well.

It is hard now to imagine a young man in his early twenties sitting at dawn or twilight at a desk or table, dashing off these exuberant, profound essays, thinly disguised as epistles and sending them out to astonish their readers. There were six postal deliveries in London at that time, spread from early morning to late evening, so his friends were able to know, almost from hour to hour, the passionate views that accompanied his development. But shadows were gathering. In 1818 one brother, George, left for the United States. Late in the year another, Tom, died of tuberculosis. His own health was showing ominous signs of deterioration. By now, he also had caught tuberculosis.

In the Autumn of 1818 reviews of his first volumes were published. They were savage. In *Blackwood's Edinburgh Magazine,* the notorious John Gibson Lockhart admonished the young writer: "It is a better and a wiser thing to be a starved apothecary than a starved poet; so back to the shop Mr John, back to plasters, pills, and ointment boxes, &c." Keats was devastated. His letters would become more sober, more wary, but still possessing that lilt of eloquence and common sense that made them unique, and revealing a profound sense of his own worth. To his publisher in 1818, following the attacks, he wrote: "The Genius of Poetry must work out its own salvation in a man."

The genius of poetry. It remains hard to define. Each era has had a stake in identifying it. And yet now a young poet, just twenty-three years of age, was about to add his luminous witness to this difficult and elusive concept. The early Autumn of 1818 ushered in the great year of Keats's writing. "Most of the poetry by which he is remembered," wrote a twentieth-century commentator, "follows in the comet's tail of this brilliant effort." None

of it came easily. The sketches of the time show a keen, intense profile. They display a young man who still loved conversation, friendship, harvest walks, and the great poems of the past. But reality was darkening all around him. The letters show a lovesick suitor — he had just met Fanny Brawne, his first and last love — and a distraught brother: Tom was dying. They also show the new maturity of the poet, setting out on his last trial of strength.

First came *Hyperion.* The poem in its first incarnation — there are in fact two parts — is a story of fallen gods. No longer is Keats's subject the decorative gods of his earlier poems. The boundary between his inner and outer worlds had started to shimmer and dissolve. Now his inner life, with its fears and hopes, is itself epic, and his epic characters speak with the intensity of his own experience. The idiom and music of the poem are full of austere power. All at once, the young poet so accused of self-indulgence and sentimentality is writing with a new assurance:

Deep in the shady sadness of a vale
Far sunken from the healthy breath of morn,
Far from the fiery noon, and eve's one star,
Sat gray-hair'd Saturn, quiet as a stone.

In early December he broke off writing. His brother's death left him wretched. "My pen seems to have grown too gouty for verse," he wrote a friend. But in January he completed the splendid and ornamental "Eve of St. Agnes," using the narrative of young lovers to weave a rare charm of language and image. By the time the lovers have "fled away into the storm" at the end of the poem, the reader has been enchanted.

Now, at last, came the great odes, the poems Keats had awaited. An English spring of rain, shadow, and sunlight forms the background to almost all of them. There are six: the odes to Psyche, Melancholy, the Nightingale, and Indolence, the "Ode on a Grecian Urn," and, later in the year, the ode "To Autumn." Except the last, they were written in the spring of 1819. The odes stand at the center of Keats's achievement. They are sentinels of the last year of his writing life, gathering in and guarding everything he had learned about poetry and loss. Three of them — "Ode to a Nightingale," "Ode on a Grecian Urn," and "To Autumn" — remain among the greatest poems of the nineteeth or any century.

Each is worth comment, but perhaps "Ode on a Grecian Urn" is the most marvelous and surprising in structure. This is the play-within-a-play poem. In it the poet addresses a Grecian urn, painted with a frieze of men and women. The poem is a work of art about a work of art. It turns the craft of a new civilization on the artifact of an old one. Part of the magic comes from the fact that the Grecian vase in the poem just will not keep still. It begins as a "Cold Pastoral" and a "foster-child of silence and slow time." But suddenly the barrier between life and art disappears: the empty town, the lost people, the human moment are all utterly real at the same moment that they are lyrically realized:

What little town by river or sea-shore,
  Or mountain-built with peaceful citadel,
    Is emptied of its folk, this pious morn?
And, little town, thy streets for evermore
  Will silent be; and not a soul to tell
    Why thou art desolate, can e'er return.

The "Ode to a Nightingale," written only weeks apart from it, continues this brilliant conversation between life and fear, art and

mortality. Keats was staying at the time with Charles Brown, in whose garden a nightingale had built her nest. Brown describes Keats coming in from the garden, putting down his scraps of paper with their notes and scribbling modestly out of sight. Written on them was a testament of terror and acceptance:

Darkling I listen; and, for many a time
  I have been half in love with easeful Death,
Call'd him soft names in many a musèd rhyme,
  To take into the air my quiet breath.

Keats's *annus mirabilis* was moving toward its close. Each month brought new achievements, a new reach of style and power. But his health was deteriorating. He could not shake a sense of an approaching doom.

In August 1819 he came to Winchester. Here, in the valley of the river Itchen, under chalk hills and with water meadows on every side, lay the peace of a legendary England. In the late light of summer this old seat of the wool and cloth trade seemed a respite as well as a destination. Here he finished one of the signature works of his career, the narrative poem *Lamia*. It is different, gorgeous, and disturbing. It tells the story of a young woman who is in fact a serpent. She is loved by Lycius, a youth of Corinth. Their marriage ceremony takes place and is marred by the presence of Apollonius, Lycius's old master of logic and philosophy. He stares intensely at Lamia, revealing her sinister reality. She dies and Lycius joins her, broken by grief and love on his wedding day.

The improbable plot covers a powerful allegory and a nagging question. What tolerance has truth for beauty? What place has the imagination in a logical world? The question is partly resolved by style. As a young man, Keats had been impatient of eighteenth-century poetry. Yet *Lamia* could never have been written without the snap and hiss of the Augustan couplet. Through it, Keats embarks on a consideration of poetry, which is enabled by the eighteenth century, but travels well beyond its powers of reference.

At the end of *Lamia,* the weak lover and the powerful serpent and the determined philosopher face one another. Each drains and undermines the others' powers.

> What wreath for Lamia? What for Lycius?
> What for the sage, old Apollonius?
> Upon her aching forehead be there hung
> The leaves of willow and of adder's tongue;
> And for the youth, quick, let us strip for him
> The thyrsus, that his watching eyes may swim
> Into forgetfulness; and, for the sage,
> Let spear-grass and the spiteful thistle wage
> War on his temples. Do not all charms fly
> At the mere touch of cold philosophy?

In September 1819, still at Winchester, Keats wrote to a friend, "How beautiful the season is — How fine the air. A temperate sharpness about it." Then the poet continued, "Somehow a stubble plain looks warm — in the same way that some pictures look warm. This struck me so much in my Sunday's walk that I composed on it."

The poem he composed is "To Autumn." It is full of the beautiful peace of acceptance.

In the words of one critic, "each generation has found it one of the most nearly perfect poems in English." Its surface is the invocation to a tranquil autumn, heavy with the warmth and fruition of the harvest. But below the surface of the poem is the acceptance of more than the end of the year. The beautiful, feminized figure of the season suggests completion:

> Sometimes whoever seeks abroad may find
> Thee sitting careless on a granary floor,
>   Thy hair soft-lifted by the winnowing wind;
> Or on a half-reap'd furrow sound asleep,
>   Drowsed with the fumes of poppies, while thy hook
>   Spares the next swath and all its twinèd flowers;
> And sometimes like a gleaner thou dost keep
>   Steady thy laden head across a brook.

And yet the poem is also a tough-minded acceptance of the end. Ahead of Keats lay his failing health, his ebbing of strength, above all the loss of his ability to go further with the craft he so loved. In this poem, and in all the poems of his great year of writing, lay his tolerance for the extraordinary paradox of art: that an artist can make everything safe from time except himself. John Keats was not safe. He died of tuberculosis in Rome in February 1821. He was twenty-five years of age. His achievement — so rapid, so courageous — did more than place him among the English poets after his death. It redefined the sense of what is possible in poetry.

John Keats

*"On First
Looking into
Chapman's
Homer"*

Much have I travell'd in the realms of gold,
    And many goodly states and kingdoms seen;
    Round many western islands have I been
Which bards in fealty to Apollo hold.
Oft of one wide expanse had I been told
    That deep-brow'd Homer ruled as his demesne;
    Yet did I never breathe its pure serene
Till I heard Chapman speak out loud and bold:
Then felt I like some watcher of the skies
    When a new planet swims into his ken;
Or like stout Cortez when with eagle eyes
    He star'd at the Pacific — and all his men
Look'd at each other with a wild surmise —
    Silent, upon a peak in Darien.

····:····

"Sonnet to Sleep"

O soft embalmer of the still midnight,
    Shutting with careful fingers and benign
Our gloom-pleas'd eyes, embower'd from the light,
    Enshaded in forgetfulness divine:
O soothest Sleep! if so it please thee, close,
    In midst of this thine hymn, my willing eyes,
Or wait the Amen ere thy poppy throws
    Around my bed its lulling charities.
Then save me or the passed day will shine
    Upon my pillow, breeding many woes:
Save me from curious conscience, that still hoards
    Its strength for darkness, burrowing like the mole;
Turn the key deftly in the oiled wards,
    And seal the hushed casket of my soul.

····:····

Fanatics have their dreams, wherewith they weave
A paradise for a sect; the savage too
From forth the loftiest fashion of his sleep
Guesses at heaven: pity these have not
Trac'd upon vellum or wild Indian leaf
The shadows of melodious utterance.
But bare of laurel they live, dream, and die;
For Poesy alone can tell her dreams,
With the fine spell of words alone can save
Imagination from the sable charm
And dumb enchantment. Who alive can say
"Thou are no poet; may'st not tell thy dreams"?
Since every man whose soul is not a clod
Hath visions, and would speak, if he had lov'd
And been well nurtured in his mother tongue.
Whether the dream now purposed to rehearse
Be poet's or fanatic's will be known
When this warm scribe my hand is in the grave.

"The Fall of Hyperion: A Dream," canto 1, lines 1–18

····⫶····

She was a gordian shape of dazzling hue,
Vermilion-spotted, golden, green, and blue;
Striped like a zebra, freckled like a pard,
Eyed like a peacock, and all crimson barr'd;
And full of silver moons, that, as she breathed,
Dissolv'd, or brighter shone, or interwreathed
Their lustres with the gloomier tapestries.

"Lamia," Part I, lines 47–53

Nathaniel Hawthorne

························≈≪≫≈≪≫≈≪≫≈························

BY DANIEL MARK EPSTEIN

He soared to Parnassus in his early thirties and has maintained his perch there, preening his glorious wings, while other writers have come and gone. To appraise Hawthorne's uncanny powers is to revive a discussion — a paean, really — as old as the author's second published book, *Twice-Told Tales* (1837, 1841). Edgar Allan Poe, probably the only critic qualified to make

such a judgment in 1842, called Hawthorne "one of the few men of indisputable genius to whom our country has yet given birth." Poe was echoing the opinion of a great writer of disputable genius, Longfellow, who in 1837 had declared that the first edition of Hawthorne's stories "comes from the hand of a man of genius."

Herman Melville added his voice to the chorus in 1850, in an essay comparing his contemporary to Shakespeare. Henry James took up the torch for a new generation, in 1879 devoting an entire book to Hawthorne, wherein James, like Melville, used the term "genius" unsparingly. "Hawthorne," James wrote, "is the most valuable example of the American genius."

Poe, Melville, James — what more could a novelist ask for in the way of blurbs? And none begrudged that term hoarded up for those rare authors whose artistry is transcendent. How did they, how do we, decide upon works of genius? Longinus's checklist *On the Sublime* (a Greek

treatise circa the first century A.D.) is useful. Certain "sublime" elements of Hawthorne's tales and novels — their precise language, powerful figures of speech, effective structure and organization — are imperishable. Other qualities that Longinus calls for — significant thoughts and emotional intensity — may have wizened, here and there, with the passage of decades and a way of life.

One example of the effect of social change upon a novel's strength is our children's response to *The Scarlet Letter*, long required reading in high schools. When I read the book as a student in 1964, I was deeply moved by the plight of Hester Prynne and her daughter, so cruelly treated by the Puritan community because Hester refused to identify her child's father. And I was not insensitive to the unwed mother's guilt. Girls I knew who "got in trouble" disappeared for half a year, and returned childless and sad. Then in the 1980s a teacher informed me, drolly, that it had

Hawthorne was born on July 4, 1804, in Salem, Massachusetts. He died in Plymouth, New Hampshire, on May 19, 1864.

become impossible to discuss *The Scarlet Letter* with high-school juniors because "they just don't see what all the fuss is about."

In twenty years sexual behavior had changed so drastically that a main theme of Hawthorne's masterpiece came unplugged. As far as those youngsters were concerned, the book lacked significant thought and intensity of emotion. Longinus, standing at the blackboard, might have looked at his checklist, frowned, and judged *The Scarlet Letter* no longer a work of genius, having failed the test of time. Let us argue that the book was not written for adolescents and that an equally important theme in it is the sin of Roger Chillingworth in blighting Arthur Dimmesdale's soul. Yet it is a fact that a change in morals has robbed *The Scarlet Letter* of much of its heat.

It is not fine language that wins Hawthorne the laurel; it is the intensity of feelings his stories evoke, and what Longinus calls the "grandeur" or elevation of thought.

Assigning those flint-hearted teenagers the duty of reading Hawthorne's great novel was ill-advised, when for the same price and less trouble they could have read a dozen of his tales, in which his prowess is so striking no thoughtful person is likely to deny it.

In "The Snow Image" two children make a fairy girl out of snow, as their mother looks on. "She stood an instant on the threshold, hesitating whether she ought to ask the child to come in, or whether she should even speak to her. Indeed she almost doubted whether it were a real child after all, or only a light wreath of the new-fallen snow, blown hither and thither about the garden by the intensely cold west wind. . . . All this while the mother stood on the threshold, wondering how a little girl could look so much like a flying snowdrift, or how a snowdrift could look so very like a little girl."

Worried about the girl's scanty attire, the woman calls out to her children, asking if the stranger comes from the neighborhood. They insist they have made her out of snow. As if to confirm her origins, a flock of snowbirds "flew at once to the white-robed child, fluttered eagerly about her head, alighted on her shoulders. . . . She, on her part, was evidently as glad to see these little birds . . . and welcomed them by holding out both her hands. Hereupon, they each and all tried to alight on her two palms and ten small fingers and thumbs, crowding one another off, with an immense fluttering of their tiny wings."

Hawthorne was an avowed allegorist, whose models were Spenser, Dante, and Bunyan. While the precision of Hawthorne's description makes this "snow sister" as vivid and sympathetic as the flesh-and-blood characters in the story, the metaphors and similes lead us to the pith of an allegory. The child is seen as "a light wreath" of snow blown hither and thither "by the intensely cold west wind," and likened to "a flying snowdrift." Thus "The Snow Image" allegorizes the conflict between the imagination and the inhospitable world of facts. The wreath represents the crown of poetry as well as the evanescence of beauty; the cold wind of reality blows the flying snowdrift where it will.

Mama, whose character has "a strain of poetry in it," half-believes the children, and would not interfere with their creative play. But Papa is an "exceedingly matter-of-fact sort of man, a dealer in hardware." He takes one look at the snow child and, fearing she will catch her death of cold, insists — over his children's loud objections — that she come inside and sit by the stove. The result, much to be expected, is nonetheless disturbing.

A synopsis cannot convey Hawthorne's subtlety. Allegory attains the status of high art when it engages a human or metaphysical paradox; otherwise it belongs to the theater of melodrama or the pulpit. The snow child, very charming, is also faintly sinister. One fears she will freeze the real children. Papa is not an ogre but a kind man with good intentions. Even the symbols of cold and heat are not circumscribed: the seductive snow can inspire or kill, and so can the warmth of hearth and home.

We need not read long in any Hawthorne story to find jeweled phrases and perfectly balanced periods. Clifford, the addled recluse in *The House of the Seven Gables,* passes his time blowing soap bubbles. "Behold him, scattering airy spheres abroad, from the window into the street! Little impalpable worlds, were those soap-bubbles, with the big world depicted, in hues bright as imagination, on the nothing of their surface." In "Lady Eleanor's Mantle," the haughty owner of the poisonous cape arrives in New England to find a crazed admirer "offering his person as a footstool" for her to tread upon as she alights from her carriage. She pauses to consider if he is worthy. "Then, though as lightly as a sunbeam on a cloud, she placed her foot upon the cowering form, and extended her hand to meet that of the Governor." In "The Great Carbuncle," on the dawn of discovering the long-sought, fabulous gem, the newlyweds awake to a sight more precious by far. "She and her husband fell asleep with hands tenderly clasped, and awoke from visions of unearthly radiance to meet the more blessed light of one another's eyes."

Yet it is not fine language that wins Hawthorne the laurel; it is the intensity of feelings his stories evoke, and what Longinus calls the "grandeur" or elevation of thought. Hawthorne's brooding temperament was well suited to a fashion of the time, the Gothic romance. Starting with Horace Walpole in 1764, gathering momentum in the popular stories of Ann Radcliffe and Charles Maturin before being imported to America by Charles Brockden Brown, the genre was a dependable moneymaker by the time Hawthorne and Poe took it up. The Gothic tale features horror, physical or psychological violence, and supernatural events that the author contrives to reconcile with the laws of nature. The story is usually set in a faraway time or place, often in an old mansion or castle with a skeleton (real or figurative) in the closet.

Hawthorne had a knack for illuminating lovers in the gloom. The young hero of "Rappacini's Daughter" goes to study in Padua, "very long ago," and takes a room "in a high and gloomy chamber of an old edifice" overlooking a walled garden tended by a famous wizard and his beautiful daughter. Giovanni falls in love despite his professor's warning that Beatrice's flowers are poisonous, that she is a victim of her father's dark science, and that her immunity to poison has isolated her from the world. This plot is a perfect recipe for Gothic melodrama, or Poe's elaboration of

the grotesque. But in Hawthorne's gentle hands the lovers' yearning and dread, and their struggle against fate, raise the little romance to the level of tragedy.

At the story's end Beatrice murmurs, "I would fain have been loved, not feared." It is by the grace of Hawthorne's art — so different from Poe's — that the motif of love often subdues horror, even when the lovers are doomed. In *The House of the Seven Gables,* it is young Phoebe's love for the unfortunate Clifford and Hepzibah Pyncheon and their boarder Holgrave that breaks the curse on that ancient house, and makes way for a happy ending.

There is horror aplenty in Hawthorne, from the skeleton reduced to snow-white lime in "Ethan Brand" to the accidental killing of a youth in "Roger Malvin's Burial." But the shock value is never an end in itself; it always arises in service of the moral. Throughout the master's books this moral — a caution against estrangement — is so pervasive that a few carpers have accused Hawthorne of monotony.

Rigorously applied, Hawthorne's major precept, his *moral,* if you will, challenges the intellect to the highest degree possible in a work of literature. In "Wakefield," a story fleshing out a news item, a Londoner on a whim rents an apartment a block from home. On the pretext of going on a weeklong journey, he bids farewell to his good wife and then hides away around the corner for twenty years. Hawthorne's psychological review of the case, non-judgmental, wryly humorous, prefigures the portraiture of Henry James and Edith Wharton. But when time comes to end his ironic study, which in every other way is bracingly modern, Hawthorne does not resist the impulse to "lend its wisdom to a moral."

"Amid the seeming confusion of our mysterious world, individuals are so nicely adjusted to a system, and systems to one another and to a whole, that, by stepping aside for a moment, a man exposes himself to a fearful risk of losing his place forever. Like Wakefield, he may become, as it were, the Outcast of the Universe."

This statement of Hawthorne's chief moral appeals to today's reader because of its existential purity. The concept of Sin has practically disappeared from current secular discourse; in its place we often use a term Hawthorne would have recognized as nearly identical — alienation. It comes without the religious and ethical qualifications that give weight to the Gothic stories at the heart of Hawthorne's oeuvre. The vain and selfish Wakefield, like the protagonists of *Oedipus Rex, Hamlet, The Scarlet Letter,* and *The Stranger,* has made himself an outcast.

Readers sometimes mistake Hawthorne for a Puritan or a Calvinist. He was neither. Like most great writers he was a critic of ideas and a servant of none. Although he moralizes, Hawthorne is no moralist in the old-fashioned sense. His moralizing is auspiciously progressive: he condemns behavior that separates the individual from society, and society that unfairly isolates the exceptional individual. Much has been made of the etiology of guilt in Hawthorne; it is no more than an effect of alienation.

So Lady Eleanor's arrogance brings a plague upon her city. "The curse of Heaven hath stricken me," she cries from her deathbed, "because I would not call man my brother, nor woman my sister." Rappaccini's pride in his science walls him and his beloved daughter away from society in Padua, virtually entombing them. In both *The Scarlet Letter* and "The

Minister's Black Veil," zealotry and obsessive guilt raise the ministers so far above their congregations that, while the men apparently excel as priests, they lose the personal capacity to love and be loved. And in the comic "Peter Goldthwaite's Treasure" the lust for gold so completely removes Peter from the practical world that he tears down his house in search of the imagined hoard. It is always the Sophoclean isolation of the protagonist that precipitates disaster.

Finally, it was Hawthorne's destiny to create, in the humbler medium of prose fiction, the Ur-myth of a nation, a task the Muses usually assign to narrative and dramatic poets such as Homer, Aeschylus, Virgil, and Shakespeare. The Gothic served Hawthorne well. By setting his stories in Colonial times, he evoked the legendary while avoiding novelty, which Longinus observed can reduce the sublime to the ridiculous. Young Goodman Brown's fateful encounter with the witches, in the story that bears his name, seems real in that faraway time. Likewise does the magical resurrection of the Colonial hero, "The Gray Champion," when a British tyrant takes over the Governor's mansion.

"The Maypole of Merry Mount" is perhaps Hawthorne's most illustrious effort to forge a "foundation myth." In the happy colony of Merry Mount the citizens live for pleasure. Dancing around the Maypole, dressed in animal hides, the revelers celebrate the harmony of man and nature. But nearby dwells "a settlement of Puritans, most dismal wretches, who said their prayers before daylight, and then wrought in the forest or the cornfield till evening made it prayer time again. Their weapons were always at hand to shoot down the straggling savage.... Woe to the youth or maiden who did but dream of a dance!"

"Jollity and gloom were contending for an empire," Hawthorne prophesies. "The future complexion of New England was involved.... Should the grizzly Saints establish their jurisdiction over the gay sinners, then would their spirits darken all the clime." The outcome is not so important as Hawthorne's having defined the terms of the conflict: grim Puritans against happy pagans, propriety versus nature, settlers against natives, an armed community forcing its way of life upon a vulnerable but worthy minority. The antagonism has been constant in American history.

Equally significant is the complex allegory "My Kinsman, Major Molineux," in which a youth travels to a distant town to seek his fortune in the form of a wealthy cousin's patronage. After a frustrating, Kafkaesque search for his patron, the young man finds that Molineux is no longer in any position to help him, having fallen afoul of imperial politics. The tale is a pocket-sized American Bildungsroman, in which the seeker learns that nothing is quite what it seems, that a man is at the mercy of his community, and that spirited self-reliance — in compliance with the *system* — is the key to worldly success.

Separately, each of these Gothic tales — and I include *The Scarlet Letter* and *The House of the Seven Gables* among them — is sublime. Taken together, they comprise a foundation myth of the New World, as eloquent in explaining a nation to itself as are the works of Homer and Virgil.

Nathaniel Hawthorne

From The Scarlet
Letter, *chapter 11*

[Mr. Dimmesdale's] inward trouble drove him to practices more
in accordance with the old, corrupted faith of Rome than with the better light of the church in which he had been born and bred. In [his]
secret closet, under lock and key, there was a bloody scourge.
Oftentimes, this Protestant and Puritan divine had plied it on his own
shoulders, laughing bitterly at himself the while, and smiting so much
the more pitilessly because of that bitter laugh. It was his custom, too,
as it has been that of many other pious Puritans, to fast — not, however, like them, in order to purify the body and render it the fitter medium of celestial illumination, but rigorously, and until his knees trembled beneath him, as an act of penance. He kept vigils, likewise, night
after night, sometimes in utter darkness; sometimes with a glimmer-
ing lamp; and sometimes, viewing his own face in a looking glass, by
the most powerful light which he could throw upon it. He thus typi-
fied the constant introspection wherewith he tortured, but could not
purify, himself. In these lengthened vigils, his brain often reeled and
visions seemed to flit before him; perhaps seen doubtfully, and by a
faint light of their own, in the remote dimness of the chamber, or more
vividly, and close beside him, within the looking glass. Now it was a
herd of diabolic shapes that grinned and mocked at the pale minister,
and beckoned him away with them; now a group of shining angels,
who flew upward heavily, as sorrow-laden, but grew more ethereal as
they rose. Now came the dead friends of his youth, and his white-
bearded father, with a saintlike frown, and his mother, turning her face
away as she passed by. Ghost of a mother — thinnest fantasy of a
mother — methinks she might yet have thrown a pitying glance
toward her son! And now, through the chamber which these spectral
thoughts had made so ghastly, glided Hester Prynne, leading along
little Pearl in her scarlet garb, and pointing her forefinger, first at the
scarlet letter on her bosom, and then at the clergyman's own breast.

None of these visions ever quite deluded him. At any moment,
by an effort of his will, he could discern substances through their
misty lack of substance, and convince himself that they were not

solid in their nature, like yonder table of carved oak, or that big, square, leather-bound and brazen-clasped volume of divinity. But, for all that, they were, in one sense, the truest and most substantial things which the poor minister now dealt with. It is the unspeakable misery of a life so false as his, that it steals the pith and substance out of whatever realities there are around us, and which were meant by Heaven to be the spirit's joy and nutriment. To the untrue man, the whole universe is false — it is impalpable — it shrinks to nothing within his grasp. And he himself, in so far as he shows himself in a false light, becomes a shadow, or, indeed, ceases to exist.

····∷····

In the latter part of the last century there lived a man of science, an eminent proficient in every branch of natural philosophy, who not long before our story opens had made experience of a spiritual affinity more attractive than any chemical one. He had left his laboratory to the care of an assistant, cleared his fine countenance from the furnace smoke, washed the stain of acids from his fingers, and persuaded a beautiful woman to become his wife. In those days when the comparatively recent discovery of electricity and other kindred mysteries of Nature seemed to open paths into the region of miracle, it was not unusual for the love of science to rival the love of woman in its depth and absorbing energy. . . . We know not whether Aylmer possessed this degree of faith in man's ultimate control over Nature. He had devoted himself, however, too unreservedly to scientific studies ever to be weaned from them by any second passion. His love for his young wife might prove the stronger of the two; but it could only be by intertwining itself with his of science, and uniting the strength of the latter to his own.

Such a union accordingly took place, and was attended with truly remarkable consequences and a deeply impressive moral. One day, very soon after their marriage, Aylmer sat gazing at his wife with a trouble in his countenance that grew stronger until he spoke.

"Georgiana," said he, "has it never occurred to you that the mark upon your cheek might be removed?"

From "The Birthmark"

111

Charles Dickens

....

BY A. N. WILSON

Does Dickens reflect the world as it is, or create a world of his own into which we are drawn, as into some phantasmagoric sideshow at a fairground, such as the Punch and Judy puppet show of Codlin and Short or the waxworks of Mrs. Jarley in *The Old Curiosity Shop,* or the overblown dramatics of Mr. Vincent Crummles in *Nicholas Nickleby?*

Dickens, more than any writer, asks us to take the world on his own comical terms. And yet, again and again, we discover that what appears to be most fantastical in his pages turns out to be most realistic. The melodramas of Crummles are as nothing to the real-life school dramas of Squeers and Smike. Jarley's waxworks contain no one so alarming as Quilp. And, as with Russian dolls, each one containing another identical but smaller than itself, this process of discovering the realism of Dickens extends outside the novels themselves. Non-Dickensians, or anti-Dickensians, believe that his novels themselves are like the pantomimes, fairgrounds, waxwork shows, and melodramas that he so enjoyed — overcolored, exaggerated joke-versions of reality — but lay no claim to being serious reflections of the way that we as human beings truly are, the way we live, suffer, love. Others, myself decidedly among them, would say that Dickens is supreme among novelists, not just as a superb entertainer, not merely as a

great lord of language, nor as a pantomimic manipulator of tears and laughter, but as a great artist.

Dickens, who was immediately popular from the periodical publication of the first part of *The Pickwick Papers,* remains more than ever popular, and more than ever read. Many reasons could be adduced for this. Great genius, such as that of Dickens, cannot be reduced to simple one-line explanations. But one central fact that explains his survival is that at some very deep level, he was writing about what Wordsworth calls

the very world, which is the world
Of all of us, — the place where in the end,
We find our happiness, or not at all.

The financial chaos into which England and Europe were plunged by the Napoleonic wars — followed by immense industrial and financial developments in England, far outsoaring the rest of the world in commercial and

Dickens was born on February 7, 1812, in Portsmouth, Hampshire, England. He died in Gad's Hill, near Chatham, Kent, England, on June 9, 1870.

113

industrial terms — led to the world that historians see through the eyes of Malthus, Hegel, and Marx. Rural poverty in Ireland, and in the rest of Great Britain, and the expansion of the industrial cities led to huge population movements, vastly overcrowded and unsanitary conurbations. The world of Mr. Pickwick's stage coaches was obsolete even as Dickens wrote about it: that was a part of the comedy's appeal. Survival itself, in that overcrowded and industrialized world, became a much fiercer battle than it had ever been in the days when London — the London of Samuel Johnson, let us say — numbered a few hundred thousand souls. Dickens's world was one of cholera-infested slums, a river that was so thick with human ordure that the nearby Houses of Parliament had to close during the summer months because of the unendurable smell, and — this, surely is the most distinctive feature of early nineteenth-century London, the feature that would strike any visitor from the twenty-first century as most distressing — it was a world where tens of thousands of poor children were at large, clothed in rags, and expected, just as much as the grown-ups, to earn their own keep.

In a scene that he worked up for use in *David Copperfield,* Dickens recollected his own boyhood experience, when working in the blacking-warehouse off the Strand, of entering a public house:

I was such a little fellow, with my poor white hat, little jacket, and corduroy trowsers, that frequently, when I went into the bar of a strange public-house for a glass of ale or porter to wash down the saveloy and the loaf I had eaten in the street, they didn't like to give it to me. I remember one evening (I had been somewhere for my father, and was going back to the borough over Westminster-bridge) that I went into the public-house

in Parliament-street, which is still there though altered, at the corner of the short street leading into Cannon-row, and said to the landlord behind the bar, "What is your very best — the VERY *best* — ale, a glass?"

He recollected how the landlord and his wife came round from behind the bar to look at him and questioned him about who he was and what he did, "To all of which, that I might commit nobody, I invented appropriate answers."

The beginnings of Dickens's fictions — and not merely their beginnings, but their essence and their end! He had much to hide, much to invent. The reason he crossed Westminster Bridge to see his father was that John Dickens's debts were not settled, and in that early capitalist world where money was God, debtors were imprisoned. The blacking factory and the Marshalsea prison were the universities in which Dickens learned his art and nurtured his genius. The young Shakespeare's life is wholly mysterious to us, and when he began to write his plays, he drew invariably from other people's story-books, or from the chronicle-histories of England. When Dickens began to write, the overpopulation and industrialization of Britain had already provided him with his theme of themes: that is, children who have suffered separation from their families and who long in some way or another to get back to them, either to actual families or to substitutes who provide the warmth and innocence of home.

In our world of late capitalist liberalism, prison is for thieves and felons. In Dickens's world, such people were often hanged or deported. Long-term prison sentences were reserved not for those who had taken money but who had lost it, through bad luck or improvidence. Mr. Micawber's celebrated dictum — "Annual income twenty pounds, annual expenditure nineteen nineteen and six, result happiness" — was the defining creed of the Victorian middle class. Dickens grew up in the shadow, as so many at the lower and unfortunate end of that class would do, of debt: the mainstay of Western economy in our day but, for them, the ultimate disgrace. As has often been observed, Mr. Dorrit represents the dark side, Mr. Micawber the sunny side, of the same phenomenon — Dickens's reinvention of his father, his reliving of early humiliations and separations.

If the patterns of the economic life of the West have changed, the inner anxieties and fears of childhood have not changed at all. In our era of divorce and unmarried parentage, the "Dickensian" fears are deeper than ever for a modern child. The remarriage of David Copperfield's mother to Mr. Murdstone is the ultimate severance: it makes home itself strange. "Ah, what a strange feeling it was to be going home when it was not home, and to find every object I looked at, reminded me of the happy old home, which was like a dream I could never dream again!" David defines the presence in his mother's house of the cruel stepfather and his sister, Miss Murdstone, as "a monstrous load I was obliged to bear, a daymare that there was no possibility of breaking in, a weight that brooded on my wits, and blunted them!" David Copperfield, through the death of his father and the unwise marriage of his mother to Mr. Murdstone, is thrust out of the comforting world of family and home and becomes a whipped, tearful exile in boarding-schools (the sort of waif tortured by Wackford Squeers in *Nicholas Nickleby*).

Oliver Twist's story is a version of the same thing but in reverse. He was born by a hideous accident in a workhouse and drawn into the street-life of Fagin and the Artful Dodger, yet by the chance of picking Mr. Brownlow's pocket, he was led back to the family that had lost him before he even came into the world. In *Dombey and Son*, Florence Dombey and her cold-hearted father are both victims of the materialism that is always the villain in Dickens's fiction. It is only Mr. Dombey's broken-hearted lonely daughter who knows what really counts in life. Mr. Dombey thinks, until the very end, that the best sort of house is a counting-house. He longs for his house to be Dombey and Son, because love of money has blinded him to what a real father-son relationship should be like. Only through bereavement and loss and humiliation does he learn the true state of his alienation. So it is that Dickens, child of the debtor's jail, stands the values of capitalism on their heads, not by advocating a Marxist alternative, but by opposing love to Mammon.

Dickens's greatness shows itself in great scenes, great characters, and unimprovable sentences, but the books themselves, taken as a whole, very often collapse as you feel him speeding toward the deadline. The plot of *Little Dorrit,* for example, is all but self-defeating. When the story starts, Arthur Clennam, upon the death of his father, returns from twenty years trading in the family firm in China. He asks his mother whether his father's death-agonies had been caused by the knowledge that the house of Clennam owed its prosperity to some great wrong, "Is it possible, mother, that he had unhappily wronged any one and made no reparation?" If Clennam's suspicions had turned out to be groundless, then much of the power of the story would be lost. But this, for some unfathomable reason,

is what happens. Clennam discovers that the tiny, childlike woman who comes to serve Mrs. Clennam and help with the sewing is known as "Little Dorrit" and resides in the debtor's prison, the Marshalsea. He finds out that she was born there, and so we are introduced to two of the most extraordinary *mise en scenes* created in English fiction: Mrs. Clennam's self-imposed imprisonment in her crumbling house, and old Mr. Dorrit's imprisonment for debt. The Dorrits, it turns out, are not debtors at all but very rich; they have an inheritance, discovered by the redoubtable Pancks, which enables them to leave the Marshalsea in style and step from the wonderfully evoked prison to a thinly sketched series of caricatures and feeble scenes in foreign hotels. And Mrs. Clennam turns out not, in fact, to be Arthur's mother. She adopted him, the result of a union between his father and a chorus girl in the employ of Frederick Dorrit, and has been employing Little Dorrit to make "reparation" to the Dorrits, who should by rights have received some money for this exchange.

Yet by now, we all know that Dickens has somehow or other, through carelessness or willfulness, departed from the perfect novel and left behind the true novel, the one we have been reading, shall reread, and will always remember as one of the wondrous reading experiences of our lives. The relationship between Arthur and Mrs. Clennam is one of the great mother-son portraits of literature. Its painfulness, the stifled pride and anger, and mutually inexpressible yearning for love will be recognized by many a stiff Englishman whose childhood has separated him from the maternal bosom and who has tried to maintain a friendship with his mother in adult life.

One of the key reasons that *Great Expectations,* by contrast with *Little Dorrit,* is so keenly and poignantly the most successful of all Dickens's novels is that the dislocation is self-inflicted. Unlike Florence Dombey, Oliver Twist, or David Copperfield, Pip has, in a fashion, a loving home. True, his sister has a foul temper, and his parents are dead, which is certainly not a very good start in life. But, in the saddest and truest sentence he ever wrote, Dickens notes, "It is a most miserable thing to feel ashamed of home." The tormented love for Miss Havisham's niece Estelle leads Pip into more than a morbid infatuation with a woman. It teaches him snobbery, whose poison eventually makes him completely indifferent to the hurt feelings of the truest friends he has in the world: his honest, unfailingly faithful brother-in-law Joe Gargery ("What larks, Pip!") and Joe's second wife, Biddy. The mysterious inheritance that makes him into a gentleman comes not, as he vainly supposes, from Miss Havisham and the comparatively genteel fortune of a brewery but from a convict. He thinks he is being rewarded for social climbing, whereas, in fact, he, like the virtuous in St. Matthew's Gospel, did so much for the least of his brethren — he stole a pie and a file for a chained escaped prisoner. In the end, Pip is bailed out from the debtor's jail by Joe, who leaves him in his chambers with the note: "Not wishful to intrude I have departed fur you are well again dear Pip and will do better without Joe. P.S. Ever the very best of friends." What is great about the novel is that it completely refuses to compromise. Pip is contemptuous of Joe for his low manner, but by the time he comes to despise himself for being so, it is too late, as Joe has the emotional intelligence to recognize.

Pip's miserably sad relationship with Joe is thrown into ever more painful contrast by the near-perfection and comedy of Wemmick's relationship with the Aged P. down in the miniature fortress of Walworth. When Pip first sees the tiny, fantastical bower, Wemmick explains to him:

> I am my own engineer, and my own carpenter, and my own plumber, and my own gardener, and my own Jack of all trades. . . . Well, it's a good thing, you know. It brushes the Newgate cobwebs away and pleases the Aged.

In so far as Dickens has a political creed, translatable into modern terms, Wemmick has expressed it in those words. The novels are all hymns of hate to collectivism in any form, to nannyism and Benthamite busybodydom, to churches or states wishing to mind the business of individuals, or to confuse their duty — that of alleviating the suffering of the poor — with their odious hunger to improve the poor themselves. For if Dickens's novels are so often about the pains of dislocation within families and the trauma of isolation, they are also hymns of praise to the glory of individualism.

Men, women, and children survive by being wonderfully and ridiculously themselves. It may be that at some supposedly sophisticated phase of one's reading life, perhaps in adolescence or one's early twenties, one thinks it is smart to sneer at Dickens for his drawing of caricatures. In maturity one comes to see that, although he can indeed be said to draw caricatures, so can nature. People in real life do repeat themselves, parody themselves, and overdraw themselves — and in just the way that Dickens's characters so frequently do.

Dickens often allows us glimpses of characters alone, being themselves, and doing nothing much in particular. One thinks, for example, of the marvelously funny descriptions of Dick Swiveller's domestic arrangements at the beginning of *The Old Curiosity Shop* or of Quilp's life in his shack of a counting-house on Quilp's Wharf, taking a cat-nap by lying down on his desk. Balzac takes the trouble to fill in the minutiae of minor characters' lives in this way: it is one of the things that the two novelists have in common, and it is one of the things that makes novels abidingly readable. When we have half-forgotten the plots or the grand themes of a book, it is often these minor details that stay in the head, like the unforgettable details of a great painting.

Dickens, too, has details that are painterly when his imagination is most fully engaged: "When I neared home the light on the spit of sand off the point on the marshes was gleaming against a black night sky, and Joe's furnace was flinging a path of fire across the road." Of all English novelists, Dickens is the best stylist, the most penetrating and sympathetic psychologist, the closest to a great poet. Like such a poet, he refashions the world in his own terms and persuades us that what we have seen is not Dickens's world but the true world.

Charles Dickens

From Great
Expectations,
chapter 14

It is a most miserable thing to feel ashamed of home. There may be black ingratitude in the thing, and the punishment may be retributive and well deserved; but, that it is a miserable thing, I can testify.

Home had never been a very pleasant place to me, because of my sister's temper. But, Joe had sanctified it, and I believed in it. I had believed in the best parlour as a most elegant saloon; I had believed in the front door, as a mysterious portal of the Temple of State whose solemn opening was attended with a sacrifice of roast fowls; I had believed in the kitchen as a chaste though not magnificent apartment; I had believed in the forge as the glowing road to manhood and independence. Within a single year all this was changed. Now, it was all coarse and common, and I would not have had Miss Havisham and Estella see it on any account.

How much of my ungracious condition of mind may have been my own fault, how much Miss Havisham's, how much my sister's, is now of no moment to me or to any one. The change was made in me; the thing was done. Well or ill done, excusably or inexcusably, it was done.

Once, it had seemed to me that when I should at last roll up my shirt-sleeves and go into the forge, Joe's 'prentice, I should be distinguished and happy. Now the reality was in my hold, I only felt that I was dusty with the dust of the small coal, and that I had a weight upon my daily remembrance to which the anvil was a feather. There have been occasions in my later life (I suppose as in most lives) when I have felt for a time as if a thick curtain had fallen on all its interest and romance, to shut me out from anything save dull endurance any more. Never has that curtain dropped so heavy and blank, as when my way in life lay stretched out straight before me through the newly-entered road of apprenticeship to Joe.

I remember that at a later period of my 'time,' I used to stand above the churchyard on Sunday evenings, when night was falling, comparing my own perspective with the windy marsh view, and making out some likeness between them by thinking how flat and low both were, and how on both there came an unknown way and a dark mist and then the sea. I was quite as dejected on the first working-day of my apprenticeship as in that after-time; but I am glad to know that I never breathed a murmur to Joe while my indentures lasted. It is about the only thing I *am* glad to know of myself in that connection.

For, though it includes what I proceed to add, all the merit of what I proceed to add was Joe's. It was not because I was faithful, but because Joe was faithful, that I never ran away and went for a solider or a sailor. It was not because I had a strong sense of the virtue of industry, that I worked with tolerable zeal against the grain. It is not possible to know how far the influence of any amiable honest-hearted duty-doing man flies out into the world; but it is very possible to know how it has touched one's self in going by, and I know right well that any good that intermixed itself with my apprenticeship came of plain contented Joe, and not of restless aspiring discontented me.

What I wanted, who can say? How can *I* say, when I never knew? What I dreaded was, that in some unlucky hour I, being at my grimiest and commonest, should lift up my eyes and see Estella looking in at one of the wooden windows of the forge. I was haunted by the fear that she would, sooner or later, find me out, with a black face and hands, doing the coarsest part of my work, and would exult over me and despise me. Often after dark, when I was pulling the bellows for Joe, and we were singing Old Clem, and when the thought how we used to sing it at Miss Havisham's would seem to show me Estella's face in the fire, with her pretty hair fluttering in the wind and her eyes scorning me, — often at such a time I would look towards those panels of black night in the wall which the wooden windows then were, and would fancy that I saw her just drawing her face away, and would believe that she had come at last.

After that, when we went in to supper, the place and the meal would have a more homely look than ever, and I would feel more ashamed of home than ever, in my own ungracious breast.

Walt Whitman

BY JUSTIN KAPLAN

Nearing seventy, "gossiping in the early candle-light of old age," Walt Whitman looked back over the long and often arduous road that led from the first publication of *Leaves of Grass* in 1855. "I had my choice when I commenc'd," he wrote. "I have had my say entirely my own way." The work of an unknown and untried thirty-six-year-old poet, his book arrived in a largely indifferent world not as a trial venture, a merely "promising" work, but as a stylistically and substantively achieved masterpiece. *Leaves of Grass* was both the fulfillment of American literary romanticism and the beginnings of American literary modernism. It established Whitman as his country's chief poet of international standing. His imperial voice asserts itself in the work of Wallace Stevens, William Carlos Williams, Ezra Pound, Hart Crane, the generation of Allen Ginsberg and Jack Kerouac, and poets of today. Along with Benjamin Franklin, Abraham Lincoln, and Mark Twain, Whitman has become a god-like presence in the American consciousness. D. H. Lawrence called him "the first white aboriginal."

Whitman wrote his unrhymed poetry in a revolutionary free-verse form that derived its cadences from the King James Bible but in every other way defied the literary conventions and practices of his century. He shunned and discarded what he saw as the baggage of classical, medieval, and foreign allusions. The poetry of *Leaves of Grass* is ecstatic and down-to-earth, expansive and laconic, colloquial and lyrical, boastful and modest, solemn and playful, grandiose and self-mocking, and altogether original. Its idiom and language were native and populist. Common grass, universal, growing "wherever the land is and the water is," was his constitutive and enclosing metaphor. It was also the flag of his disposition, "out of hopeful green stuff woven." The new poet's meters were lawless, his morals elastic, and his program heretical and subversive, celebrating the sexual, unbound, and unashamed in human behavior.

I am the poet of the body,
And I am the poet of the soul.

Whitman created a radical poetry voicing a radical consciousness and even a messianic purpose: "For I confront peace, security, and all the settled laws, to unsettle them." The poet of "Song of Myself," the major poem in the 1855

Whitman was born on May 31, 1819, in West Hills, Long Island, New York. He died in Camden, New Jersey, on March 26, 1892.

edition, even seems at times to appoint himself a latter-day Christ and deliver his own Sermon on the Mount. He intended *Leaves of Grass* to be nothing less than a "new Bible" for his century and for the America to come. He was a prophet but also the tenderest, most loving of lyric poets, and he celebrated moments of oneness with all of creation.

Poets of ecstasy through the ages rendered the consummated marriage of the soul with God in sexual imagery. But sexuality as sexuality — "the root of roots," "the desire to copulate" — is an unmuted force in *Leaves of Grass*. Whitman sanctifies the democratization of the whole person, the liberation of impulse and instinct from involuntary servitude to society and convention. The explicit sexuality of the love between man and man is one of the driving forces of his poetry, together with the love between man and woman. Fluid in sexual identity, lover of men and women, multi-gendered, the poet-hero of *Leaves of*

Grass is sometimes "she who adorn'd herself and folded her hair expectantly, My truant lover has come, and it is dark." He merges his identity with his reader's:

It is I you hold and who holds you,
I spring from the pages into your arms....
O how your fingers drowse me,
Your breath falls around me like dew....

There is nothing quite like it in literature, Whitman at his best. Even when he is at his awful worst — windy, bombastic, repetitious, self-imitative, fumbling with French words to naturalize them — you may love him for that, too. ("Only a man with the most extraordinary feel for language, or none whatsoever," Randall Jarrell wrote, "could have cooked up Whitman's worst messes.") The poet of *Leaves of Grass* is unworried, nonchalant, and variable: prophet, stump orator, loafer, sexual athlete. He celebrates the open road and the modern city, its "glories strung like beads on my smallest sights and hearings." But he is also a free, naked, and natural creature of the outdoors:

I think I could turn and live with the animals ...
        they are so placid and self-contained,
I stand and look at them sometimes half the day long.
They do not sweat and whine about their condition,
They do not lie awake in the dark and weep for their sins,
They do not make me sick discussing their duty to God,
Not one is dissatisfied ... not one is demented with the
        mania of owning things,
Not one kneels to another nor to his kind that lived
        thousands of years ago,
Not one is respectable or industrious over the whole
        earth.

Whitman's great work ran upstream against the literary taste and practice of his time. The year *Leaves of Grass* first appeared, the Cambridge poet-scholar Henry Wadsworth Longfellow published his foray into genteel primitivism, *The Song of Hiawatha,* an immediate sensation in both England and at home. Longfellow's eclectic and cosmopolitan epic had an Ojibway Indian hero and was written in the manner and meters of the Finnish national epic, *Kalevala.* Whitman dismissed Longfellow's hybrid as "a pleasing ripply poem." On the other side of the Atlantic in 1855 William Wordsworth's successor as Poet Laureate, Alfred Tennyson, published *Maud: A Monodrama* ("tedious and affected, with some sweet passages," Whitman said) and was writing *Idylls of the King,* a protracted commemoration of medievalism and Arthurian legend.

The setting, subject, and matrix of Whitman's poetry were the United States in the booming and turbulent nineteenth century, an age of iron, steam, science, and democracy — "The Modern Man I sing." In style, substance, and presentation *Leaves of Grass* stood in opposition to the poetry of Whitman's day, conspicuously the work of upper-class, cultivated New England eminences with triple-barreled names that thundered authority and respectability: William Cullen Bryant, John Greenleaf Whittier, Henry Wadsworth Longfellow, Oliver Wendell Holmes, James Russell Lowell. Following the populist examples of Kit Carson and Davy Crockett, the new poet called himself "Walt." The frontispiece portrait facing the title page of *Leaves of Grass* in 1855 showed a vigorous man of the streets and wharves. He is dressed like a sailor or a laborer, coatless and bare-necked. Casually, even defiantly, he stands with his pelvis thrust forward, his left hand in his pants pocket, the other on his hip, and he is clearly a stranger to parlors, clubs, and libraries. As readers learned about midway into the long poem later titled "Song of Myself," this man so confidently advancing on them from his position on the printed page, is

Walt Whitman, an American, one of the roughs,
    a kosmos,
Disorderly fleshy and sensual . . . eating drinking
    and breeding,
No sentimentalist . . . no stander above men and women
    or apart from them . . . no more modest than
    immodest.

This was a new sort of persona for the poet in nineteenth-century America. In his thirties, the former schoolteacher, house-builder, hack-fiction writer, newspaper editor, and journalist had begun to write astonishing poems of ecstasy and illumination, celebrations of nature and vital impulse, of pain, grief, tenderness, sexual longing, and surreal journeyings:

I dream in my dreams all the dreams of the
    other dreamers,
And I become the other dreamers.

He wrote with a unique admixture of wit, humor, clowning, Western brag, Yankee laconism, deliberate absurdity, and colossal egotism.

Unscrew the locks from the doors!
Unscrew the doors themselves from their jambs!
The scent of these arm-pits is aroma finer than
prayer. . . .

I dote on myself, there is that lot of me and all so
    luscious . . .

I discover myself on the verge of a usual mistake.

I do not say these things for a dollar or to fill up
    the time while I wait for a boat. . . .

I sound my barbaric yawp over the roofs of the
    world.

In its first appearance *Leaves of Grass* was a privately printed book of eighty-three pages of seemingly undisciplined verse and ten pages of eccentrically structured and punctuated prose, a preface that served as a storehouse of ideas for poems in subsequent editions. The author, who never missed an opportunity to promote his book, had sent a copy to Ralph Waldo Emerson, mid-century America's reigning sage and arbiter. The celebrated letter Emerson wrote to the as-yet unknown author, a stranger to him, right away recognized a decisive event in the nation's literature. "I find it the most extraordinary piece of wit and wisdom that America has yet produced. I am very happy in reading it, as great power makes us happy," he wrote to Whitman. "I find incomparable things said incomparably well, as they must be. I find the courage of treatment, which so delights us, and which large perception only can inspire. I greet you at the beginning of a great career." Another work of insurgency, Henry Thoreau's *Walden*, published the summer before, had drawn only qualified praise from Emerson. But it was *Leaves of Grass* that answered the Concord sage's passionate call for a native genius gifted with "nerve and dagger" and a "tyrannous command" of "our incomparable materials."

Almost up to the day of his death on March 26, 1892, Whitman continued to add single poems and "clusters" of poems to his book, including his Civil War cycle, *Drum-Taps*. By the time *Leaves of Grass* arrived at its final stage in the so-called "Deathbed" edition (1891–92), it had grown to more than four hundred pages. Along the way he compared his modern epic with a tree of many growth-rings, a cathedral, a great city like his million-footed Manhattan. In the prose of *Specimen Days,* published in 1882, Whitman wrote a profoundly intimate autobiography that he described as "the most wayward, spontaneous, fragmentary book ever printed." He provided a few glimpses of his family and his early years, but mostly he wrote about his experiences as a hospital nurse in wartime Washington's military hospitals, the bustle of the cities and the suffering of the war, his breakdown and illness as a consequence of overwork caring for the wounded and dying, and his eventual return to an inner equilibrium. Taken together, *Leaves of Grass, Specimen Days,* and the miscellaneous essays, recollections, and ruminations in his *Complete Prose Works* (1892) established him as a sort of national oversoul and conscience. The unbridled and bardic hero of "Song of Myself" had aged and mellowed into "The Good Gray Poet." Despite his claims of public neglect, Whitman's canny recognition of the value of publicity, self-promotion, and photographic portraiture made him almost as conspicuous and immediately recognizable as Mark Twain. He engineered controversy, planted news stories, and managed to make himself famous for his alleged obscurity.

Whitman's work as poet and prose writer is a running epic of American democracy, at the time still regarded by many in England, even some of his admirers there, as a dubious experiment in the optative mood. He had been born in a Long Island farmhouse in 1819 during the administration of James Monroe, a Virginian

Along with Benjamin Franklin, Abraham Lincoln, and Mark Twain, Whitman has become a god-like presence in the American consciousness. D. H. Lawrence called him "the first white aboriginal."

of the old school who had served under Washington at Valley Forge and still wore silk breeches, a survival of the eighteenth century. A scattering of other Revolutionary War veterans — Whitman called them "the sacred army" — were still alive, along with bitter memories of the British occupation of New York and of Americans rotting away in British prison ships moored in the East River. When Whitman died in 1892, the president was Benjamin Harrison, a successful corporation lawyer, obedient to business interests. The United States had meanwhile become a rich, increasingly industrial nation that proved the durability of the Union by surviving the Civil War — "America brought to hospital in her fair youth."

Perhaps only Herman Melville in the poetry of *Battle Pieces* was as responsive as Whitman in *Drum-Taps* to the tragedy and high drama of the Civil War. Melville, however, had had none of Whitman's direct experience of the daily horrors of battlefields, surgical tents, and hospitals, where amputation was the favored medical option. *Specimen Days* was in large part Whitman's record of the war both as witness and participant in his role of "wound-dresser." "The real war will never get into the books," he wrote. That history had been too passionate, too incredible and sacred, to be violated by telling. It could only be indicated, in poems of mourning over the transfigured dead and dying:

Young man I think I know you — I think this face is the
    face of the Christ himself,
Dead and divine and brother of all, and here again he lies.

Only after the guns were silenced did Whitman keen over "the dead, the dead, the dead — our dead" of both South and North. Insofar as there was a redeemer, for him it was the martyred Abraham Lincoln, a symbolic figure who transcended politics, leadership, and victory. Lincoln is not named, nor was there need to name him, in "When Lilacs Last in the Dooryard Bloom'd," Whitman's threnody for the murdered president: "the sweetest, wisest soul of all my days and lands." The Civil War was the central event of Whitman's middle life, a test not only of Union but of the democratic principle undergirding his poetry.

Having survived the tests of secession and disunion, the United States entered what Whitman, critic and moralist, called the era of "hollowness of heart" and "hypocrisy throughout." This was the postwar period, the era of Reconstruction turned sour and cynical that Mark Twain called the Gilded Age. Whitman anatomized that era in a long and unflinching prose essay, *Democratic Vistas*. "We had best look our times and lands searchingly in the face," he wrote, "like a physician diagnosing some deep disease." He came away appalled and saddened. "Our New World democracy," he wrote, "is, so far, an almost complete failure in its social aspects, and in really grand religious, moral, literary, and esthetic results." A century and a half later, the United States was the world's sole and indisputable superpower, with material interests and power outposts spread over the entire globe. But already in Whitman's day, as he wrote in *Democratic Vistas,* the nation's reach had expanded beyond its original territorial limits and even the ambitious limits of manifest destiny. The United States was on its way to achieving "empire so colossal, outvying the antique, beyond Alexander's, beyond the proudest sway of Rome. In vain have we annex'd Texas, California, Alaska, and reach north for Canada and south for Cuba. It is as if we were somehow being endow'd with a vast and more and more thoroughly appointed body, but then left with little or no soul."

The once sunlit poet of 1855 had matured and broadened in vision, his early exuberance tempered by loneliness, the horrors of the Civil War, and a degree of resignation and disappointment. The center of his life, even his reason for being, had been the creation, defense, and promotion of *Leaves of Grass.* But his sacred book had as yet failed to gain the broad acceptance he had hoped for in the country from which it had sprung. *Leaves of Grass* in 1892 had its partisans at home and abroad, but it was still something of an outlaw book, a present disappointment of his high hopes for it. But with justified confidence he called it "a candidate for the future" that would continue to live "on its own blood." Today, Whitman's *Leaves of Grass* is a cornerstone of his nation's literature and read in virtually every written and spoken language.

Walt Whitman

I celebrate myself,
and what I assume you shall assume,
For every atom belonging to me as good belongs to you.

From Leaves of Grass *(1855)*

I loafe and invite my soul,
I lean and loafe at my ease .... observing a spear of summer grass.

Houses and rooms are full of perfumes .... the shelves are crowded with
    perfumes,
I breathe the fragrance myself, and know it and like it,
The distillation would intoxicate me also, but I shall not let it.

The atmosphere is not a perfume .... it has no taste of the distillation .... it is
    odorless,
It is for my mouth forever .... I am in love with it,
I will go to the bank by the wood and become undisguised and naked,
I am mad for it to be in contact with me.

The smoke of my own breath,
Echos, ripples, and buzzed whispers .... loveroot, silkthread, crotch and vine,
My respiration and inspiration .... the beating of my heart .... the passing of
    blood and air through my lungs,
The sniff of green leaves and dry leaves, and of the shore and darkcolored sea-
    rocks, and of hay in the barn,
The sound of the belched words of my voice .... words loosed to the eddies of
    the wind,
A few light kisses .... a few embraces .... a reaching around of arms,
The play of shine and shade on the trees as the supple boughs wag,
The delight alone or in the rush of the streets, or along the fields and hillsides,
The feeling of health .... the full-noon trill .... the song of me rising from bed
    and meeting the sun.

Have you reckoned a thousand acres much? Have you reckoned the earth
    much?
Have you practiced so long to learn to read?
Have you felt so proud to get at the meaning of poems?

Stop this day and night with me and you shall possess the origin of all poems,
You shall possess the good of the earth and sun . . . . there are millions of suns
    left,
You shall no longer take things at second or third hand . . . . nor look through
    the eyes of the dead . . . . nor feed on the spectres in books,
You shall not look through my eyes either, nor take things from me,
You shall listen to all sides and filter them for yourself.

····:¦:····

Trippers and askers surround me,
People I meet . . . . . the effect upon me of my early life . . . . of the ward and city
    I live in . . . . of the nation,
The latest news . . . . discoveries, inventions, societies . . . . authors old and
    new,
My dinner, dress, associates, looks, business, compliments, dues,
The real or fancied indifference of some man or woman I love,
The sickness of one of my folks — or of myself . . . . or ill-doing . . . . or loss or
    lack of money . . . . or depressions or exaltations,
They come to me days and nights and go from me again,
But they are not the Me myself.

Apart from the pulling and hauling stands what I am,
Stands amused, complacent, compassionating, idle, unitary,
Looks down, is erect, bends an arm on an impalpable certain rest,
Looks with its sidecurved head curious what will come next,
Both in and out of the game, and watching and wondering at it.

Backward I see in my own days where I sweated through fog with linguists
    and contenders,
I have no mockings or arguments . . . . I witness and wait.

····:¦:····

I believe in you my soul . . . . the other I am must not abase itself to you,
And you must not be abased to the other.

Loafe with me on the grass . . . . loose the stop from your throat,
Not words, not music or rhyme I want . . . . not custom or lecture, not even
the best,
Only the lull I like, the hum of your valved voice.

I mind how we lay in June, such a transparent summer morning;
You settled your head athwart my hips and gently turned over upon me,
And parted the shirt from my bosom-bone, and plunged your tongue to
my barestript heart,
And reached till you felt my beard, and reached till you held my feet.

Swiftly arose and spread around me the peace and joy and knowledge that
pass all the art and argument of the earth;
And I know that the hand of God is the elderhand of my own,
And I know that the spirit of God is the eldest brother of my own,
And that all the men ever born are also my brothers . . . . and the women my
sisters and lovers,
And that a kelson of the creation is love;
And limitless are leaves stiff or drooping in the fields,
And brown ants in the little wells beneath them,
And mossy scabs of the wormfence, and heaped stones, and elder and
mullen and pokeweed.

Herman Melville

························∞∞∞∞∞∞························

BY WILLIAM H. PRITCHARD

Melville shares with those American writers who are his peers — Emerson, Hawthorne, Thoreau, Twain, James, Faulkner — a stylistic aggressiveness that takes hold of us when we first read him and, over the course of further encounters, intensifies rather than relaxes its grip. Such aggressiveness is of course unmistakable in the tumult, sometimes the blatancy, of his most ambitious novels, *Moby-Dick* and *Pierre,* but is also there in the quieter subtleties of his memorable shorter fictions: "Bartleby the Scrivener," "Benito Cereno," and *Billy Budd, Sailor.*

Yet the perceived difficulty and complication of Melville's work, along with its evident intent to say something important about human ultimates — good and evil, life and death — have tempted both professional critics and ordinary readers to search for, and always find, metaphysical profundities in it. Thus they argue about what Melville was *really* getting at, rather than paying attention to the literary performance as it unfolds over pages of sentences and paragraphs. Searchers for profundity also tend to push aside or ignore the very large ingredient of humor — of comedy, satire, parody — that informs so many of Melville's sequences. For among other things he is, along with Twain and Frost, the most mischievous of American writers, concerned with engaging his audience in seriously play-ful colloquy, sometimes to the point where we lose our bearing and wonder if we've got the narrator's tone of voice just right or somewhat wrong. There is no doubt that Melville was an overreacher, a most ambitious writer with a yen to plumb the mysteries of human behavior. But the writerly ways he goes about this enterprise are never less than centrally active, and they invite our responsive cooperation.

In understanding his career and reputation as a writer, two biographical facts are of note. The first is that, although Melville lived into his seventy-third year, the writing for which he will be remembered was almost wholly the product of the eleven years that began with his highly successful "Peep at Polynesian Life," *Typee* (1846), and ended with his final novel, *The Confidence-Man: His Masquerade* (1857), published to less than acclaim. Only his poems and the posthumously published *Billy Budd* post-date those years. The second, perhaps even more surprising fact is that at the time

Melville was born on August 1, 1819, in New York, New York. He died there on September 28, 1891.

of his death he was virtually forgotten as a writer; it would be another thirty years before he was rediscovered by his first full-length biographer, Raymond Weaver, and the Melville revival got under way. Over the past nine decades that revival has been marked by a never-ceasing flow of biographical and critical studies, many of them convinced they have the "secret" to Melville's extraordinary — and extraordinarily troubled — creative powers, this secret to be explained or exposed in one or another historical, socio-economic, or psychoanalytic vocabulary. On the evidence of Herschel Parker's enormous two-volume biography, there is no American writer for whom we have a more factually documented year-by-year record.

Yet the interesting fact, at least in my experience of the writer, is that, unlike Hawthorne, Twain, or William Dean Howells, the more you read Melville and read about him, the more strange and finally unaccountable his genius becomes. The very fact that we have recourse to that word "genius" — which we don't think to do with, say, Howells — is probably a guarantee of this unaccountability. We may remember Captain Ahab's words in his great speech about the white whale where he urges himself and his men to "strike through the mask" of visible objects, like the whale, that are propelled by invisible powers: "He tasks me; he heaps me; I see in him outrageous strength, with an inscrutable malice sinewing it." Ahab's attempt to summon up adequate language to express the inexpressible or "inscrutable" power of *Moby-Dick* may be applied, in a somewhat milder tonality, to the reader's attempt to take in, to follow, to keep up with, Melville the writer.

He lived in many places: New York City; upstate New York near Albany; on Pacific islands and on the decks of whaling ships and man-of-war frigates; on a farm near Pittsfield, Massachusetts, called Arrowhead, during his most productive years; and, for his last decades, again in New York City. But most of all he lived in a city of words that, as the critic James Wood put it, "no other nineteenth-century novelist writing in English lived in." "They were suburbanites by comparison," Wood adds. Sometimes he abused the privilege of living in that city of words; at least D. H. Lawrence thought so when, in one of his two essays on Melville in *Studies in Classic American Literature,* he wrote, "Nobody can be more clownish, more clumsy and sententiously in bad taste, than Herman Melville, even in a great book like *Moby-Dick.*" Lawrence thought it was because Melville was unsure of himself, and thus again and again had to "hold forth, often so amateurishly."

But how should we come to terms with a writer who inhabits, as did Melville, a vast city of words (critics have studied closely the coinages and improvisations of his language) and at the same time — in Lawrence's word — is "unsure" of himself? We may think of other Romantic and post-Romantic writers — Shelley, Faulkner, and Wallace Stevens come to mind — whose ventures in striking through the mask have to be repeated endlessly since they never succeed on any particular occasion in making language live up to their aspirations for it. (Think of Faulkner's page-long sentences or of Stevens's endless endeavor to say something in every manner of way.) Melville's unsureness was once memorably put into words by his friend Hawthorne when Melville visited him five years after *Moby-Dick* appeared: "He can neither believe, nor be comfortable in his unbelief, and he is too honest and courageous not to try to do one or the other." In other words, he refused to or was unable to adopt the second-best consolations of ironic skepticism, as Hawthorne, by contrast, managed to do.

At the end of the "Cetology" chapter in *Moby-Dick,* after Ishmael, or Melville, has presented us with a seemingly exhaustive classification of the various kinds of whales, we are told that this "Cetological System" must remain, like "the great Cathedral of Cologne," unfinished:

For small erections may be finished by their first architects; grand ones, true ones, ever leave the copestone to posterity. God keep me from ever completing anything. This whole book is but a draught — nay, but the draught of a draught. Oh, Time, Strength, Cash, and Patience!

The fear is of "succeeding" by writing a sentence — a book — that isn't sufficiently a "mighty book" because it's too finished. "To produce a mighty book, you must choose, a mighty theme," he says elsewhere in the novel. This means that there can be no end to expression since the whale — since the world out there — is inexpressible. To be "unsure" then is a guarantee of one's seriousness as a man and a writer; it brings with it, however, more than a measure of torment.

In this connection there is a revealing passage in *Pierre,* Melville's most tormented piece of writing and the novel that, following hard on the heels of *Moby-Dick* (which also sold poorly), did so much to sink his reputation. After meeting his mysterious, presumed half-sister Isabella and deciding to throw in his lot with her by pretending to marry her — thus protecting the memory of his father, of whom Isabella is the presumed illegitimate fruit — Pierre, or Melville, speculates on the difference between novels and the "life" they claim to embody. Pierre had read more novels than most youths, we are told,

but their false, inverted attempts at systematizing eternally unsystematizable elements; their audacious, intermeddling impotency in trying to unravel and spread out and classify the more than thin gossamer threads that make up the complex of life, these things over Pierre had no power now.

We are told that he "pierced" straight through the "helpless miserableness" of fiction and saw that, like God, human life partakes of his "unravellable inscrutableness." Although novels pretend to clear up and resolve the mysteries they present,

yet the profounder emanations of the human mind, intended to illustrate all that can be humanly known of human life; they never unravel their own intricacies and have no proper endings, but in imperfect, unanticipated, and disappointing sequels (as mutilated stumps), hurry to abrupt intermergings with the eternal tides of time and fate.

(No wonder he subtitled his novel "The Ambiguities.")

However much of Melville's intent in the novel was to correct the illusions of his romantic hero, the above sentences, in their tortuous contortions, suggest that the author himself had discovered the trumped-up banalities of most novels and was determined not to fall into them. One of his most quoted remarks was made in June of 1851 when he was finishing *Moby-Dick* and worried whether the book — or any of his books — would "pay": "What I feel most moved to write, that is banned — it will

not pay. Yet, altogether, write the other way I cannot. So the product is a final hash, and all my books are botches." He wrote his father-in-law, with reference to his attempts in the novels directly preceding *Moby-Dick* — *Redburn* and *White-Jacket* — "My only desire for their 'success' (as it is called) springs from my pocket, and not from my heart. So far as I am individually concerned, and independent of my pocket, it is my earnest desire to write those sort of books which are said to 'fail.'" It is probably, then, something more than a historical coincidence that Melville's "botches" only began to be seriously read and criticized at the same time as modernist texts such as Joyce's *Ulysses* and Eliot's *The Waste Land* appeared. Like them and like other twentieth-century work, Melville's most powerful fiction, whether at its peak of brilliance in *Moby-Dick* or at its peak of miscalculation in *Pierre*, carries on a debate with itself: questioning, revising, playing with its own formulations to the extent that naïve readers then or now, looking for a good book to read on an airplane, will be disappointed if not disgusted. It was with such readers that Melville was destined to "fail."

Yet in fact he is wonderfully hospitable to those who are willing to become active, since reading, as Walt Whitman put it memorably, "is not a half-sleep, but, in highest sense, a gymnast's struggle . . . the reader is to do something for himself, must be on the alert, must himself or herself construct indeed the poem, argument, history, metaphysical essay — the text furnishing the hints, the clues, the start or framework." From beginning to end, Melville's work is remarkable for the vigor and variety of its "texts," which we're invited to listen to, and often to struggle with. In what is perhaps the best of all books on him as writer, *The Example*

of Melville, Warner Berthoff insists that Melville's storytelling demands "direct collaboration between the teller and his audience." This is especially the case when we are given in some of Melville's tales — *Billy Budd* foremost among them — a recital of something that has already taken place, rather than a "dramatic" presentation of something happening before our eyes.

But whether the storyteller is Melville-the-author or an imagined character standing in for him, there is a humor in the voice sometimes approaching the quality of gusto. Such humor has been underappreciated in his writing: *Moby-Dick,* much admired for the power of its rhetorical flights whether conducted through Ahab or Ishmael, is also laced with a genial, devil-may-care humor — a "wayward mood," Ishmael tells us, that "comes over a man only in some time of extreme tribulation . . . so that what just before might have seemed to him a thing most momentous, now seems but a part of the general joke." Ishmael says there is nothing like whaling to produce this "genial, desperado philosophy," and it often seems to come over Melville when he contemplates life in its range, from ultimates like the "blackness of darkness" all the way down to the dumplings served on the *Samuel Enderby,* a ship encountered by the *Pequod.* Accompanying "bull beef" they are

small, but substantial, symmetrically globular and indestructible dumplings. I fancied that you could feel them, and roll them about in you after they were swallowed. If you stooped over too far forward you risked their pitching out of you like billiard-balls.

To my knowledge no one has emphasized this passage as an example of Melville's philosophy, and for good reason, since it is but one of innumerable satisfying touches in which "philosophy," ideas about ultimate concerns, is replaced by wayward, mischievous verbal activity expended on the meanest of particulars.

When Melville visited Hawthorne in Liverpool in 1857, on his way to the Holy Land, he struck Hawthorne as, in Melville's own words, "pretty much determined to be annihilated," and it is possible that such a desperado attitude was provoked by his increasing sense of life as a "general joke." The years Melville spent after his retirement from writing fiction (he did publish volumes of poems, including a fantastically long one, *Clarel*), first attempting a career as lecturer, then securing employment as District Inspector of the Customs in New York City, suggest that the joke became an increasingly bitter one. (During these years two of his four children died; one was probably a suicide.) But the shorter pieces he wrote in the six years following *Moby-Dick* invariably display what Wyndham Lewis called "the curse of humor." It is found in extravagant sketches like "The Lightning-Rod Man" and "I and My Chimney," in which a stubborn householder — Melville under light disguise — successfully resists attempts on the part of others to "improve" his premises. Then there is the dark comedy, anticipating Kafka, of his great story "Bartleby the Scrivener," in which the mysterious clerk who "prefers not to" — not to do his work or vacate the premises of the lawyer who employs him — eventually prefers not to eat and not to live. *The Confidence-Man* is a vigorous if perhaps too relentless satire of all sorts of optimistic attitudes toward life: "confidence" in this or that remedy or palliative is exposed as just another kind of confidence ("con") game. And in his least-read fiction, the short novel *Israel Potter,* we follow the picaresque adventures of a young man from western Massachusetts who fights at the battle of Bunker Hill, is impressed into the British Navy, escapes and undertakes an undercover mission for Benjamin Franklin and becomes quartermaster under John Paul Jones on the *Bon Homme Richard.* It is a very good boy's book and an impressive instance of Melville's humorous creation.

W. H. Auden's fine poem, "Herman Melville," begins, "Toward the end he sailed into an extraordinary mildness, / And anchored in his home and reached his wife, / And rode within the harbor of her hand." It ends with the old man sitting down at his desk to write his last story, *Billy Budd.* Auden sees Melville as finally reconciling himself to "the ambiguities" — paternal, familial, psycho-sexual — in the name of the "goodness" of Billy, the "Handsome Sailor," "an Angel of God" as his Captain Vere calls him, who, for striking dead the evil mate Claggart, must hang. Auden's poem is only one of many and conflicting interpretations of *Billy Budd,* but all readers agree, I think, on the perfect way the tale ends, with a poem supposedly written by another foretopman, "rudely printed" and titled "Billy in the Darbies" ("darbies" are handcuffs). The poem's closing lines give words to Billy's dream of his burial at sea, "fathoms down," and they may also be read as a version of Melville's own epitaph, composed by himself but spoken in the voice of his art:

I feel it stealing now. Sentry, are you there?
Just ease these darbies at the wrist,
And roll me over fair!
I am sleepy, and the oozy weeds about me twist.

Herman Melville

From Moby-Dick, *chapter 36*

"All visible objects, man, are but as pasteboard masks. But in each event —
in the living act, the undoubted deed — there, some unknown but still
reasoning thing puts forth the mouldings of its features from behind the
unreasoning mask. If man will strike, strike through the mask! How can
the prisoner reach outside except by thrusting through the wall? To me,
the white whale is that wall, shoved near to me. Sometimes I think there's
naught beyond. But 'tis enough. He tasks me; he heaps me; I see in him
outrageous strength, with an inscrutable malice sinewing it. That
inscrutable thing is chiefly what I hate; and be the white whale agent, or be
the white whale principal, I will wreak that hate upon him. Talk not to me
of blasphemy, man; I'd strike the sun if it insulted me. For could the sun do
that, then could I do the other; since there is ever a sort of fair play herein,
jealousy presiding over all creations. But not my master, man, is even
that fair play. Who's over me? Truth hath no confines."

····⁘····

From Moby-Dick, *chapter 49*

There are certain queer times and occasions in this strange mixed
affair we call life when a man takes this whole universe for a vast practical
joke, though the wit thereof he but dimly discerns, and more than suspects
that the joke is at nobody's expense but his own. However, nothing dispir-
its, and nothing seems worth while disputing. He bolts down all events, all
creeds, and beliefs, and persuasions, all hard things visible and invisible,
never mind how knobby; as an ostrich of potent digestion gobbles down
bullets and gun flints. And as for small difficulties and worryings,
prospects of sudden disaster, peril of life and limb; all these, and death
itself, seem to him only sly, good-natured hits, and jolly punches in the side
bestowed by the unseen and unaccountable old joker. That odd sort of
wayward mood I am speaking of, comes over a man only in some time of
extreme tribulation; it comes in the very midst of his earnestness, so that
what just before might have seemed to him a thing most momentous, now
seems but a part of the general joke. There is nothing like the perils of
whaling to breed this free and easy sort of genial, desperado philosophy;
and with it I now regarded this whole voyage of the Pequod, and the great
White Whale its object.

····⁘····

140

From Israel Potter, *chapter 1*

The traveller who at the present day is content to travel in the good old Asiatic style, neither rushed along by a locomotive, nor dragged by a stage-coach; who is willing to enjoy hospitalities at far-scattered farmhouses, instead of paying his bill at an inn; who is not to be frightened by any amount of loneliness, or to be deterred by the roughest roads or the highest hills; such a traveller in the eastern part of Berkshire, Mass., will find ample food for poetic reflection in the singular scenery of a country, which, owing to the ruggedness of the soil and its lying out of the track of all public conveyances, remains almost as unknown to the general tourist as the interior of Bohemia.

Travelling northward from the township of Otis, the road leads for twenty or thirty miles towards Windsor, lengthwise upon that long broken spur of heights which the Green Mountains of Vermont send into Massachusetts. For nearly the whole distance, you have the continual sensation of being upon some terrace in the moon. The feeling of the plain or the valley is never yours; scarcely the feeling of the earth. Unless by a sudden precipitation of the road you find yourself plunging into some gorge; you pass on, and on, and on, upon the crests or slopes of pastoral mountains, while far below, mapped out in its beauty, the valley of the Housatonic lies endlessly along at your feet.

····:¦:····

"Monody"

To have known him, to have loved him
    After loneness long;
And then to be estranged in life,
    And neither in the wrong;
And now for death to set his seal —
    Ease me, a little ease, my song!

By wintry hills his hermit-mound
    The sheeted snow-drifts drape,
And houseless there the snow-bird flits
    Beneath the fir-tree's crape:
Glazed now with ice the cloistral vine
    That hid the shyest grape.

George Eliot

BY PAULA MARANTZ COHEN

In 1873, when George Eliot was at the height of her fame, she accepted an invitation to visit the critic F. W. H. Myers at Cambridge. He describes the most dramatic moment during their meeting as follows: "Taking as her text the three words which have been used so often as the inspiring trumpet-calls of men, — the words of *God, Immortality,* and *Duty,* — [she] pronounced,

with terrible earnestness, how inconceivable was the *first,* how unbelievable the *second,* and yet how peremptory and absolute the *third.*"

Although Eliot's successors, the Edwardians, would snicker at such "terrible earnestness," the statement goes to the heart of Eliot's greatness. Many Victorians had begun to lose faith in Christian salvation, but what did they have to replace it? Matthew Arnold in "Dover Beach" wistfully invokes love as the raft to cling to. But Eliot presents a more practical solution. Her novels explore how the cultivation of moral character can serve as a source of meaning, even in the absence of belief in God.

Eliot began her career with all sorts of obstacles in her way: she was not rich; she was not pretty; she had no pedigree or social standing. She broke with her family and scandalized her society by choosing to live with a married man, George Henry Lewes, whose wife refused to divorce him. She wrote and developed as a writer, even at a time when women were dis-

couraged from intellectual work (hence the assumption of her pen name, George Eliot, in place of her real one, Marian Evans).

What is especially impressive about Eliot's literary career is the way it widened in scope as new projects provided more room for the exercise of her intellect and imagination. She began by doing translations of German philosophy and theology, "soul-stupefying work" that nonetheless taught her respect for the meticulousness required for good writing. She then moved to editing and reviewing, staying in the shadow of others but becoming versed in literary styles and contemporary issues. Finally, she began writing fiction, first short stories then novels.

Among her most notable early novels is the autobiographical *The Mill on the Floss* (1860), which is both a Wordsworthian paean to childhood joy and an unsettling exploration of childhood trauma. Starting in the mid-1860s came her big books, which Henry James would refer

George Eliot was the pen name of Marian Evans. She was born on November 22, 1819, at South Farm, Arbury, Warwickshire, England, and died in London on December 22, 1880.

143

to as "baggy monsters": *Romola,* a monumental historical novel, exploring the religious and artistic ferment of fifteenth-century Florence, and *Felix Holt, the Radical,* a novel of social engagement, set against the background of the British labor movement of the 1830s. Her most important novels were her two final ones: *Middlemarch* (1871–72), a sprawling anatomy of English society, and *Daniel Deronda* (1874–76), an attempt to reach beyond English society to embrace larger issues of identity and nationalism. While *Middlemarch* established Eliot's place as the foremost literary figure of her age, *Daniel Deronda* tested her reputation by raising issues that many of her readers preferred to ignore. Deronda is an English aristocrat who discovers, midway through the novel, that he was born a Jew. With this personal revelation comes a more general awareness of British intolerance, and this prompts him, at the end of the book, to leave England for Palestine.

When the novel appeared, many readers were offended by the idea of a Jewish hero and by the criticism of Britain central to the plot. Others faulted the novel's structure, arguing that its "Jewish parts" lacked the coherence and realism of its "British parts." But Eliot's overreaching in this final novel — her determination to attempt more than her society or even her talent could encompass — reflects the enormous ambition that had propelled her career from the beginning.

A BBC adaptation of *Daniel Deronda* was broadcast a few years ago, so that more people

What is especially impressive about Eliot's literary career is the way it widened in scope as new projects provided more room for the exercise of her intellect and imagination.

are now familiar with the plot. Yet the adaptation had nothing to do with the book. Unlike Jane Austen, where so much of what counts resides in the dialogue, making her easily adaptable to the screen, Eliot's greatness lies not in her dialogue (which Virginia Woolf noted was the weakest aspect of her fiction) but in her style, an element that cannot be separated from the written word.

Eliot's style has three principal facets. There is her use of startlingly original metaphors to encapsulate her characters and foreshadow their destinies. Thus, we get a vivid premonition of marital disaster, when Casaubon, the dry-as-dust scholar in *Middlemarch,* is said to woo his bride with a "frigid rhetoric . . . as sincere as the bark of a dog or the cawing of an amorous rook." And there is a similar sense of problems in store when, in the same novel, the superficially charming Rosamond Vincy is described as someone who "acted her own character, and so well, that she did not know it to be precisely her own."

Also central to Eliot's style is her phrasing, which often follows the path of her characters' pretensions, rising high, then falling in a heap at the end: "Mrs. Glegg paused, for speaking with much energy for the good of others is naturally exhausting" (*The Mill on the Floss*). "Some attributed [Mr. Sampson's] reticence to a wise incredulity, others to a want of memory, others to simple ignorance" (*Felix Holt*). "[Dorothea] felt that she enjoyed [riding] in a pagan, sensuous way, and always looked forward to renouncing it" (*Middlemarch*).

The most important — though most derided — aspect of Eliot's style is her narrative voice, which frequently breaks into the action to philosophize or cast judgment. In the following celebrated passage from *Middlemarch,* we are alerted to the countless sorrows that transpire around us without our noticing them:

The element of tragedy which lies in the very fact of frequency has not yet wrought itself into the coarse emotion of mankind; and perhaps our frames could hardly bear much of it. If we had a keen vision and feeling of all ordinary human life, it would be like hearing the grass grow and the squirrel's heart beat, and we should die of that roar which lies on the other side of silence. As it is, the quickest of us walk about well wadded with stupidity.

The second sentence of this passage is often quoted alone, diluting the force of Eliot's meaning: for it is not only humanly impossible to absorb the tragedy of everyday life; it is also a function of human stupidity that this tragedy goes unnoticed. Eliot's genius is to show that the two ideas are both connected and distinct.

Many critics, even those as discerning as Henry James, have criticized her narrative voice as overly intrusive and sententious. But their criticism seems entirely wrong-headed. Eliot's voice, in its assumption of a wiser, juster, more all-encompassing perspective, is the ligament of her novels. It elevates them from ingenious storytelling to divine comedy.

I am not the first to compare Eliot to Dante (her contemporary Lord Acton also did), for all that these two epic imaginations delineated different worlds. Dante accepted a system of medieval hierarchy and predetermination while pointing toward a humanistic concept of character. Eliot clung to a humanistic conception while pointing toward a more modern, relativistic one. She was, after all, a precursor of Sigmund Freud: as D. H. Lawrence put it: "It was really George Eliot who started it all. It was she who started putting action inside." But what Eliot shared with Dante was a compulsion to describe and evaluate the moral nature of human beings. And for all her understanding of interior, unconscious action, she retained a belief in the power of the human will to shape character.

Of all Eliot's novels, *Middlemarch,* about everyday life in a rural community around the time of the first Reform Bill of 1832, is the most comprehensive in creating a moral taxonomy of character that can serve as a guide for living. Set in a period some forty years before it was written, its characters fall into established groups. There are the entrenched rich: the silly but enthusiastic Mr. Brooke; the solid if unimaginative Sir James Chettam; and the morally energetic but naïve Dorothea Brooke. There are the industrious middle class: the honest workman, Caleb Garth; the sanctimonious banker, Bulstrode; and the potential recruit to committed work, Fred Vincy. And there are the creative (or allegedly creative) spirits: the scientific Lydgate, the scholarly Casaubon, and the poetic Ladislaw. These are only a sampling of the vast and variegated cast of *Middlemarch.*

While many of these characters are simple sketches, meant to exemplify a singular trait or moral attribute, the most interesting ones — Lydgate, Fred Vincy, Dorothea, Ladislaw, Bulstrode — have mixed natures. Eliot seems to have conceived of human character as resembling a chemical reaction in which a large

number of potentially important variables are present but only some are activated. The direction of a life is a function of which variables are activated and which are not, an outcome which we have it in our power to control. "The strongest principle of growth lies in human choice," she asserts in *Daniel Deronda*.

And here is where Eliot's greatest value lies for a culture. As one of the most clear-sighted inhabitants of Middlemarch, the clergyman Farebrother, points out to the idealistic Dorothea: "Character is not cut in marble — it is not something solid and unalterable. It is something living and changing, and may become diseased as our bodies do." Eliot shows how a character's resolve can be weakened and aspects of human nature, endearing or harmless in youth, can become toxic later in life. By the same token, she also demonstrates the reverse, expressed in Dorothea's rejoinder to Farebrother: "Then [character] may be rescued and healed." The novels acknowledge the possibility of change for the better.

Moreover, Eliot presents these insights using situations recognizable in any time and place. When Fred Vincy's father urges him to pursue a career in the church despite his unsuitability for this work, the impulse is as misguided but as understandable now as it was then. And when Dorothea Brooke marries the austere scholar, Casaubon, seeking to find meaning for her own life through his, she learns the lesson, as true now as it was then, that it is impossible to live through another person.

The novel contains other insights into the power dynamics of relationships. Lydgate, seduced by the seemingly pliant Rosamond, discovers that her will is stronger than his, though her intellectual and moral judgment are weaker. Fred Vincy is also mastered by his wife, Mary Garth, but with positive results, since she saves him from his weaker nature and gives his life solidity and direction. (The idea of being "saved" by a good woman, a hackneyed staple of so much Victorian literature, seems entirely convincing in this case.)

Eliot does not directly critique the idea of male superiority in her novels, but there are times when her narrative voice becomes biting on the subject: "a man's mind — what there is of it — has always the advantage of being masculine," she comments acidly at one point, "— as the smallest birch-tree is of a higher kind than the most soaring palm — and even his ignorance is of a sounder quality." Mary Garth's love for Fred Vincy, though tender and steadfast, is not unmixed with scorn: "Husbands are an inferior class of men, who require keeping in order," she tells her father at one point. Likewise, Dorothea chooses for a second husband a man who has none of the mental or spiritual superiority that she imagined in her first.

But despite such hints at social critique, the novels never go so far as to attack established authority or convention. Eliot knew that revolutions could be dangerous — an awareness central to both *Felix Holt* and *Romola*. She plants germs of new ideas, under the assumption that a change in perception in small things is the safest and surest way to change large ones. Ultimately, her tentativeness and moderation with respect to social reform reflects her belief in the complex interconnectedness of private and public worlds: to pull too hard in one direction is to rend the fabric in the other. Life is a balancing act between what we desire and what we can do (here again, she anticipates Freud).

Her careful attitude toward change also relates to her attachment to the past. "There is no sense of ease like the ease we felt in those scenes where we were born, where objects

What Eliot shared with Dante was a compulsion to describe and evaluate the moral nature of human beings. And for all her understanding of interior, unconscious action, she retained a belief in the power of the human will to shape character.

became dear to us before we had known the labor of choice," she writes in *The Mill on the Floss*. We find meaning in the past, according to Eliot, because it is the world we know. By the same token, that world contains only the seeds of our future lives; their potential may or may not be realized. Mary Garth explains that she loves Fred Vincy "because I have always loved him," but refuses to marry him until he can realize in some concrete way the potential goodness that inspired her early love. The tragic destinies in Eliot's novels are reserved for those who try to compartmentalize past and present, private and public. Lydgate never achieves his scientific aspirations because he is trapped in a marriage with a woman who cannot respect his work. Bulstrode is eventually toppled from his position of influence because his present piety is built on a denial of the past.

One of the harshest indictments of contemporary society, as I see it, is that there seems to be no place in it for George Eliot's novels. The Edwardians rejected Eliot as a sensibility against which they needed to rebel: she was the antithesis of the experimental styles and iconoclastic politics of modernism. But our society has not rejected her on esthetic or ideological grounds. Her moral seriousness simply doesn't register on our cultural landscape; most people don't have the time or patience to read her "baggy monsters."

Ironically, she still appears in the one place she ought not to be: the high school curriculum, which often insists on assigning *Silas Marner* to tenth graders (when it is not performing the greater error of assigning Edith Wharton's *Ethan Frome*). As Virginia Woolf observed, Eliot wrote novels for grown-ups. To put them into the hands of children is to diminish the possibility for future appreciation — assuming, that is, that these same children will grow up to have time to open one of her books at all. What a loss to the esthetic, intellectual, and moral fiber of a society to have no time or inclination to know the genius of George Eliot.

George Eliot

From Adam Bede, *chapter 41*

"It is not for us men to apportion the shares of moral guilt and retribution. We find it impossible to avoid mistakes even in determining who has committed a single criminal act, and the problem how far a man is to be held responsible for the unforeseen consequences of his own deed, is one that might well make us tremble to look into it. The evil consequences that may lie folded in a single act of selfish indulgence, is a thought so awful that it ought surely to awaken some feeling less presumptuous than a rash desire to punish."

·····:¦:·····

From The Mill on the Floss, *book 1, chapter 2*

Mrs. Tulliver was what is called a good-tempered person — never cried when she was a baby on any slighter ground than hunger and pins, and from the cradle upwards had been healthy, fair, plump, and dull-witted, in short, the flower of her family for beauty and amiability. But milk and mildness are not the best things for keeping, and when they turn only a little sour they may disagree with young stomachs seriously. I have often wondered whether those early Madonnas of Raphael, with the blond faces and somewhat stupid expression, kept their placidity undisturbed when their strong-limbed, strong-willed boys got a little too old to do without clothing. I think they must have been given to feeble remonstrance, getting more and more peevish as it became more and more ineffectual.

·····:¦:·····

From The Mill on the Floss, *book 2, chapter 1*

There is no sense of ease like the ease we felt in those scenes where we were born, where objects became dear to us before we had known the labour of choice, and where the outer world seemed only an extension of our own personality: we accepted and loved it as we accepted our own sense of existence and our own limbs. Very commonplace, even ugly, that furniture of our early home might look if it were put up to auction: an improved taste in upholstery scorns it; and is not the striving after something better and better in our surroundings, the grand characteristic that distinguishes man from the brute — or, to satisfy a scrupulous accuracy of definition, that distinguishes the British man from the foreign brute? But heaven knows where that striving might lead us, if our affections had not a trick of twining round those old inferior things, if the loves and sanctities of our life had no deep immovable roots in memory.

····:····

From Middlemarch, *chapter 24*

[Caleb Garth's] early ambition had been to have as effective a share as possible in this sublime labour, which was peculiarly dignified by him with the name of "business"; and though he had only been a short time under a surveyor, and had been chiefly his own teacher, he knew more of land, building, and mining than most of the special men in the county.

His classification of human employments was rather crude and, like the categories of more celebrated men, would not be acceptable in these advanced times. He divided them into "business, politics, preaching, learning, and amusement." He had nothing to say against the last four; but he regarded them as a reverential pagan regarded other gods than his own. In the same way, he thought very well of all ranks, but he would not himself have liked to be of any rank in which he had not such close contact with "business" as to get often honourably decorated with marks of dust and mortar, the dam of the engine, or the sweet soil of the woods and fields. Though he had never regarded himself as other than an orthodox Christian, and would argue on prevenient grace if the subject were proposed to him, I think his virtual divinities were good practical schemes, accurate work, and the faithful completion of undertakings: his prince of darkness was a slack workman. But there was no spirit of denial in Caleb, and the world seemed so wondrous to him that he was ready to accept any number of systems, like any number of firmaments, if they did not obviously interfere with the best land-drainage, solid building, correct measuring, and judicious boring (for coal). In fact, he had a reverential soul with a strong practical intelligence. But he could not manage finance: he knew values well, but he had no keenness of imagination for monetary results in the shape of profit and loss: and having ascertained this to his cost, he determined to give up all forms of his beloved "business" which required that talent. He gave himself up entirely to the many kinds of work which he could do without handling capital, and was one of those precious men within his own district whom everybody would choose to work for them, because he did his work well, charged very little, and often declined to charge at all. It is no wonder, then, that the Garths were poor, and "lived in a small way." However, they did not mind it.

····:·····

Men can do nothing without the make-believe of a beginning. Even Science, the strict measurer, is obliged to start with a make-believe unit, and must fix on a point in the stars' unceasing journey when his sidereal clock shall pretend that time is at Nought. His less accurate grandmother Poetry has always been understood to start in the middle; but on reflection it appears that her proceeding is not very different from his; since Science, too, reckons backwards as well as forwards, divides his unit into billions, and with his clock-finger at Nought really sets off *in medias res*. No retrospect will take us to the true beginning; and whether our prologue be in heaven or on earth, it is but a fraction of that all-presupposing fact with which our story sets out.

From Daniel Deronda, *chapter 1*

····:·····

But the fervour of sympathy with which we contemplate a grandiose martyrdom is feeble compared with the enthusiasm that keeps unslacked where there is no danger, no challenge — nothing but impartial midday falling on commonplace, perhaps half-repulsive, objects which are really the beloved ideas made flesh. Here undoubtedly lies the chief poetic energy: — in the force of imagination that pierces or exalts the solid fact, instead of floating among cloud-pictures. To glory in a prophetic vision of knowledge covering the earth, is an easier exercise of believing imagination than to see its beginning in newspaper placards, staring at you from a bridge beyond the corn-fields; and it might well happen to most of us dainty people that we were in the thick of the battle of Armageddon without being aware of anything more than the annoyance of a little explosive smoke and struggling on the ground immediately about us.

From Daniel Deronda, *chapter 33*

Emily Dickinson

BY BRUCE FLOYD

"What I assume you shall assume," boasted Walt Whitman, the other great American poet of the nineteenth century. Emily Dickinson wrote in a letter to Thomas Wentworth Higginson that she had never read Whitman but that she had heard that he was "disgraceful." We will never know whether she ever read Whitman, but if she had, she surely would have puzzled over Whitman's assertion that whatever he assumed, others would assume. Dickinson thought she perceived the world with a singular vision, thought that perhaps no one else saw the way she did. Whatever it was that Dickinson assumed, she undoubtedly thought that she assumed it alone. She never spoke for anyone but herself, through what she called her "consciousness":

This Consciousness that is aware
Of Neighbors and the Sun
Will be the one aware of Death
And that itself alone

Is traversing the interval
Experience between
And most profound experiment
Appointed unto Men —

How adequate unto itself
Its properties shall be
Itself unto itself and none
Shall make discovery.

Adventure most unto itself
The Soul condemned to be —
Attended by a single Hound
Its own identity.

Consciousness, she writes, is the "awful mate / The soul cannot be rid." It is her consciousness, her way of responding to the world, that she sometimes longs "to banish." She wishes she had "the art" to do so. She asks, "How can I have peace / Except by subjugating / Consciousness?" Of course she understands, and she understood before she wrote this clever poem, that she can't: "How this be / Except by Abdication — Me — of Me?" In another poem she intimates that consciousness is a burden:

To flee from memory
Had we the Wings
Many would fly
Inured to slower things
Birds with surprise
Would scan the cowering Van
Of men escaping
From the mind of man.

Those who know Emily Dickinson only superficially, by a handful of her often-anthologized poems, take one of two positions on her. Some see her as the elfin belle of Amherst, the

Dickinson was born on December 10, 1830, in Amherst, Massachusetts. She died there on May 15, 1886.

slightly daffy woman wandering about in her white dress or diligently attending to her flowers. In this view she is a harmless eccentric, one who from time to time bakes cookies for the neighborhood children and writes poems about birds and other creatures, a woman hopelessly naïve, somehow "too fragile" for the hard truth of life, certainly not one we take seriously. The other standard view is that Emily Dickinson was a mad woman, obsessed with death, crazed with thwarted love — again, not to be taken seriously. Neither view grants her the status of major poet, let alone genius.

The origin of the standard views derives from a few heavily italicized facts. In 1862, she began her habit of wearing only white. She never left her father's house after 1865. Mabel Loomis Todd, who considered herself Dickinson's friend, never saw the poet in person until Dickinson had died and lay in her casket, that little body, one may assume, finally emptied of its troublesome consciousness, that relentless sensibility at last laid to rest. If one is seeking bizarre behavior in Dickinson's actions, examples abound, but nothing is served, it seems to me, by trotting out the anecdotes dealing with Dickinson's behavior. Besides, we know, don't we, that "Much Madness is divinest sense — / To a discerning eye"? Go along with things and you are deemed "sane," but if you "Demur — you're straightway dangerous — / And handled with a chain." One doesn't have to live in Amherst in the middle of the nineteenth century to know the cost of nonconformity.

But what of those who read Dickinson in depth, who have spent much of their lives reading her poetry? Lewis Mumford, who calls the years between 1865 and 1895 the "Brown Decades," capturing in the phrase a time of almost unparalleled mediocrity, with a literature barren and stale, says that these "sterile years are redeemed by the silent presence of Emily Dickinson."

Most of the critical studies on Dickinson work outward from a few facts. Depending on whom you read, Dickinson wrote roughly between 1,800 and 2,200 poems. We know that about two thirds of her poems were written in seven feverish years. They were sewn in packets and put into her desk, where they were discovered after her death.

Biographers and critics have taken many of these poems and tried to link them with events in Dickinson's life. Much has been written about whether Dickinson had a love affair and, if she did, how much of it was merely in her head and whom the person was she loved. Speculation runs a wild gamut. Was Dickinson a lesbian? Was the object of her love Christ? William Shurr writes that Dickinson may have become pregnant by Charles Wadsworth, adding that Wadsworth abandoned Dickinson, and Dickinson may have either miscarried or aborted the baby. John Cody suggests that Dickinson had a full-blown psychotic episode. What is one to believe? One can argue almost anything, it seems, when explaining Dickinson.

Much of Dickinson's life is a mystery, and it's understandable that we want to find connections between her poetry and the events in her life. But the biographical approach misses the major point about Dickinson. It is not so much what happened in Dickinson's life that generates her best poetry as it is her astonishing awareness of life itself. Make no mistake about it: the "tooth" that fed on her soul was the awe and terror of existence, the truth about

life. Dickinson's sensibility was such that no exterior change in her life would have changed her way of seeing the world. It is hard to say why she saw the world the way she did, only that she seemed to lack the filter most of us have to screen out the bitter realities of life. It was as if she had been born with an exposed heart that could not defend itself against the dark truths of human existence.

Dickinson's best poetry, her deepest poetry, her most searingly honest poetry, deals with a single self-conscious and mortal creature — herself, Miss Emily Dickinson — confronting infinity, the existential paradox of "individuality within finitude." Here there is none of Whitman's merging into the great float; it is the solitary individual standing against the immensity and complexity and silence of the universe — it is the human creature standing alone under the stars and knowing she must die.

Dickinson's art is an act of personal heroism, a way of finding a solution to life when the collective solution fails. For some reason, none of the illusions of nineteenth-century American life gave her comfort. Since her culture could not assuage her anxiety, she rejected it. When she did, she was confronted by the most dreadful thing a human being can face: she was isolated. And to be isolated in Amherst in the middle of the nineteenth century is to be alone in ways we perhaps cannot now comprehend.

Unlike the other members of the community, Dickinson could not find solace in religion. What they readily accepted, she questioned. All she had to do was look from her window at the world:

Apparently with no surprise
To any happy Flower
The Frost beheads it at its play —
In accidental power —
The blonde Assassin passes on —
The Sun proceeds unmoved
To measure off another Day
For an Approving God.

In another poem she says that once the dying "knew where they went": "They went to God's right Hand — / That hand is amputated now / And God cannot be found." When Dickinson sat at her window and peered out, she saw a perishable world, the "heavens stitched shut."

Had she not been exceedingly bright and imaginative, not to mention courageous, she would have sunk into a withering neurosis. Instead she set about creating an artistic personality, out of which she would make art. She consciously called herself a poet. "This is my letter to the world," she says, hardly modest. The poet is one who "Entitles us — by Contrast — / to ceaseless poverty." He is

"exterior to time." What does she think of the rank of poet?

I reckon — when I count at all —
First — Poets — Then the sun —
Then Summer — Then the Heaven of God —
And then — the List is done —

But, looking back — the First so seems
To Comprehend the Whole —
The Others look a needless Show —
So I write — Poets — All —

Poetry, she believes, will endow her with a kind of immortality:

The Poets light but Lamps —
Themselves — go out —
The Wicks they stimulate —
If vital Light

Inhere as do the Suns —
Each Age a Lens
Disseminating their
Circumference —

Although she often sank into despair, Emily Dickinson, as bright a poet as ever lived in the United States, was never less than acutely aware of what she was doing. She was about the creation of her poetic persona. Her poetry was the medium by which she shaped and controlled the world, which she faced alone. Things didn't seem so bad once written down, "under rule." She made a conscious effort to disentangle herself from a counterfeit culture, knowing well the restrictions she simply had to accept. Her time and place made it almost impossible for her to leave Amherst, but none of that matters: she would have seen the world the same way regardless of where she had spent her days. "They shut me up in prose," she says, when she was a child, but she had the "will" to "abolish captivity." She makes an effort to free herself from what she perceives as a hollow and shallow society. Through the genius of her poetry she "builds" herself:

The Props assist the House
Until the House is built
And then the Props withdraw
And adequate, erect,
The House supports itself. . . .

And after she has freed herself from the restraints, she now "dwell[s] in Possibility — / A fairer house than Prose — / More numerous of Windows — / Superior — for Doors."

Emily Dickinson knew that beauty and meaning are forged in the human imagination, are the creations of the imagination. She would have agreed with William Blake, who said that a fool and a wise man don't look at the same tree. A fool and a wise man don't look at anything the same way. The profound and almost incalculable difference between Dickinson and the other citizens of Amherst was not the world outside the window but the way her imagination saw the world outside the window. She once watched the busy inhabitants of Amherst on the streets and, genuinely consternated, wondered aloud how those people managed to live without thinking. Didn't they hear the mystery and wonder in the song of a bird? If she let her "Countenance disclose / The Subterranean freight / The Cellars of the soul," "What Terror would enthrall the Street"? They understood Emily Dickinson less, though it now seems that she was undoubtedly the sanest person in Amherst. Her imagination took the most common things and transformed them into things rich and strange.

To hear an Oriole sing
May be a common thing —
Or only a divine.

It is not of the Bird
Who sings the same, unheard,
As unto Crowd —

The Fashion of the Ear
Attireth that it hear
In Dun, or fair —

So whether it be Rune,
Or whether it be none
Is of within.

The "Tune is in the Tree —"
The Skeptic — showeth me —
"No sir! In Thee."

Emily Dickinson knew, too, that this imagination, which can be the source of beauty and meaning, reveals the beginning of terror. She always accepted the "price," knowing "For each ecstatic instant / We must an anguish pay." She had to learn to live with ghosts:

One need not be a Chamber — to be Haunted —
One need not be a House —
The Brain has Corridors — surpassing
Material Place —

Far safer, of a Midnight Meeting
External Ghost
Than its interior Confronting —
That Cooler Host.

Far safer, through an Abbey gallop,
The Stones a'chase —
Than Unarmed, one's a'self encounter —
In lonesome Place —

Ourself behind ourself, concealed —
Should startle most —
Assassin hid in our Apartment
Be Horror's least.

The Body — borrows a Revolver —
He bolts the Door —
O'erlooking a superior spectre —
Or More.

Dickinson once wrote that men said "What?" when she spoke. Her psychological insight was beyond the ken of most of those she knew. They could not fathom the freshness of her expression, the blazing intensity of her mind, and the formulations of her imagination. "What do you mean?" they asked of her.

Robert Frost said that had Emily Dickinson overseen the publication of her poems, she would have eliminated many of those found in the *Complete Poems*. Perhaps. She wrote some trite and sentimental poems, some of them maddeningly obscure. Like Wallace Stevens, she wrote too many poems, but if these two poets had to write the bad poems to find the superb ones, that seems a small price to pay. In the end we rightly judge a poet by his or her best work.

One could argue that Dickinson and Stevens were the two deepest poets our country has produced, both New England recluses, poets who kept the world at bay, who sat at windows and transformed the quotidian into something rich and strange, a woman and a man whose imaginative lives were rich beyond telling. Dickinson knew what Stevens knew: "Poetry is a purging of the world's poverty and change and evil and death. It is a present perfecting, a satisfaction in the irremediable poverty of life."

Dickinson knew who she was: she was a poet. And what to her is a poet?

This was a Poet — It is That
Distills amazing sense
From ordinary Meanings —
And Attar so immense

From the familiar species
That perished by the Door —
We wonder it was not Ourselves
Arrested it — before —

Of Pictures, the Discloser —
The Poet — it is He —
Entitles Us — by Contrast —
To ceaseless Poverty —

Of Portion — so unconscious —
The Robbing — could not harm —
Himself — to him — a Fortune —
Exterior — to Time —

Emily Dickinson was able to distill amazing sense from ordinary things, showing us that nothing is really ordinary, that there is nothing beautiful in life except life itself, the world outside her window. In her genius, she reminds us that our awareness of the world, the simple fact that there is anything at all, is miracle enough to fill us with awe and make us tremble.

Emily Dickinson

No Rack can torture me —
My Soul — at Liberty —
Behind this mortal Bone
There knits a bolder One —

You cannot prick with saw —
Nor pierce with Scimitar —
Two Bodies — therefore be —
Bind One — The Other fly —

The Eagle of his Nest
No easier divest —
And gain the Sky
Than mayest Thou —

Except Thyself may be
Thine Enemy —
Captivity is Consciousness —
So's Liberty.

····:····

This World is not Conclusion.
A Species stands beyond —
Invisible, as Music —
But positive, as Sound —
It beckons, and it baffles —
Philosophy — don't know —
And through a Riddle, at the last —
Sagacity, must go —
To guess it, puzzles scholars —
To gain it, Men have borne
Contempt of Generations
And Crucifixion, shown —

384

501

159

Faith slips — and laughs, and rallies —
Blushes, if any see —
Plucks at a twig of Evidence —
And asks a Vane, the way —
Much Gesture, from the Pulpit —
Strong Hallelujahs roll —
Narcotics cannot still the Tooth
That nibbles at the soul —

····:·····

683

The Soul unto itself
Is an imperial friend —
Or the most agonizing Spy —
An Enemy — could send —

Secure against its own —
No treason it can fear —
Itself — its Sovereign — of itself
The Soul should stand in Awe —

····:·····

997

Crumbling is not an instant's Act
A fundamental pause
Dilapidation's processes
Are organized Decays.

'Tis first a Cobweb on the Soul
A Cuticle of Dust
A Borer in the Axis
An Elemental Rust —

Ruin is formal — Devil's work
Consecutive and slow —
Fail in an instant, no man did
Slipping — is Crash's law.

····:·····

He scanned it — staggered —
Dropped the Loop
To Past or Period —
Caught helpless at a sense as if
His Mind were going blind —

Groped up, to see if God was there —
Groped backward at Himself
Caressed a Trigger absently
And wandered out of Life.

1062

····:⁞:····

Tell all the Truth but tell it slant —
Success in Circuit lies
Too bright for our infirm Delight
The Truth's superb surprise

As Lightning to the Children eased
With explanation kind
The Truth must dazzle gradually
Or every man be blind —

1129

····:⁞:····

We never know how high we are
Till we are asked to rise
And then if we are true to plan
Our statures touch the skies —

The Heroism we recite
Would be a normal thing
Did not ourselves the Cubits warp
For fear to be a King —

1176

Mark Twain

⸻⸻⸻⸺◦◦◦◦◦◦⸺⸻⸻⸻

BY DAVID CARKEET

Mark Twain makes us laugh — instantly, reflexively, unselfconsciously. Very few writers can do this. Fewer still can do it and achieve the rank of their nation's most widely read author. Twain's comic gift was matched by a preference for plain expression. He favored short sentences, and if he did write a long one, he made sure, as he once said, "that there are no folds in it, no vaguenesses. . . . It won't be a sea-serpent, with half its arches under the water, it will be a torchlight procession." I have never had to read a Mark Twain sentence twice, though I have often chosen to. A third salient characteristic related to Twain's directness: he proclaimed an agenda of getting at the truth of things, especially when the truth was obscured by prevailing opinion. "Sham" and "humbug" were among his favorite words.

These qualities, evident in his good works, stand out in his best work, *Adventures of Huckleberry Finn* (1884). What is odd about *Huckleberry Finn*, though, is that the novel is strong in areas where Twain often failed. Characterization, for example. While nobody can best him for a quick sketch of a flat character, the indisputably round characters he created consist of only one: Huck. Or consider his handling of internal conflict. A Twain character mentally debating a course of action soon exhausts the reader's interest in the subject, but Huck's strug-

gles with his conscience are among the most memorable passages in the novel. Knowing when to shut up could also be a problem for Twain, but when Huck rouses Jim for their escape from Jackson's Island, a single pronoun signals the bond at the heart of the novel — "They're after us," Huck says, even though they're pursuing only Jim. It's an intuitive utterance that comes from the boy's mouth as unthinkingly as it must have come from the author's pen. Nothing is belabored in *Huckleberry Finn*, nothing unnecessarily repeated, until the end, alas, in the scenes on the Phelps plantation, which are best treated not with interpretive cartwheels to justify them but as evidence of how easily this author could run off the rails.

What would Mark Twain's reputation be if he had never written *Huckleberry Finn*? In his own lifetime, the subtraction from his fame would be slight; he was nearly fifty years old and a national treasure when the novel was published, with much more work and notoriety still

Mark Twain was the pen name of Samuel Langhorne Clemens. He was born on November 30, 1835, in Florida, Missouri, and died in Redding, Connecticut, on April 21, 1910.

ahead. But take away *Huckleberry Finn* and his current literary reputation would rest on a body of work distinguished for its volume and originality but with no single major work of genius on the list: a children's book (*The Adventures of Tom Sawyer*), some uneven adult novels with plots premised on "stretchers" (*The Prince and the Pauper, A Connecticut Yankee in King Arthur's Court, Pudd'nhead Wilson*), several too-long travel books, a dozen or so striking short stories, essays, and autobiographical chapters, and half a dozen aphorisms. To be sure, practically everything Twain wrote flashes with brilliance. But the brilliance of *Huckleberry Finn* is blinding.

How did Twain, a writer who so often got in his own way, manage to stay out of his way when he wrote his masterpiece? Much of the achievement of the novel flows from Huck's narrative voice. Consider these two passages, both describing a moment of quiet before sunrise on the river: "There was a delicious sense of repose and peace in the deep pervading calm and silence of the woods. Not a leaf stirred; not a sound obtruded upon great Nature's meditation." "Then we set down on the sandy bottom where the water was about knee deep, and watched the daylight come. Not a sound, anywheres — perfectly still — just like the whole world was asleep, only sometimes the bull-frogs a-cluttering, maybe." The first is from *Tom Sawyer* (chapter 14), a book inspired by Twain's Hannibal boyhood and told in a formal, third-person style. The second is from *Huckleberry*

> *Huck's language is much more than a collection of dialect features. It is a rhythm, a penchant for italics, a set of favored idioms, and a lightly comic tendency to restate a point until it has reached satisfactory expression.*

Finn (chapter 19), which begins in the same small town but is narrated altogether differently — by Huck in the first person. Tom's dutifully pleasant Nature is an object of distant contemplation, while Huck's language pulls us right into the river with him. Twain's creative spirit was a restless one, and his eagerness to try different forms for presenting this river material that was so important to him led him to a unique experiment — a first-person dialect narration by an ignorant boy.

Although Twain's choice of narrator for *Huckleberry Finn* freed him from conventional language, it exposed him to a danger of a different kind. Dialect writers of the period often packed their language with so many odd features that reading their stories can be a word-by-word torture. But Twain knew that the fewer apostrophes, the better. Huck doesn't even drop the *g* in *-ing*, which his real-life counterpart surely would have done. The dialect in *Huckleberry Finn* is carried by mildly nonstandard grammar (*we was*) and colorful vocabulary (*smouch* or *hook* for "steal"), and the reader masters it early and easily.

But Huck's language is much more than a collection of dialect features. It is a rhythm, a penchant for italics, a set of favored idioms, and a lightly comic tendency to restate a point until it has reached satisfactory expression. Twain had been carrying this style in his head for some time before *Huckleberry Finn,* using it here and there in short works predating the novel, like "Jim Smiley and His Jumping Frog" and several sketches in *Roughing It,* as well as in stories written while *Huckleberry Finn* was in progress, like the hilarious "The Invalid's Story." In each of these tales, a character takes the stage away from a formal English-speaking narrator and holds forth in a rustic dialect with signature phrases: "by and by," "*he* was satisfied," "he warn't particular," "no slouch," "down on," "as much as to say," "as you please," "too many for me," "laid over any [noun] that ever *I* see," and a fondness for the word "modest" in incongruous attributions, as in "You never see a frog so modest and straightfor'ard as he was, for all he was so gifted." Most of these appear in Huck's dialect.

Who are these proto-Hucks? Significantly, they are all adults. Many of them are Westerners from Twain's years in California and Nevada, a time of freedom, adventure, and self-discovery. They are strong, opinionated people. They don't give a damn — they say what they have to say without regard for what anyone else might think of them. In the mysterious process of literary creation, Twain gave young Huck the dialect of these people — toned down in slang and digressiveness — and with it he gave Huck some of their peculiar personality features, which he mixed with the traditional attributes of a child. Yes, Huck loves what any boy loves — swimming, fishing, the circus. But he is also precociously independent, both economically and in the psychological sense of being inner-directed. Unlike his pal Tom Sawyer, who is consumed with his public image, Huck does what he wants to do, in small ways and in one large way: he defies the established order and helps a runaway slave escape.

To this point in Twain's career, Huck's style had been used for the telling of short tales by middle-aged Westerners about outlandish creatures — a frog filled with buckshot, a cat who can spot promising gold diggings, a woman whose borrowed glass eye falls out in society. How would he use this style in a full novel? The early chapters of *Huckleberry Finn* feel a bit like a *Tom Sawyer* shadow play, stuck as they are in St. Petersburg, Missouri. But Twain found the beginning of his true plot in one perfectly crafted scene: Huck's escape from the cabin where his father holds him captive (chapter 7). All of the elements are right. As for motive — always a concern to Twain as a fierce critic of others' work — Huck simply has no choice: his drunken father has tried to kill him and will try again. For suspense, Huck must act quickly: he has as long as it will take Pap to cross the river, sell some lumber for whiskey money, and return to the shanty. The boy's plan evolves with impromptu naturalness — he'll escape on foot into Illinois; no, he'll go downriver; no, *he'll fake his death,* then go downriver. He creates a crime scene with chilly concentration: the axe-smashed door to suggest a break-in, the slaughtered pig's blood spilled on the cabin floor, the plucked hair attached to the blood-smeared axe blade, the sack of rocks to simulate the trail of a boy's body dragged to the river's edge.

Huck steals away when darkness falls, and the chapter concludes with a short canoe voyage to Jackson's Island — five stunning paragraphs charged with suggested feeling. Huck has obliterated his identity and severed all ties to his friends and his hometown, whose twinkling lights he sees from the island. But instead of dwelling on what he has wrought, he records a sample of river humanity — the incidental words he overhears from men on the ferry landing and a passing lumber raft. When a raftsman

gives an order to the oarsman, Huck says, "I heard that just as plain as if the man was by my side." But the man is not by his side. Huck is alone. The chapter closes, "There was a little gray in the sky, now; so I stepped into the woods and laid down for a nap before breakfast." With a fugitive's consciousness of daylight, Huck withdraws from view. Here Twain knew that no further words could add to the power of the scene.

When I read a novel, I often find a point of engagement, an emotional moment that draws me in and commits me to the work. The escape from Pap's cabin is such a moment for me. Authors, too, can experience a point of engagement with an unfolding novel — a passage where they discover some crucial aspect of the work they are writing: its tone, or the heart of a character, or the embarkation point for the main story line. The escape scene could well have been such a point for Twain. Along with its releasing the story from St. Petersburg and binding Huck's fate with Jim's, some tantalizing correspondences between Twain's and Huck's careers suggest an unconscious authorial investment in the episode. Early in Twain's life, deaths and near-deaths set him on a course to become a writer, at least as he interpreted events. In a late memoir, "The Turning Point of My Life," he tells how, unable to stand the suspense over a measles epidemic sweeping through Hannibal, he crawled into bed with an afflicted chum to contract the disease, succeeded, and nearly died. This happened not long after his father's death — and because of it, in his mother's eyes. Once the

Twain shares all of Huck's salient qualities but one, humorlessness, and he certainly knew how to put that one on in public performance, wearing it on the stage like a costume.

young boy had recovered, she found new paternal structure for him in a printer's apprenticeship, and from that point the author outlines the steps to his literary life. Thus we have a literary career triggered by the son's near-death on the heels of the father's actual death. In the novel, Huck's main career — his journey downriver — begins with his feigned death, and early in the river journey Jim finds Huck's father dead in a floating house. Although Huck doesn't learn the identity of the dead man until the end of the novel, the reader experiences the news of Pap's death as a release of the son into the world.

When he escapes from Pap, Huck exhibits a trait that he shares with another epic water traveler, *resourcefulness,* one we will see again and again when he lies to protect himself and Jim, for Huck can lie almost faster than the reader can read. The boy hero has other memorable qualities, often enumerated by scholars in their attempts to capture the magic of his appeal.

Huck is *good*, although he thinks he is bad, and his low estimate of himself ("ignorant and so kind of low-down and ornery") awakens a protective instinct in the reader. Kindness to others is the boy's natural impulse, as when he expresses sorrow for two scoundrels, the king and the duke, who have treated him badly.

Huck is *naïve*. Twain usually plays this feature for laughs in single sentences, but in one passage that should be a model text for naïve narration in every fiction writing handbook, we get an extended view of the world through

Huck's eyes. This is the circus scene (chapter 22), a masterpiece of misreporting that speaks for itself.

Although his narrative style and innocence create most of the book's comedy, Huck himself is *humorless.* From St. Petersburg to Arkansas, he doesn't laugh once. Often he is the only somber one in the crowd. During the drunk's circus ride, the crowd roars with delight, but Huck is "all of a tremble to see his danger." Later, when the rightful English claimants to the Wilks fortune arrive to challenge the fraudulent claims of the king and the duke, the townspeople rejoice in celebration of this rampant depravity. Huck's reaction sums up his whole temperament: "I didn't see no joke about it."

Earlier, I linked Twain and his young hero with regard to the role of deaths in initiating their careers. There are many other Twain-Huck connections. Huck is an uncouth outsider resisting the attempts of society to civilize him. Insert "Mark Twain" in that sentence and you have a description of the author's ambivalent relationship with culture. Of the human capacity for moral agony, Huck says, "If I had a yaller dog that didn't know no more than a person's conscience does, I would pison him." Twain's life was similarly guilt-wracked over offenses real and imagined. Huck is also an acute observer committed to getting at the truth. Does prayer get you what you ask for? If you rub a lamp, will a genie appear? His fervent investigations cast doubt on received opinion. Like his creator, Huck is humbug's foe.

In fact, Twain shares all of Huck's salient qualities but one, humorlessness, and he certainly knew how to put that one on in public performance, wearing it on the stage like a costume. As for Huck's goodness, Twain would cringe at the comparison, but his life is a record of broad concern for humanity and acts of charity at the individual level. As for naïveté, we have portraits matching Huck's in *The Innocents Abroad* and the early chapters of *Life on the Mississippi.* The narrator of these is sometimes a Hannibal chucklehead, and an author cannot render himself as an innocent unless he was one in the past and remains one in some basic self-conception.

A final shared quality is that, although he was a notorious hater of the human race, Twain's descriptions of people, both in his literary work and private papers, frequently evince what can only be called love of individual specimens of humanity, especially ones who are unique or off-center (his luckless brother Orion, though he often exasperated Twain, was one such). Twain had a recurring style for these character appreciations in his notebooks and letters: He would describe some peculiar bit of behavior — a shtick — and then give a resounding endorsement so rich you can almost hear his laughter. Huck, too, reports on likeable, oddball characters, though with a sobriety befitting his character, like the absent-minded Silas Phelps ("the innocentest best old soul I ever see") and the undertaker presiding over the Wilks funeral ("there warn't no more smile to him than there is to a ham"). A similar respect for eccentricity informs the language of Huck's precursors — the quaint Western narrators of Twain's earlier dialect tales.

I make these Twain-Huck connections because I see them as fundamental to the achievement in the characterization of Huck.

To write a profound work, an author must tap into the core of his or her being. Nothing less will do. In rendering Huck, Twain rendered a close version of himself.

Twain must have known that *Huckleberry Finn* was a success, because he tried to repeat it. His notebooks after the novel's publication are peppered with ideas for Huck and Tom, and some of these made it into print in *Tom Sawyer Abroad* and *Tom Sawyer, Detective,* dull tales in which nothing is at stake. It's noteworthy that though Tom is in these titles, Huck provides the first-person narration. Tom's name might have been more marketable, but Huck's consciousness was the author's preferred one.

After finishing *Tom Sawyer,* Twain wrote about the novel to his friend William Dean Howells, "I perhaps made a mistake in not writing it in the first person." He began *Huckleberry Finn* the following year, and if it was his atonement, we should all be glad of the mistake. By intuitively making the right point-of-view choice for the novel, Twain protected himself against the fatal pull of propriety. Because his starting point was so deliciously low, in the heart of Huck, he could never stray far from his own heart.

Mark Twain

From Adventures of Huckleberry Finn, *chapter 33*

. . . I told Tom all about our Royal Nonesuch rapscallions, and as much of the raft-voyage as I had time to; and as we struck into the town and up through the middle of it — it was as much as half after eight, then — here comes a raging rush of people, with torches, and an awful whooping and yelling, and banging tin pans and blowing horns; and we jumped to one side to let them go by; and as they went by, I see they had the king and the duke astraddle of a rail — that is, I knowed it *was* the king and the duke, though they was all over tar and feathers, and didn't look like nothing in the world that was human — just looked like a couple of monstrous big soldier-plumes. Well, it made me sick to see it; and I was sorry for them poor pitiful rascals, it seemed like I couldn't ever feel any hardness against them any more in the world. It was a dreadful thing to see. Human beings *can* be awful cruel to one another.

We see we was too late — couldn't do no good. We asked some stragglers about it, and they said everybody went to the show looking very innocent; and laid low and kept dark till the poor old king was in the middle of his cavortings on the stage; then somebody give a signal, and the house rose up and went for them.

So we poked along back home, and I warn't feeling so brash as I was before, but kind of ornery, and humble, and to blame, somehow — though *I* hadn't done nothing. But that's always the way: it don't make no difference whether you do right or wrong, a person's conscience ain't got no sense, and just goes for him *anyway*. If I had a yaller dog that didn't know no more than a person's conscience does, I would pison him. It takes up more room than all the rest of a person's insides, and yet ain't no good, nohow. Tom Sawyer he says the same.

····:⋮:····

From Adventures of Huckleberry Finn, *chapter 22*

It was a real bully circus. It was the splendidest sight that ever was, when they all come riding in, two and two, a gentleman and a lady, side by side, the men just in their drawers and undershirts, and no shoes nor stirrups, and resting their hands on their thighs, easy and comfortable, — there must a been twenty of them — and every lady with a lovely complexion, and perfectly beautiful, and looking just like a gang of real sure-enough queens, and dressed in clothes that cost millions of dollars, and just littered with diamonds. It was a powerful fine sight; I never see anything so lovely. And then one by one they got up and stood, and went a-weaving around the ring so gentle, and wavy and graceful, the men looking ever so tall and airy and straight, with their heads bobbing and skimming along, away up there under the tent-roof, and every lady's rose-leafy dress flapping soft and silky around her hips, and she looking like the most loveliest parasol.

And then faster and faster they went, all of them dancing, first one foot stuck out in the air and then the other, the horses leaning more and more, and the ring-master going round and round the centre-pole, cracking his whip and shouting "Hi! — hi!" and the clown cracking jokes behind him; and by and by, all hands dropped the reins, and every lady put her knuckles on her hips and every gentleman folded his arms, and then how the horses did lean over and hump themselves! And so, one after the other they all skipped off into the ring, and made the sweetest bow I ever see, and then scampered out, and everybody clapped their hands and went just about wild....

By and by a drunk man tried to get into the ring — said he wanted to ride; said he could ride as well as anybody that ever was. They argued and tried to keep him out, but he wouldn't listen, and the whole show come to a standstill. Then the people begun to holler at him and make fun of him, and that made him mad, and he begun to rip and tear; so that stirred up the people, and a lot of men begun to pile down off of the benches and swarm toward the ring, saying, "Knock him down! throw him out!" and one or two women begun to scream. So, then, the ring-master he made a little speech, and said he hoped there wouldn't be no disturbance, and if the man would promise he wouldn't make no more trouble, he would let him ride, if he thought he could stay on the horse. So everybody laughed and said all right, and the man got on. The minute he was on, the horse begun to rip and tear and jump and cavort around, with two circus men hanging on to his bridle trying to hold him, and the drunk man hanging onto his neck, and his heels flying in the air every jump, and the whole crowd of people standing up shouting and laughing till the tears rolled down. And at last, sure enough, all the circus men could do, the horse broke loose, and away he went like the very nation, round and round the ring, with that sot laying down on him and hanging to his neck, with first one leg hanging most to the ground on one side, and then t'other one on t'other side, and the people just crazy. It warn't funny to me, though; I was all of a tremble to see his danger. But pretty soon he struggled up astraddle and grabbed the bridle, a-reeling this way and that; and the next minute he sprung up and dropped the bridle and stood! and the horse agoing like a house afire too. He just stood up there, a-sailing around as easy and comfortable as if he warn't ever drunk in his life — and then he begun to pull off his clothes and sling them. He shed them so thick they kind of clogged up the air, and altogether he shed seventeen suits. And then, there he was, slim and handsome, and dressed the gaudiest and prettiest you ever saw, and he lit into that horse with his whip and made him fairly hum — and finally skipped off, and made his bow and danced off to the dressing room, and everybody just a-howling with pleasure and astonishment.

Then the ring-master he see how he had been fooled, and he *was* the sickest ring-master you ever see, I reckon. Why, it was one of his own men! He had got up that joke all out of his own head, and never let on to nobody. Well, I felt sheepish enough, to be took in so, but I wouldn't a been in that ring-master's place, not for a thousand dollars. I don't know; there may be bullier circuses than what that one was, but I never struck them yet. Anyways, it was plenty good enough for *me*; and wherever I run across it, it can have all of *my* custom, every time.

Henry James

BY JOSEPH EPSTEIN

"I have never beheld, for my part, any creature who struck me as to his degree assailed by the perceptions," Ethel Colburn Mayne remarked after meeting Henry James. What she can only have meant is that in no one she had previously met had she noted such powers of sensitivity to his environment, wherever that environment might be. In his preface to the "New York Edition" of *The Awkward Age,* James writes about being "infinitely addicted to 'noticing.'" The goal, for James the novelist and for those of his characters he most loved, was always to be someone "on whom nothing was lost." Marcel Proust may have had social radar quite as powerful as Henry James's, but in Proust the subjective element was always foremost. James was more objective, and objectivity carried to a high power, as Schopenhauer notes, "is genius."

"For an old idiot who notices as much as I," the character Mr. Longdon in *The Awkward Age* remarks, "something particular is always happening. If you're a man of imagination." A man of imagination Henry James, as he himself might have put it, immitigably, irretrievably, indefatigably was. He saw and felt more than the rest of us; perhaps more than anyone who ever chose to record his thoughts. A being organized for literature, his was a mind whose sensitive receptors were turned off only by death.

If genius is in any substantial part genetic, then Henry James could scarcely have been better born. His father, Henry James Sr., was a Swedenborgian befriended by many of the Boston Transcendentalists; his brother was William James, the philosopher so often cited as the founder of American pragmatism. Comparisons between the Brothers James, William and Henry, increase the mystery of intellectual inheritance. The older William had one of the boldest, firmly outlined minds of his time, all blue and sunburst; Henry's mind was subtle, fine-meshed, lit in the chiaroscuro manner, delicately cross-hatched and with endless shadings of grey. Henry always spoke admiringly of William; William purported to be puzzled by the complications explicit in Henry's later fiction.

George Santayana, who had taught in the department of philosophy at Harvard with William James, met Henry James late in the novelist's life, and wrote that Henry, on their

James was born on April 15, 1843, in New York, New York. He died in London, England, on February 28, 1916.

only meeting, made him feel more at home than William after long acquaintance ever had. "Henry was calm," Santayana writes in his autobiography, "he liked to see things as they are, and be free afterwards to imagine how they might have been. . . . He was of course subtle and bland, appreciative of all points of view, and amused at their limitations."

To be "appreciative of all points of view," and yet "amused at their limitations" — what better prescription can there be for the novelist? Yet how James attained this aesthetic condition has nothing to do with genes and everything to do with sedulous self-training. For if Henry James was a genius, he was not a genius born but one made through unrelenting observation and analysis, discipline, and rigor. A character in *The Tragic Muse,* his novel about the theater, says: "Genius is only the art of getting your experience fast, of stealing it, as it were." As a young man, he quickly realized that, as he put it, "life is effort, unremittingly repeated." To read Henry James is to discover a talent that deepens over time, coming into full power at maturity, and then sailing beyond into what, in "The Next Time," his story about a man who hungered for commercial success and could only produce unwanted literary masterpieces, he called "the country of the blue."

A reader of Henry James's early work would not, I think, have recognized in it the writer that he was to become. There are, it is said, no Mozarts in literature, by which is meant that

James saw and felt more than the rest of us; perhaps more than anyone who ever chose to record his thoughts. A being organized for literature, his was a mind whose sensitive receptors were turned off only by death.

literary genius, unlike musical and visual arts genius, takes much more time to ripen, though a few poets — Rimbaud and Keats notable among them — sent blazing comets into the empyrean at an early age.

"Talent without genius comes to little," wrote Paul Valery. "Genius without talent is nothing." James's early talent showed up in an impressive verbal athleticism. He could toss language around in an artful way from the outset. At twenty, he would describe to his friend Thomas Sergeant Perry the unavailing efforts of a local clergyman: "The brimstone fizzles up in the pulpit but fades away into the musk and cologne water in the pews." The humor, nicely dipped in irony, was also there from an early age. At the end of another letter to Perry, this one written when James was seventeen, he notes: "According to my usual habit, having fully satisfied my egotism, I turn to humbler themes. Pray how may *you* be?" From the outset James's was in good part a comic genius; and the comic view was always at the center of his vision. The heavy overlays of irony — of saying one thing and meaning another, usually subtler thing — in James's work are in good part his way of making plain the absurdity of much human behavior. Only in a Henry James novel, *The Europeans,* would a young woman "be inconvenienced with intelligence."

James could have been a highly successful literary or art critic, and, under the lash of having to earn his living as a professional writer, he did a fair amount of both, but he hadn't any doubt

about his true vocation. "To produce," he wrote to his friend Grace Norton, "some little exemplary works of art is my narrow and lowly dream." In reality, the dream was neither narrow nor lowly. One of his early culture heroes was Balzac, who himself set out in his novels to write the full story of French society in his time. Not long after settling permanently in England — having found nineteenth-century America anemic in the arterial flow of social detail necessary to a novelist of his proclivities — James announced that he hoped one day to be the country's "moral portrait-painter." To qualify as a writer at the level of genius, he knew it would take what it called for from Michelangelo, "energy, positiveness, courage, call it what you will." No more self-conscious literary artist has perhaps lived than Henry James, who, sometime after this thirtieth birthday, wrote, "Mysterious and incontrollable (even to one's self) is the growth of one's mind. Little by little, I trust, my abilities will catch up with my ambitions."

To make his abilities commensurate with his ambitions was the sole work of the remainder of Henry James's life. "Genius," Somerset Maugham wrote to his friend the painter Gerald Kelly, "is a combination of talent and character, but character to a certain extent — I do not know how but I believe enormously — can be acquired." No one worked harder at the task of literary self-development than James. From his merely interesting early novels — *The Reverberator, Roderick Hudson, The American* — James pressed on, deepening his investigations as he went from novel to novel.

Owing to the rarified subject matter of his fiction — the work-free rich at play, usually in the elysian fields of Europe — not many people realize that Henry James himself had to work very hard to earn his own keep. That he earned his living through his writing makes James's career seem all the more valiant. The valor comes through his refusal to compromise — to lower his sights in any sense, even if it meant more in the way of remuneration. When his brother William complained that his novel *The Golden Bowl* was hard going, and asked if he couldn't write in a more easygoing way, James shot back that perhaps one day he would "write you your book on the two-and-two-make-four system on which all the awful truck that surrounds us is produced." But, somehow, he never got around to it. He couldn't have done even if he had desperately tried. As W. H. Auden has said of him, there can be no controversy whatsoever "about the consistent integrity displayed both in the work and the man."

James was what Arnold Bennett called "a small public writer," though not by his own choosing. Like caviar, like certain kinds of music, his writing, especially his later writing, is an acquired taste and as such not for everyone. His prose may not even be successfully translatable into other languages. He was especially disappointed to learn that this was so even for French, a language that he knew so well as to pass for a Frenchmen himself when in France. (T. S. Eliot remarked that James had succeeded in turning himself into a European, but of no known country.) He was disappointed again when the New York edition of his collected (and self-selected and often substantially revised) fiction proved yet another commercial failure. None of these things were as Henry James wished. They were merely inevitable given the nature of his genius.

This genius called for James to drill ever deeper into the bedrock of human consciousness and motivation. He began as a straight enough writer, though always with a high purpose: that purpose being to explore social and personal behavior through his own powerful moral imagination. In an early novel such as *Washington Square,* one sees him meticulously

> *James announced that he hoped one day to be the country's "moral portrait-painter." To qualify as a writer at the level of genius, he knew it would take what it called for from Michelangelo, "energy, positiveness, courage, call it what you will."*

exploring the monstrousness of a heart closed by reason and the deep vice of attempting to control the lives of others, even one's own children. In a novella such as *The Aspern Papers,* he worked through the corruption inherent in the too-deep desire for possession; in this instance, possession of the papers of a famous dead poet, a cause that makes an otherwise civilized man as ruthless as any hunter after precious prey. In *Daisy Miller,* which was famous in its day, one learns the steep fine paid for social conformity leading on to social cowardice. The English critic Desmond MacCarthy said, of Henry James's characters, that only the good are beautiful and that in a James novel there is no shortcut to being good. Henry James is perhaps the only novelist who could invest resignation in his characters with grandeur. But all this is part of what one thinks of as Early James.

Genius, by its nature, grows and deepens. Such was the case with what is known as Henry James's Middle Phase. James wrote of the novelist George Du Maurier that "he saw mystery, reality, irony, in everything," but it was even truer of him. As he grew older, his phrasing became more exact, his eye more precise, his range of subject widened. His abilities, in other words, had fully caught up with his ambition. The old accusations against him — that he cut things too fine, that he chewed much more than he had bit off — were put to rest in *The Bostonians, The Portrait of a Lady,* and

The Princess Casamassima, all novels anchored in a firmly detailed world.

Anyone who might think Henry James an over-refined snob and a writer of greatly limited range will do a strong double-take upon reading *The Princess Casamassima,* James's political novel of 1886. The beginning of that novel provides an extended description of the dark, dank London women's prison in which the mother of the novel's hero gives birth to him on what will also be her deathbed. Not Dickens, not Zola, could have done it better. Later in that same novel, one Madame Grandoni, a character who clearly speaks for James, remarks: "An honorable nature, of any class, I always respect." And the most honorable natures in this novel are all of the working class.

"You are rich when you can realize the dreams of your imagination," James has his character Ralph Touchett say in *The Portrait of a Lady.* Financially, James himself never came close to realizing his own dreams. He had great hopes that these three novels of his middle period would resoundingly ring the commercial gong for him — hopes that, like many another of his hopes in this realm, were dashed by apathy on the part of the public and ignorance on part of reviewers (though *The Portrait of a Lady* at least earned critical acclaim). Even today many people feel that these novels represent James's genius at its most attractive, and wish he had been able to continue to work further in this vein.

But financial pressure forced him to turn, in 1890, with the hope of achieving "fame and shekels," to the theater, the most serious misstep of his career. I say misstep, but debacle is closer to it. Although the theater is nothing but talk, James's manner was altogether too talky for the stage, and as a playwright he may be likened to the man who was given an unlimited budget and exceeded it. *Guy Domville,* the one play of his that made it to the London stage, was roundly booed. For a man of James's refined sensibility this was a disaster, and one that led him to the precipice of a serious breakdown.

Henry James was fifty-two at the time of his theatrical failure. He knew that the only way out was through his art. "Produce again," he wrote, "produce, produce better than ever, and all will yet be well." As he was later to write to Paul Bourget: "For myself, more than ever, our famous 'Art' is the one refuge and sanatorium." With the resilience of genius, he wrote his way back to sound health.

For a superior writer nothing is ever, finally, wasted. And so it was that James claimed to have taken from his theatrical failure what he called his new "scenic" method of composing his novels: the notion that novels, like plays, ought to work toward key scenes, carefully preparing for them all along the way. Around this time, too, a severe case of writer's cramp caused him to begin dictating his novels. Dictating, many feel, is what changed Henry James's style as he now entered what the critics call his Major Phase.

In the style of his Major Phase, James sentences roll on, in the manner of a great but highly loquacious talker, which James himself in fact was, laden with irony, merriment — the merriment of malice, his friend Edith Wharton called it — richly elaborate metaphors, and astonishingly subtle observations. Here is a sentence from *The American Scene,* James's travel book of 1907, that, in describing the wintry landscapes of the

United States, provides a characteristically ornate late-style Jamesian sentence:

The spread of this single great wash of winter from latitude to latitude struck me in fact as having its analogy in the vast vogue of some infinitely selling novel, one of those happy volumes of which the circulation soars, periodically, from Atlantic to Pacific and from great windy state to state, in the manner as I have heard it vividly put, of a blazing prairie fire; with as little possibility of arrest from 'criticism' in one case as from the bleating of lost sheep on the other.

The quotient of throw-away *aperçus* is very high in the later James. In *The Awkward Age,* one of the novels of the Major Phase, you will find a character remarking that he doesn't really believe "in the existence of friendship in big societies — in great towns and great crowds. [Friendship's] a plant that takes time and space and air; and London society is a huge 'squash,' as we elegantly call it — an elbowing, pushing, perspiring mob." Another character in the same novel is "a master of two kinds of urbanity, the kind that added to distance and that kind that diminished it." Like the young heroine of this novel — and of all the novels of the Major Phase — James seems to "take things in at [his] pores."

"He had a mind so fine," T. S. Eliot said of Henry James, "that no idea could violate it." Eliot meant that Henry James, in his art, operated above the level of ideas, on sensibility, where nuanced feeling trumped abstract thought. Instinct, feeling, the heart in conflict with itself — this is what interested Henry James. Sensibility was for him as oxygen is for the rest of us.

James's *modus operandi* is to set out the materials that allow his readers to make important judgments, which he chose, by deliberation, not to make for them. Inevitably these judgments are moral, for reading Henry James exercises above all the faculty of moral imagination. "Without exception," as Auden noted, "so far as I know, the characters in Henry James are concerned with moral choices; they may choose evil, but we are left in no doubt about the importance of their having chosen it. . . ." Why should it matter, if, as in *The Wings of the Dove,* a young man courts a rich and dying heiress, comforting her in the final wan years of her life, even if his motive is to gain her money after her death so that he can later marry someone else? If the question seems of small interest, reading Henry James is probably not the best way for you to spend your time. No other writer calls for quite such concentrated effort; strict attention must at all times be paid. But for those who can stay the course the reward is entrée to a world of aesthetic subtlety and moral refinement that one is otherwise unlikely to have known existed. It won't do to call Henry James a universal genius. The dazzlingly complex game played out in his novels is not for everyone. But for those prepared to make the effort, there is no more exhilarating game in town.

Henry James

From The Sacred Fount, *chapter 1*

It was an occasion, I felt — the prospect of a large party — to look out at the station for others, possible friends and even possible enemies, who might be going. Such premonitions, it was true, bred fears when they failed to breed hopes, though it was to be added that there were sometimes, in the case, rather happy ambiguities. One was glowered at, in the compartment, by people who on the morrow, after breakfast, were to prove charming; one was spoken to first by people whose sociability was subsequently to show as bleak; and one built with confidence on others who were never to reappear at all — who were only going to Birmingham. As soon as I saw Gilbert Long, some way up the platform, however, I knew him as an element. It was not so much that the wish was father to the thought as that I remembered having already more than once met him at Newmarch. He was a friend of the house — he wouldn't be going to Birmingham. I so little expected him, at the same time, to recognise me that I stopped short of the carriage near which he stood — I looked for a seat that wouldn't make us neighbours.

I had met him at Newmarch only — a place of a charm so special as to create rather a bond among its guests; but he had always, in the interval, so failed to know me that I could only hold him as stupid unless I held him as impertinent. He was stupid in fact, and in that character had no business at Newmarch; but he had also, no doubt, his system, which he applied without discernment. I wondered, while I saw my things put into my corner, what Newmarch could see in him — for it always had to see something before it made a sign. His good looks, which were striking, perhaps paid his way — his six feet and more of stature, his low-growing, tight-curling hair, his big, bare, blooming face. He was a fine piece of human furniture — he made a small party seem more numerous. This, at least, was the impression of him that had revived before I stepped out again to the platform, and it armed me only at first with surprise when I saw him come down to me as if for a greeting. If he had decided at last to treat me as an acquaintance made, it was none the less a case for letting him come all the way. That, accordingly, was what he did, and with so clear a conscience, I hasten to add, that at the end of a minute we were talking together quite as with the tradition of prompt intimacy. He was good-looking enough, I now again saw, but not such a model of it as I had seemed to remember; on the other hand his manners had distinctly gained in ease. He referred to our previous encounters and common contacts — he was glad I was going; he peeped into my compartment and thought it better than his own. He called a porter, the next minute, to shift his things, and while his attention was so taken I made out some of the rest of the contingent, who were finding or had already found places.

This lasted till Long came back with his porter, as well as with a lady unknown to me and to whom he had apparently mentioned that our carriage would pleasantly accommodate her. The porter carried in fact her dressing-bag, which he put upon a seat and the bestowal of which left the lady presently free to turn to me with a reproach: "I don't think it very nice of you not to speak to me." I stared, then caught at her identity through her voice; after which I reflected that she might easily have thought me the same sort of ass as I had thought Long. For she was simply, it appeared, Grace Brissenden. We had, the three of us, the carriage to ourselves, and we journeyed together for more than an hour, during which, in my corner, I had my companions opposite. We began at first by talking a little, and then as the train — a fast one — ran straight and proportionately bellowed, we gave up the effort to compete with its music. Meantime, however, we had exchanged with each other a fact or two to turn over in silence. Brissenden was coming later — not, indeed, that that was such a fact. But his wife was informed — she knew about the numerous others; she had mentioned, while we waited, people and things: that Obert, R.A., was somewhere in the train, that her husband was to bring on Lady John, and that Mrs. Froome and Lord Lutley were in the wondrous new fashion — and their servants too, like a single household — starting, travelling, arriving together. It came back to me as I sat there that when she mentioned Lady John as in charge of Brissenden the other member of our trio

182

had expressed interest and surprise — expressed it so as to have made her reply with a smile: "Didn't you really know?" This passage had taken place on the platform while, availing ourselves of our last minute, we hung about our door.

"Why in the world *should* I know?"

To which, with good nature, she had simply returned: "Oh, it's only that I thought you always did!" And they both had looked at me a little oddly, as if appealing from each other. "What in the world does she mean?" Long might have seemed to ask; while Mrs. Brissenden conveyed with light profundity: "*You* know why he should as well as I, don't you?" In point of fact I didn't in the least; and what afterwards struck me much more as the beginning of my anecdote was a word dropped by Long after someone had come up to speak to her. I had then given him his cue by alluding to my original failure to place her. What in the world, in the year or two, had happened to her? She had changed so extraordinarily for the better. How could a woman who had been plain so long become pretty so late?

Joseph Conrad

....................∽∽∞∞∞∞∞∞∞∞∞∽∽....................

BY ELIZABETH LOWRY

English readers have always had an uneasy relationship with Conrad. H. G. Wells, ever pragmatic between flights of science fiction, was famously irritated by what he called Conrad's "florid mental gestures." In his reviews of Conrad's early novels Wells complained that "only greatness could make books of which the detailed workmanship is so copiously bad, so well worth

reading, so convincing, and so stimulating," concluding rather waspishly, "Conrad 'writes.' It shows." Leonard Woolf was harsher still, grumbling after finishing *Suspense* that "I had the feeling which one gets on cracking a fine, shining, new walnut . . . only to find that it has nothing inside it." He added despondently, "most of the later Conrads give one this feeling." Toward the end of Conrad's life, E. M. Forster confessed to having a similar suspicion that Conrad's eloquence was all a sleight of hand when he hazarded that, far from having anything specific to say, "he is misty in the middle as well as at the edges . . . the secret casket of his genius contains a vapour rather than a jewel."

It was not until F. R. Leavis unequivocally ranked Conrad in *The Great Tradition* (1948), his groundbreaking reappraisal of the English novel, as "among the very greatest novelists in the language — or any language," that the question was settled. Yet even Leavis had to concede that he felt a certain "exasperation"

that the greatness attributed to Conrad "tended to be identified with an imputed profundity" — a profundity that Leavis considered not just "the reverse of a strength," but even "a disconcerting weakness or vice." There is clearly a problem with Conrad: as Leavis pointed out, he has "long been generally held to be among the English masters," but we do not really understand him or quite trust him. It is an irony that Conrad himself, with his instinctive tendency to contradiction, his love of absurdity, and his appreciation of the relativism of human perceptions, would have relished.

Woolf and Forster were right, up to a point. There *is* a puzzle, a paradox, at the heart of Conrad's work. In tackling the popular themes of his day — imperial expansion, political intrigue, ships and the sea — he invested them with an anxiety and a complexity that was entirely new. As Conrad explained in a letter to the *New York Times,* his chief aim was "the courageous recognition of all the irreconcilable

Conrad was born Teodor Józef Konrad Korzeniowski on December 3, 1857, in Berdychiv, Ukraine. He died in Canterbury, Kent, England, on August 3, 1924.

antagonisms that make our life so enigmatic, so burdensome, so fascinating, so dangerous — so full of hope." His work is always predicated on a binary conflict, a simultaneous insistence on opposites: reason and emotion, moral corruption and redemption, idealism and skepticism, loyalty and betrayal, belonging and isolation, heroism and pragmatism. And his prose strives for a corresponding form, a form that will do justice to this "struggle of contradictions." It is linguistically complex but warns about the inadequacy of language to give a true account of the world, and its philosophical sophistication goes hand in hand with a fear that excessive reflection can paralyze the will. Small wonder that Conrad liked to call himself *homo duplex*, the double man. His yielding to his instinct for fracture and paradox led him to reject traditional methods of narration in his fiction wherever possible.

The tenacity with which Conrad, although stung to the quick by critical carping at his "haze of sentences" (Wells again), initially resisted the pressure to "normalize" his style can be gauged by his fierce defense of his methods in the preface to *The Nigger of the 'Narcissus'*: "My task . . . is, above all, to make you see." By this he meant that he did not simply want to achieve a vivid surface impression, but to offer an insight into the radical instability of appearances themselves. Conrad's suspicion of language, of the act of narration itself, is a deeply seated anxiety and troubles every level of his fiction. It troubles his fiction to the extent that it must have troubled his life, his very sense of who and what he was. For originally he was not really Joseph Conrad, or an Englishman — or even an English speaker, for that matter, at all.

Conrad's home language, in an area where the predominant language was Ukrainian, was Polish; his second language was French. In 1861 his patriotic Polish parents were found guilty of subversive activities against the Russian state and the four-year-old child followed them into exile to Vologda in northern Russia. By the time he was eleven Conrad was an orphan — both parents died of tuberculosis, the result of their Siberian exile — and went first to Switzerland to live with an uncle, and then back to Kraków for his schooling. At the age of sixteen Conrad decided to go to sea and courted yet another displacement, this time leaving Poland for France, where he joined the French merchant marine in Marseilles as an apprentice. This was the start of a twenty-year career that would later take him through the ranks of the British Merchant Navy from common seaman to captain. It is an astonishing fact that until adulthood Conrad seems not to have spoken English at all. Not yet twenty-one, he taught himself the language by reading the London *Times,* Carlyle, and Shakespeare's plays. Conrad renounced his Russian citizenship and became a British subject in 1886. During his sea voyages he had begun to write in this, his third language, and — equally astonishing — his transformation into the English man of letters took place within a mere fifteen years. Although Conrad sailed to many parts of the world, including the East Indies, Java, Singapore, Australia, Mauritius, and the Congo Free State, he continued to make his home in England and settled down there to a full-time career as a novelist at the age of thirty-seven.

Conrad never lost his sense of being an outsider, of working in a foreign tongue. He later remembered that, when writing, "I had to work like a coal miner in his pit quarrying all my English sentences out of a black night." There is something irreducibly other about him; a profound foreignness not only of attitude but of idiom that makes his prose read like a translation. Wells's accusations of prolixity and vagueness are not fair, however — Conrad's style is not so much wordy and diffuse as dense. English is a language that favors end-weighted clause patterns: the typical movement in an idiomatic English sentence is from simplicity to increasing complexity, with any modifiers of the nouns being disposed toward the back. Conrad, on the other hand, heaps the modifiers onto the noun from the very beginning, resulting in a breathtaking degree of complexity. He makes free use of prepositional clauses that extend themselves through past participial phrases, of apposition and repetition. The total effect is often both copiously detailed and semantically compressed, as if we are being given as an instantaneous impression what might more naturally (to the English ear at least) have been presented as a sequence. This goes hand in hand with a sense of inversion, as if the sentence were unfolding from back to front.

Take, for example, Marlow's description of the Company's chief accountant in *Heart of Darkness:* "I sat generally on the floor, while, of faultless appearance (and even slightly scented), perching on a high stool, he wrote, wrote." Or Almayer's glimpse of the forest in *Almayer's Folly*:

As he skirted in his weary march the edge of the forest he glanced now and then into its dark shade, so enticing in its deceptive appearance of coolness, so repellent with its unrelieved gloom, where lay, entombed and rotting, countless generations of trees, and where their

successors stood as if in mourning, in dark green foliage, immense and helpless, awaiting their turn.

This is the sort of snaking periphrasis that Max Beerbohm later ruthlessly satirized in his Conradian spoof in *A Christmas Garland* ("The hut in which slept the white man was on a clearing between the forest and the river. . . ." Conrad graciously demurred that he had been "guyed most agreeably"). Conrad is most foreign, however, in his predilection for telling rather than showing, for what Leavis dismissed as an "adjectival insistence" at crucial narrative moments, where a single unambiguous picture would have settled the question. The anonymous author of *Beowulf* sets the desired standard of economy in English literature as early as the eighth century, when he tells us that Beowulf's sword was hung with chains and "all etched with poison, with battle-blood hardened." Chaucer achieves it brilliantly some centuries later when he says of his Criseyde quite simply that she was short but had no physical imperfections other than that "her eyebrows met together," as does Defoe in his matter-of-fact cataloging of Moll Flanders's tenaciously hoarded plate, linen, and "household stuff." The English tradition is full of *things,* and of choice adjectives scrupulously placed. Conrad's adjectives, however, are not so much placed as allowed to proliferate in threes, like clusters of coconuts. The primeval landscape in *Heart of Darkness* is "great, expectant, mute." When Leggatt first slips on board the *Sephora* in *The Secret Sharer* he is described as "ghastly, silvery, fish-like." The sky arching above Karain's head is "pellucid, pure, stainless" (arching, indeed, as if about to envelop "the water, the earth, and the man"). Mrs. Gould, the lonely wife in *Nostromo,* imagines the San Tomé mountain hanging over the Campo, "feared, hated, wealthy." And so on, and on (and on).

Equally tempting to the satirist — and Beerbohm, for one, gave in freely to temptation — is Conrad's love of portentous abstractions. When reading Conrad we are confronted with a cosmos that is lavishly "incomprehensible," "mysterious," "impalpable," "unaccountable," "inexplicable," "unfathomable," "impenetrable," "infinite," "vast," and "immense." Whole sentences arrive without a single concrete item for the English reader, trained in a long tradition of specifics, to latch onto. In *Heart of Darkness,* to take just one example, the stillness of the Congo estuary is "the stillness of an implacable force brooding over an inscrutable intention." Conrad himself recognized that to the English reader there was "something incomprehensible, impalpable, ungraspable" (that adjectival cluster again!) in his tendency to think in abstractions, concluding unapologetically, *"This is my Polishness."*

And yet we must remember, as Bernard Bergonzi has pointed out, that in spite of its apparent effusiveness Conrad's style is always in fact conscious and calculated. No passage is ever merely descriptive. *Pace* Woolf and Forster, Conrad's language is rich in nuances vital to its deepest meaning. Its meaning is not "revealed" like the contents of a casket or the pith of a nut, but deepens by degrees as the verbalization of his vision is varied and developed. What is this vision? The clue lies in the very tissue of words itself. "We talk with indignation and enthusiasm," the narrator of "An Outpost of Progress" tells us, "we talk about oppression, cruelty, crime, devotion, self-sacrifice, virtue, and we know nothing real beyond the words." Conrad realized that it was impossible to pinpoint "the

mysterious purpose of these illusions," that when ostensibly talking about ideas we are always really talking about words themselves. And words have no fixed or ultimate meaning; or rather, several possible meanings jostle for supremacy, depending on who is speaking. Eschewing revelation, Conrad's prose as it talks and talks sets up an infinite regress of competing subjectivities, deliberately drawing our attention to the unreliability of the very explicatory process in which we are engaged. Long before the authority of the European version of the world's story had been called into question by the independence movements of the 1950s and 1960s, Conrad had already devastatingly shown just how unreliable ideas, including the idea of civilization, were. He has been accused — most ferociously by Chinua Achebe — of racism, but the charge does not stick. Conrad shows again and again that even supposedly given areas of belief and identity are in fact artificial, culturally created; specifically, that in the imperial enterprise a quest for economic gain underpinned the cultural superstructure and its claim to bring "progress" to "the dark places of the earth."

No other writer about empire — V. S. Naipaul, Rudyard Kipling, Somerset Maugham, Leonard Woolf, Graham Greene, Olive Schreiner, and Ngugi wa Thiong'o all come to mind — has given us such a shockingly comprehensive cast of disturbed characters. "An Outpost of Progress" is typical of Conrad's method, demolishing the "pretty fictions" of imperialism by letting us into the slow self-destruction of Kayerts and Carlier, two traders, representatives of "the Great Civilizing Company" (since, as Conrad notes sardonically, "we know that civilization follows trade") in the

Congo Free State. Instead of presenting us with a Manichean opposition between backward, lazy "natives" and their heroic, energetic European "masters," Conrad dispassionately shows how the business of ivory trading at this particular center of progress degenerates into slave trading and leads to the slaughter of the local population. The story anticipates the total nihilism of *Heart of Darkness:* there, too, the legacy of the European traders is neither "light" nor "faith" nor peaceful "commerce," but a botched railroad, brutal chain gangs, and the grove of death. The "unspeakable rites" (cannibalism? human sacrifice? — the question remains tantalizingly unanswered) flourishing in Kurtz's little empire are simply an extreme reflection of the macrocosm. Significantly, Kurtz himself is not the product of a specific European nation, being part English, part French: "All Europe contributed to the making of Kurtz." Conrad's masterstroke is to make us complicit in the tale's moral confusion. It is impossible to say whether Kurtz's unnervingly ambiguous concluding cry, "The horror! The horror!" expresses repentance or a final insight into the pointlessness of all ethical judgments. Conrad insists that "the mind of man is capable of anything — because everything is in it, all the past as well as the future." Kurtz is part of all of us: none of us knows what we are capable of until we have done it.

In its probing relativism, *Heart of Darkness* predicts the confusion and anarchy of later western interventions around the globe, as Francis Ford Coppola recognized in his 1979 film *Apocalypse Now*. Conrad's apocalyptic vision of a world without moral absolutes captures the keynote of the modern age exactly. "Do you see the story?" asks Marlow. "Do you see anything?" By the end of the tale, we no longer know. And yet, in the middle of the complex verbal tissue, in the dark heart of his uncertainties, what lucid detail Conrad sometimes offers us.

Edward Garnett once recalled asking Conrad what he had particularly noticed about a heavily made-up woman who had just passed their table at the Café Royal. "The dirt in her nostril," Conrad replied instantly. This is the infallible eye that picks out the two women, "one fat and one slim, [who] sat on straw-bottomed chairs, knitting black wool" when Marlow visits the Company's Brussels office, or the "pool of blood [that] lay very still, gleaming dark-red under the wheel" after Marlow's helmsman is killed. And here, in this latent eye for the circumstantial, we might say, is Conrad's Englishness. The larger part of him, however, is engaged elsewhere, in challenging the very premises on which his fiction — and all fiction — is constructed. In his anguished and compulsive questioning of ideas Conrad is, in a very real sense, not an English but a European novelist; and in the attention that he draws to the opacity of language itself, in his tug toward entropy, toward a final dissolution of meaning, he is a far more radical writer than either Wells, Woolf, Forster, or even Leavis was able to discern. Of course there is an enigma at the center of Conrad's work. It is the enigma of the modern absurd, and it is what we go to Conrad for.

Joseph Conrad

From the preface to The Nigger of the 'Narcissus'

The sincere endeavour to accomplish that creative task, to go as far on that road as his strength will carry him, to go undeterred by faltering, weariness, or reproach, is the only valid justification for the worker in prose. And if his conscience is clear, his answer to those who, in the fullness of a wisdom which looks for immediate profit, demand specifically to be edified, consoled, amused; who demand to be promptly improved, or encouraged, or frightened, or shocked, or charmed, must run thus: My task which I am trying to achieve is, by the power of the written word to make you hear, to make you feel — it is, before all, to make you see. That — and no more, and it is everything. If I succeed, you shall find there according to your deserts: encouragement, consolation, fear, charm — all you demand — and, perhaps, also that glimpse of truth for which you have forgotten to ask....

Art is long and life is short, and success is very far off. And thus, doubtful of strength to travel so far, we talk a little about the aim — the aim of art, which, like life itself, is inspiring, difficult — obscured by mists. It is not in the clear logic of a triumphant conclusion; it is not in the unveiling of one of those heartless secrets which are called the Laws of Nature. It is not less great, but only more difficult.

····⦂····

From "Heart of Darkness"

The yarns of seamen have a direct simplicity, the whole meaning of which lies within the shell of a cracked nut. But Marlow was not typical (if his propensity to spin yarns be excepted), and to him the meaning of an episode was not inside like a kernel but outside, enveloping the tale which brought it out only as a glow brings out a haze, in the likeness of one of these misty halos that sometimes are made visible by the spectral illumination of moonshine....

"What saves us is efficiency — the devotion to efficiency. But these chaps were not much account, really. They were no colonists; their administration was merely a squeeze, and nothing more,

I suspect. They were conquerors, and for that you want only brute force — nothing to boast of, when you have it, since your strength is just an accident arising from the weakness of others. They grabbed what they could get for the sake of what was to be got. It was just robbery with violence, aggravated murder on a great scale, and men going at it blind — as is very proper for those who tackle a darkness. The conquest of the earth, which mostly means the taking it away from those who have a different complexion or slightly flatter noses than ourselves, is not a pretty thing when you look into it too much...."

····:····

[Kurtz's] was an impenetrable darkness. I looked at him as you peer down at a man who is lying at the bottom of a precipice where the sun never shines....

One evening coming in with a candle I was startled to hear him say a little tremulously, "I am lying here in the dark waiting for death." The light was within a foot of his eyes. I forced myself to murmur, "Oh, nonsense!" and stood over him as if transfixed.

Anything approaching the change that came over his features I have never seen before, and hope never to see again. Oh, I wasn't touched. I was fascinated. It was as though a veil had been rent. I saw on that ivory face the expression of sombre pride, of ruthless power, of craven terror — of an intense and hopeless despair. Did he live his life again in every detail of desire, temptation, and surrender during that supreme moment of complete knowledge? He cried in a whisper at some image, at some vision — he cried out twice, a cry that was no more than a breath:

"The horror! The horror!"

····:····

Life knows us not and we do not know life, — we don't know even our own thoughts. Half the words we use have no meaning whatever and of the other half each man understands each word after the fashion of his own folly and conceit. Faith is a myth and beliefs shift like mists on the shore: thoughts vanish: words, once pronounced, die: and the memory of yesterday is as shadowy as the hope of to-morrow....

From "Heart of Darkness"

From a letter to R. B. Cunninghame Graham, dated January 14, 1898

191

Willa Cather

......∙∙∙∙◇◇◇◇◇◇∙∙∙∙......

BY STEPHEN COX

In 1922, Willa Cather published an essay stating her literary principles. She put them in their most radical form. Novelists, she said, must clean house. They must have the courage to rid their work of elaborately "realistic" descriptions of social settings and physical sensations. They must write "the novel démeublé" — the novel with the furniture thrown out. What would be left, after all the furniture was gone, would be the fundamental thing, the human character, working out its destiny within the essential limitations of human life.

As Cather presented it, the human character was always the individual character, never the social, political, or historical category. This may seem strange, given her reputation as a great "woman writer" and a great interpreter of America's "heartland experience." But Cather was not interested in women, midwesterners, or any other *type* of human being; she was interested in individuals and their irreducibly individual choices.

Consider the crucial scene in the first novel that she regarded as a genuine expression of herself, *O Pioneers!* Alexandra Bergson, her protagonist, is the daughter of Swedish immigrants to Nebraska. Here, on the treeless prairie, the Bergson family struggles to survive. They believe in the virtue of hard work; they work their hearts out — and they fail. The father dies, leaving his miserable land to Alexandra and her brothers. The brothers want to give up. Their neighbors are clearing out; why shouldn't they? This is the point at which Alexandra makes her own, very peculiar choice. She tells her brothers that they should do what all their neighbors *aren't* doing: they should borrow money to buy more land.

To the brothers, this is a preposterous idea: they can't work the land they have now. But Alexandra argues that the purpose is *not* to work. She believes that when new, scientific methods are used, the land can be worked with much less labor and much more reward. Land that is valueless now will be very valuable then. They can sell some of it, make a profit, hire people to work for them. Her brothers gasp: think of the risk! But for Alexandra, risk is opportunity. Let other people have "a little certainty"; what she wants is "a big chance." She convinces her brothers to accept her proposal — and the family becomes rich.

Cather was born on December 7, 1873, near Winchester, Virginia. She died in New York, New York, on April 24, 1947.

193

Every great book takes chances, too. By making the heroic action of her story turn on the moment when a young woman discovers how to make money, Cather refuses to do the easy thing: to associate heroism with hard work, family solidarity, and other established values. She emphasizes, instead, economic choices that may seem amoral and unheroic, unless one understands the courage required to make them.

But a literary character is more than a moment of choice. A great character comes to life in many ways. On one level, Alexandra is simply a young farm woman. Yet beneath the commonplace surface is another, more mysterious life, the life of the unique psychological forces that make her love the land that others want to leave. Because of this deep affinity with the land, she lives also on the level of history, the level on which irreversible changes occur in the relationship of land to humanity. Describing Alexandra's decision to risk her future on an apparently worthless farm, Cather writes: "For the first time, perhaps, since that land emerged from the waters of geologic ages, a human face was set toward it with love and yearning."

As usual, Cather is sparing with words; she adds just enough to the facts of Alexandra's choice to give it the dimension of myth. A myth is a story in which the specific opens directly onto the universal. Alexandra conceives her great investment scheme while she is riding through the countryside, as such a young woman might well ride — chatting with her little brother and humming "an old Swedish hymn." But these are specifics that strike a mythic chord. They connect Alexandra with her ethnicity, her family, the world of the past, the world of the spirit. Then, in a swift transition, the pivotal event occurs: the spirit of her new country, "the great, free spirit which blows across it . . . bent lower than it ever bent to a human will before." The spirit bends to her because she has shown that she is the kind of person who can make it hers. The individual mind is only an impulse away from the realm of destiny: "The history of every country begins in the heart of a man or a woman."

Cather didn't need a big western canvas to project a myth. She could do just as well with a portrait in miniature. Her novel *My Mortal Enemy* may be the shortest actual novel ever written. Shorter than many short stories, it has all the elements of a three-volume romance — except that it reverses all romantic expectations, turning an archetypically romantic plot into a myth of dark fatality. Myra Henshawe, heir to a fortune, surrenders everything to wed a man of whom her guardian does not approve. The guardian is wrong; the man is intelligent, charming, sensitive, devoted; and Myra grows desperately unhappy with him. Her love turns to resentment; her sensibility turns to cynicism. At the end of the novel, old and dying, she sits on a cliff gazing out at the ocean, reflecting, perhaps, on the question posed by the title: who was her mortal enemy — herself, or the man she chose? We cannot know whether she finds an answer to that question, or to the larger questions of character and destiny that the book considers. We do know that Myra's story, with its implacable ambiguities, is a mythic projection of a fundamental truth — even our best choices are potentially disastrous.

Yet we must choose, and the choices are always our own, never dictated by our setting and circumstances. That was Cather's idea, and she paid a heavy price for it. She was violently criticized for her lack of social consciousness.

It wasn't that she was ignorant about social issues. In her thirties, while she was trying to save enough money to quit work and write what she wanted, she edited *McClure's Magazine,* the nation's leading organ of socially conscious, "progressive" journalism. She met many authors and critics who believed that the essential problems are those of communities, not individuals. She vigorously rejected that thesis. In her books, she threw out all "social" detail that was not embodied in individual thought and action. According to Edith Lewis, her companion during the last four decades of her life, "She always said it was what she left out that counted."

Her fiction, her critics charged, was overly concerned with private, familial, "domestic" settings. The critics would have been still more scandalized if they had realized that she chose family scenes to demonstrate the most private thing in the world, the resistant strength of individuality. In *My Ántonia,* the Shimerda family arrives from Bohemia and finds itself wholly unequipped to survive on the American frontier. Yet one of them, Ántonia, manages to build a free and happy life, to create a home that is uniquely hers. She overcomes disasters — her family's abject poverty, her father's suicide, her betrayal by a man who leaves her with child — that another author might use chiefly as examples of social problems. Cather uses them instead as an index of the individual's capacity for transcendence. Measured against the obstacles, Ántonia's victory is as great as anything in the heroic literature of the past. Her story unexpectedly reveals itself as an epic — the adventures of a culturally representative hero, alive at the center of a rich, fully rounded world, the important features of which are mirrored and magnified and revealed in their

proper significance by the challenges she faces as she journeys, like Odysseus, to her proper home. Cather includes a sly allusion to her own role as author in a reference to the epic poet Virgil as the first author to bring the Greek muse to his home country.

A rounded view of the world requires many reference points. As a child on the western frontier, Cather absorbed the formative experience of American life. She also began an extraordinarily deep and wide self-education in European literature, art, and music. She learned Greek and Latin and acquired a lifelong fascination with music and drama, science and history. Still more important, she learned to appreciate the varieties of human character. A square, solid, forthright, capable woman, a woman who knew her own mind thoroughly, she was both a brilliant talker and a brilliant listener. Her self-confidence was the basis of an intense imaginative sympathy and projection into the minds of others.

Each of her novels focuses on a particular human problem. In *The Song of the Lark,* it is the artist's need to discover her special character and then to subordinate all other aspects of the self to that. In *Lucy Gayheart,* it is the plight of the person who is almost an artist. *My Ántonia* shows how greatness of character can develop even in the humblest circumstances; *A Lost Lady* shows how greatness of character can be destroyed. *The Professor's House* assesses the power of art and character to resist the encroachment of age; *Shadows on the Rock,* set in seventeenth-century Quebec, assesses their power to sustain traditional values in a new and hostile environment. *Sapphira and the Slave Girl,* set in the antebellum South, studies traditional values that cannot be sustained.

Each of these books has its own method, appropriate to its own subject. The common element is Cather's challenge to her audience to work beside her in creating the story. A good example is *Death Comes for the Archbishop,* which recreates the life of Father Lamy, the pioneer bishop of New Mexico, in a series of snapshots that lack the normal narrative connections. The reader must identify the shape of the story by noticing the curious ways in which contrasting episodes are woven together into a single life. *The Professor's House* is another novel without the "furniture" of complete explanation. Cather first establishes her main story, which concerns the disillusionment of an intellectual who has survived the accomplishment of his great scholarly work. Then, with only a gesture at transition, she begins the story of a youth who finds the relics of an ancient civilization. After that, she proceeds, again without transition, to the conclusion of the original story, leaving it to her audience to perceive the parallels and dynamic contrasts that build, in both stories, toward a view of life as heroic endurance.

By investing so much in the intelligence of her audience, Cather is taking a risk — as big a risk, perhaps, as Alexandra Bergson takes with her remarkable real-estate scheme. Cather's literary essays indicate that she is betting on the existence of readers who will value her work enough to make in it their own deep investment of thought and feeling. It is not that her writing is obscure; she detested avant-garde artists who refused to be understood. She always gives sufficient guidance to readers who seek it. But she fully understood that a great story is both *transformative* and *reproductive*: it transforms the way in which life, even the most ordinary scenes of life, is perceived, and it enables perceptive readers to reproduce its own manner of seeing and transforming. Cather's books are poor in big, overtly dramatic scenes, but they are rich in subtle implication and underlying patterns of meaning. One learns to detect the patterns, and when one does, one learns to detect similar patterns that unfold elsewhere in life.

In Book One of *Death Comes for the Archbishop,* we see "a solitary horseman . . . pushing through an arid stretch of country somewhere in central New Mexico." The story, like the country itself, seems distinctly unpromising. That impression grows stronger when one reaches the next words: "He had lost his way." Two pages later, the situation appears even worse: we learn that the traveler is a priest without a congregation, a bishop without a bishopric. Indeed, "his own flock would have none of him." Cather provides a list of his "misadventures." But she also suggests that this is not just the story of one disaster after another. That's not the pattern that

the bishop discovers. Lost and rejected, he searches for signs of life and reconciliation. His eyes fall on a juniper tree. Worse and worse: it's the most hopeless-looking plant in the landscape: "not a thick-growing cone, but a naked, twisted trunk . . . parted into two lateral, flat-lying branches." Yet before this dead tree, the eccentric traveler stops and kneels, detecting in it the pattern of the Cross.

Perceptive readers, who are now aware that this is a man who can transform anything into a connection with his God, will not be surprised that when he rises from his devotions, "he look[s] refreshed." It is not just the tree that has been transformed; it is the man. Quietly, without announcement, Cather has begun to shape the bishop's story as the story of Christ, a story of apparent loss and actual renewal. This pattern, once identified, is confirmed by the countless episodes of fall and recovery that occur in the remainder of the novel. As a character in *Shadows on the Rock* remarks about finding one's way through the woods, "There are many little signs; put them all together and they point you right."

It is not always easy to predict how Cather's stories will turn out. But even when one can, at least half the pleasure comes from looking forward to the unexpected ways she will find of weaving her pattern. As one reads, one learns more about what to look out for; one begins, in effect, to tell the story along with her, reproducing in one's own mind her ways of perceiving.

Cather liked to show her characters learning the same kind of lessons. In *Shadows on the Rock,* an old priest — "a stubborn, high-handed, tyrannical, quarrelsome old man" — discovers a boy huddled in the snow by the wall of the new bishop's palace.

This was not an accident, he felt. Why had he found, on the steps of that costly episcopal residence built in scorn of him and his devotion to poverty, a male child, half-clad and crying in the merciless cold?

In the helpless child, the unsettling contrast, the seeming accident, the priest, like Cather, sees a meaning that needs to be worked into his story. The allusion to the Christ child does not need to be dramatized, any more than the title allusion to the Rock on which, Jesus said, he would build his church — not, at any rate, to readers who can let their imaginations work along with the author. The unmarked pattern is the substance of her art.

Her imaginative involvement with her characters was as complex as the patterning of their stories. Edith Lewis believed that Cather based most of her "great gallery of characters" on the people of Red Cloud, Nebraska, where she grew up: "Perhaps she was more interested in them even than they were in themselves." Yet, Lewis says, "she never set out to do a portrait of anyone." Her characters were grounded in objective reality, but they were also "the symbols of her own understanding of life, her loves and scorns, beliefs, appraisals, refusals." Her writing is always a four-fold work of imagination. She imaginatively recreates Red Cloud in the 1880s, New Mexico in the 1850s, Quebec in the 1690s, but she recreates them, not just as they were, but as they might be perceived and imagined by the people who lived in them. As Lewis indicates, these people are also expressions of

Cather's own way of seeing, and they are conveyed to an audience whose imagination is invited to take part with hers. "The roses," as T. S. Eliot says, have "the look of flowers that are looked at." Cather's landscapes, her plots, her characterizations are haunted by this rich and various consciousness of the self.

Like other hauntings, it is not something that every observer detects. Yet Cather is one of very few intellectual writers who appeal to readers of all stations and classes. She is also one of very few writers of the first rank for whom American readers feel genuine affection. Affection is ordinarily reserved for actors, sports personalities, and, occasionally, politicians; writers are felt to merit (at most) admiration. America's continuing and growing affection for Cather is a remarkable fact, because she did nothing whatever to court popularity. She wrote for the sake of the writing itself, caring nothing about whom she pleased or offended. It is the rare Cather story that lacks a satirical touch, and some of her stories — "Paul's Case," "The Sculptor's Funeral," "Two Friends," even *O Pioneers!* — satirize American attitudes in ways that seem calculated to offend. But there was no calculation in either her satires or her evocations of the American experience at its most heroic. Cather was simply embodying a world of imagination. And because of the way she did it, people loved her. She had been right: the individual character, the individual imagination, was the fundamental, the transcendent thing.

Willa Cather

Alexandra drew her shawl closer about her and stood leaning against the frame of the mill, looking at the stars which glittered so keenly through the frosty autumn air. She always loved to watch them, to think of their vastness and distance, and of their ordered march. It fortified her to reflect upon the great operations of nature, and when she thought of the law that lay behind them, she felt a sense of personal security. That night she had a new consciousness of the country, felt almost a new relation to it. Even her talk with the boys had not taken away the feeling that had overwhelmed her when she drove back to the Divide that afternoon. She had never known before how much the country meant to her. The chirping of the insects down in the long grass had been like the sweetest music. She had felt as if her heart were hiding down there, somewhere, with the quail and the plover and all the little wild things that crooned or buzzed in the sun. Under the long shaggy ridges, she felt the future stirring.

From
O Pioneers!,
part 1, chapter 5

····:····

It is sixteen years since John Bergson died. His wife now lies beside him, and the white shaft that marks their graves gleams across the wheat-fields. Could he rise from beneath it, he would not know the country under which he has been asleep. The shaggy coat of prairie, which they lifted to make him a bed, has vanished forever. From the Norwegian graveyard one looks out over a vast checker-board, marked off in squares of wheat and corn; light and dark, dark and light. Telephone wires hum along the white roads, which always run at right angles. From the graveyard gate one can count a dozen gayly painted farmhouses; the gilded weathervanes on the big red barns wink at each other across the green and brown and yellow fields. The light steel windmills tremble throughout their frames and tug at their moorings, as they vibrate in the wind that often blows from one week's end to another across that high, active, resolute stretch of country.

From
O Pioneers!,
part 2, chapter 1

The Divide is now thickly populated. The rich soil yields heavy harvests; the dry, bracing climate and the smoothness of the land make labor easy for men and beasts. There are few scenes more gratifying than a spring plowing in that country, where the furrows of a single field often lie a mile in length, and the brown earth, with such a strong, clean smell, and such a power of growth and fertility in it, yields itself eagerly to the plow; rolls away from the shear, not even dimming the brightness of the metal, with a soft, deep sigh of happiness. The wheat-cutting sometimes goes on all night as well as all day, and in good seasons there are scarcely men and horses enough to do the harvesting. The grain is so heavy that it bends toward the blade and cuts like velvet.

There is something frank and joyous and young in the open face of the country. It gives itself ungrudgingly to the moods of the season, holding nothing back. Like the plains of Lombardy, it seems to rise a little to meet the sun. The air and the earth are curiously mated and intermingled, as if the one were the breath of the other. You feel in the atmosphere the same tonic, puissant quality that is in the tilth, the same strength and resoluteness.

····⫶····

From My
Ántonia,
book 2,
chapter 14

We sat looking off across the country, watching the sun go down. The curly grass about us was on fire now. The bark of the oaks turned red as copper. There was a shimmer of gold on the brown river. Out in the stream the sandbars glittered like glass, and the light trembled in the willow thickets as if little flames were leaping among them. The breeze sank to stillness. In the ravine a ringdove mourned plaintively, and somewhere off in the bushes an owl hooted. The girls sat listless, leaning against each other. The long fingers of the sun touched their foreheads.

Presently we saw a curious thing: There were no clouds, the sun was going down in a limpid, gold-washed sky. Just as the lower edge of the red disc rested on the high fields against the horizon, a great black figure suddenly appeared on the face of the sun. We sprang to our feet, straining our eyes toward it. In a moment we realized what it was. On some upland farm, a plough had been left standing in the field. The sun was sinking just behind it. Magnified across the distance by the horizontal light, it stood out against the sun, was exactly contained within the circle of the disc; the handles, the tongue, the share — black against the molten red. There it was, heroic in size, a picture writing on the sun.

····:··:····

I lay awake for a long while, until the slow-moving moon passed my window on its way up the heavens. I was thinking about Ántonia and her children; about Anna's solicitude for her, Ambrosch's grave affection, Leo's jealous, animal little love. That moment, when they all came tumbling out of the cave into the light, was a sight any man might have come far to see. Ántonia had always been one to leave images in the mind that did not fade — that grew stronger with time. In my memory there was a succession of such pictures, fixed there like the old woodcuts of one's first primer: Ántonia kicking her bare legs against the sides of my pony when we came home in triumph with our snake; Ántonia in her black shawl and fur cap, as she stood by her father's grave in the snowstorm; Ántonia coming in with her work-team along the evening sky-line. She lent herself to immemorial human attitudes which we recognize by instinct as universal and true. I had not been mistaken. She was a battered woman now, not a lovely girl; but she still had that something which fires the imagination, could still stop one's breath for a moment by a look or gesture that somehow revealed the meaning in common things. She had only to stand in the orchard, to put her hand on a little crab tree and look up at the apples, to make you feel the goodness of planting and tending and harvesting at last. All the strong things of her heart came out in her body, that had been so tireless in serving generous emotions.

It was no wonder that her sons stood tall and straight. She was a rich mine of life, like the founders of early races.

From My Ántonia, *book 5, chapter 1*

Robert Frost

....∞∞∞∞∞∞∞∞∞∞∞...

BY ROBERT PACK

The genius of Robert Frost can first be found in his subtlety and surprising complexity. The surface of Frost's poems is apparently lucid and immediately accessible, based on colloquial diction (what Frost called the "sentence sound"), yet, upon scrutiny, his poems reveal themselves as elusive and allusive, complex and subtle. Just as there can be ambiguity in the suggestiveness of symbolic images, so, too, in Frost there can be ambiguity of tone — a line, say, that the poem's organization allows the reader to hear in different ways with different implications. In "Neither Out Far Nor in Deep," for example, the concluding lines describe people watching the sea, "They cannot look out far. / They cannot look in deep. / But when was that ever a bar / To any watch they keep?" can be read heroically or sarcastically, and they will still fit within the context of the poem. With Frost the poem often becomes more complex and uncertain the more one peruses it.

The range of themes and subjects in Frost's large body of work is remarkably wide, and his depiction of characters is both realistic and psychologically penetrating. Not only is Frost a poet who sees the natural world in specific detail, but he also responds to what Wordsworth called the "mighty world of eye and ear" with the Wordsworthian sense that the physical world is there to be interpreted, even reinvented through poetic apperception, a world "Both what we half create and what perceive." An image from "After Apple-Picking," for example, of the "pane of glass / I skimmed this morning from the drinking trough / And held against the world of hoary grass" has a surreal quality even though it is quite literal, and, furthermore, it carries with it the subtle biblical allusion of "looking through a glass darkly." Frost has said: "I don't like obscurity or obfuscation, but I do like dark sayings I must leave the clearing of to time."

Frost is also our preeminent nature poet, the twentieth century's true successor to Wordsworth in a way that both continues the Wordsworthian tradition and opposes it. When Wordsworth walks out into the landscape, it is always with the expectation that something of the divine will be revealed to him, and he is never disappointed. Frost too walks out into the woods to "see what we shall see," with the hope that some revelation will occur.

Frost was born on March 26, 1874, in San Francisco, California. He died in Boston, Massachusetts, on January 29, 1963.

203

On rare occasions, as in "Two Look at Two," something like revelation does indeed inform his experience so that he can conclude, "As if the earth in one unlooked-for favor, / Had made them certain earth returned their love." But usually Frost experiences what we might call an anti-revelation: it is revealed to him that nothing has been revealed, so that he can say, "One luminary clock against the sky, / Proclaimed the time was neither wrong nor right," or, in his skepticism about the evidence of an afterlife, "the strong are saying nothing until they see."

Frost's sonnet "Design" offers his darkest and most fearful vision of what the design of nature — and thus the design of the creator of nature — might be within the context of Frost's Darwinian evolutionary understanding. In this intensely compacted poem, Frost examines a minute scene in nature and asks himself what design is to be perceived there and what kind of creator, with what intent, would choose to create such a design. The poem is divided into two stanzas: the first is written in a style dependent upon similes that attempt to offer consolation by presenting images of destruction in pleasingly aesthetic terms, while the second stanza rejects the illusion that nature is benign by questioning every assertion previously made in the mode of poetic description. Thus, the central rhetorical term of the first stanza, "like," is replaced in the second stanza with the repetition of "what," a word that evokes uncertainty and bafflement.

The image of the spider sitting on a white heal-all evokes an atmosphere of innocent enchantment. Although the spider is holding up a moth, an ominous image, the poet compares this moth to a white piece of rigid satin cloth, as if to insist that this image, too, can be viewed as part of a pattern of innocent whiteness. The awareness of the moth as a dead creature is further suppressed by the simile of satin cloth, and the effect of the line is thus one of aesthetic loveliness. The word "rigid," however, undermines the poet-speaker's attempt to render the scene in comforting terms, because it functions as a breakthrough of the speaker's repressed awareness, shared by the temporarily deceived reader, of the moth's rigor mortis.

But the reality of death and blight that the poet-speaker has struggled to repress in the first stanza reasserts its power in the second as the poet's tone changes from playful to grim. Because the poet realizes that he cannot control the design of nature through consoling similes, he is left only with the unguarded honesty of asking questions. The poet now admits that the extraordinary whiteness of the scene cannot imply nature's innocence and that the attribution of innocence to the spider or the flower cannot have curative power for a mind searching for meaning in the physical world. Since the speaker can provide no answer to his own question, "What had the flower to do with being white?" he can only pose more questions that begin to acknowledge his ignorance and powerlessness. With the following line — "What brought the kindred spider to that height?" — the presence of a controlling force in a universe with its own design or intent is implied and, horrifyingly, this power may be kindred to that of the predatory spider.

Everything — so the awe-struck speaker now speculates — seems to have been determined according to a plan whose purpose, if indeed there is one, remains unknown. With the repetition of the third "what," the speaker ventures the dreadful guess: "What but design of darkness to appall?" The images of whiteness, which in the first stanza had appeared to symbolize innocence, now appear to have been a deception, a disguise for the design of darkness. The only discernible purpose of this design is to terrify those human beings who resist their need to be comforted by the belief in a benevolent and just deity. The alternatives suggested by Frost's poem are either that a God of creation is like a spider or that nature, as Darwin saw it, has evolved with no purpose at all. Frost's courage consists of his looking directly at nature, the spider, the heal-all, to be "appalled" and yet finally not to flinch. His only true comfort comes from his ability to reject any innocent or untenable form of consolation; his courage lies in his stripping away the temptations of rationalization and denial. Nature — and the God of nature if such a God exists — are both beautiful and terrible and thus the onlooker's ambivalence must be absolute. The main virtue of the poem's speaker lies in his integrity, his willingness to bear witness to a universe of unending change, not as he wishes God to have made it, but according to the testimony of his own senses and his own equivocal experience.

In the heroic skepticism of the poetry of Robert Frost, we find nature represented both as seducing and threatening, both as glorious spectacle and as the power to destroy and annihilate. In "Out, Out!" for example, Frost depicts the landscape seemingly in the mode of the Wordsworthian sublime: "And from there those that lifted eyes could count / Five mountain ranges one behind the other / Under the sunset far into Vermont." These lines become ironic, however, when lifting eyes becomes the distraction that causes the young boy to lose his hand in the buzz saw and die shortly thereafter with the onlookers unable to rescue him. And this irony deepens when the reader realizes that Frost's lines are a parody of Psalm 121, which reads, "I will lift mine eyes unto the hills, from whence cometh my help." In Frost's depiction of nature here, no help will come from the hills or from the great beyond. The final chilling lines of the poem, "And they, since they / Were not the one dead, turned to their affairs," which appear to suggest a callous or indifferent response from the boy's family, carry within them the sense that these farm people know that life must go on and that the commitment to work is inseparable from the strength of endurance in the biblical spirit of "Let the dead bury the dead."

Along with being our leading nature poet, Robert Frost is also the poet who writes most extensively about marriage, love, and desire — all in the context of loss and death. Surely, no poet since John Milton treats the theme of sexual desire and marriage more extensively or more profoundly than Frost. The dramatization of marital situations and the depiction of the fundamental separation of perspectives between men and women that need to be reconciled pervade Frost's poetry. Frost's insights

> *The main virtue of the poem's speaker lies in his integrity, his willingness to bear witness to a universe of unending change, not as he wishes God to have made it, but according to the testimony of his own senses and his own equivocal experience.*

and sympathies in exploring these universal themes contribute to his greatness as a poet as well as his remarkable craftsmanship, the integrity of each poem's organization. Frost posits a division in the natures of men and women that must be overcome through empathy, good will, and acceptance if the couple is to achieve compatibility. If they fail to "trust each other to go by contraries," as Frost says in "West-Running Brook," bitterness at the edge of potential violence will prevail as it does for the couple in "Home Burial" who grieve for their dead child.

Frost's insights and sympathies in exploring these universal themes contributes to his greatness as a poet as well as his remarkable craftsmanship, the integrity of each poem's organization.

An example of Frost's combining of lyrical and narrative techniques, together with penetrating psychological insight, can be seen in "The Death of the Hired Man." The obstacle to be overcome by the couple in this poem, Mary and Warren, is their different attitudes toward Silas, a former worker on their farm. The couple differs not simply about Silas's claim on them, but on something even more complex — their attitudes toward failure in life as exemplified by Silas. If what happens after death is a mystery — perhaps a judgment, as Frost sometimes fearfully wonders — so, too, is the cause of what makes an individual's life worthwhile or worthless. The dialogue between husband and wife presents two seemingly contradictory attitudes toward the hired man, who has returned to their farm, supposedly to work for them again, but actually to die. Although the two of them view Silas from divergent perspectives, Mary with compassion and Warren with judgment, they are in good communication with each other unlike the couple in "Home Burial."

The narrator's description of Mary is lyrical and tender, as the light of the moon "poured softly on her lap." He depicts her in an angelic image as welcoming the moonlight: "She saw it / And spread her apron to it." Then with an image of her outstretched hand — an image that will return with great significance at the poem's conclusion — the narrator in sweet incantation says: "She put out her hand / Among the harp-like morning glory strings, / Taut with the dew from garden bed to eaves." This intensely visual portrayal of Mary is brought to its lyrical height in the exquisite lines that follow: "As if she played unheard some tenderness / That wrought on him beside her in the night." At this moment, just before she addresses Warren again, some of Mary's "tenderness" passes over onto Warren and the psychological space between them narrows.

With the news of Silas's death, Warren "slipped to her side, caught up her hand and waited." Earlier, Mary had put her hand out to catch the moonlight. Later, Warren breaks a stick with his hand. And, finally, Warren takes Mary's hand, uniting himself with the moonlight as well as with some kind of universal "tenderness" that her hand can be seen to represent.

The poem concludes with Warren's simple statement of Silas's death, "'Dead,' was all he answered," not with a psychological interpretation of Mary's reaction to the cloud hitting the moon. In effect, their mourning for Silas has already taken place since their grief has concentrated on Silas's life — a concentration

that makes the question of judgment after death and Silas's ultimate worthiness seem less compelling. If there is a moral implicit in this poignant poem, it is that enough grief pervades life to exhaust our capacity for mourning. The truth that life and mourning are inseparable demands acknowledgment and acceptance. The sharing of grief may make it more bearable and even strengthen the bond between those — even across the gulf of individual differences based partly on sexual identity — who are mutually able to embrace their sorrow.

The problem that challenges the couples to reconcile their differences, to "go by contraries," in "The Death of the Hired Man" and "Home Burial" is how to deal with death. The issues that threaten to separate the couple in "West-Running Brook," by contrast, are how to accept divergent orientations in respect to the possible meaninglessness of life or the indifference of nature, which, like the stream of time, fills "the abyss's void with emptiness." So seen, as the husband philosophizes, the stream of time and flux "flows between us / To separate us for a panic moment." Frost is offering us his own version of human life as tragic, and his vision of the uses of suffering and the struggle to find meaning against the backdrop of nature's indifference. At its heart, Frost's vision consists of the sense in which the inevitability of loss can be perceived as giving life its sanctity: " 'The brook runs down in sending up our life. / The sun runs down in sending up the brook.' " Creation and destruction, order and entropy, are absolutely linked in a kind of philosophical marriage, as reconciled opposites — as contraries. This universal pattern serves as a model for the couple in "West-Running Brook," both for their relationship to each other and to their place in nature.

Even as the sharing of grief binds together the couple in "The Death of the Hired Man," so, too, does their shared vision of nature as entropic unify the couple in "West-Running Brook." The final line of the poem, " 'Today will be the day of what we both said,' " can be heard as spoken by the two of them together in a kind of duet — their affirmation of love against the backdrop of "nothingness." This entire dialogue, as the narrator's earlier interjection makes clear, has taken place in the past and given the brook its name, and so the resolving phrase, "Today will be the day," establishes the poem in a state of eternalized time that includes both past and present and thus seems to transcend the ordinary linkage of time and entropy as expressed by the husband in his earlier line, " 'Our life runs down in sending up the clock.' " And so for these married lovers "nothingness" becomes the very medium for the imagination's creation of belief in the possibility of mutual trust. Imaginative belief thus has the power to override "uncertainty" and the "panic" of separateness by virtue of its ability to conceive of the resolution of contraries as the source of an enlarged harmony.

What I take to be Frost's heroic skepticism lies precisely in his courage of uncertainty. In "For Once, Then, Something," where he taunts his critics for taunting him as a poet merely of surfaces, the poet looks down to the bottom of a well to try to discern the identity of the "something white" that is down there. He looks hard, but what he sees is "uncertain" (that key Frostian word!) and quickly he then says "I lost it." Just as in Frost's supremely enigmatic poem, "Directive," the reader is unable to distinguish between illusion and revelation, so here, too, the Frostian speaker cannot tell whether he has had a glimpse of something as large and grand as Truth or merely something physical, with no symbolic importance, like a "pebble of quartz." The poem ends in uncertainty. "My long two-pointed ladder's sticking through a tree / Toward heaven still" is the metaphor Frost uses in "After Apple-Picking" to evoke his sense of the human longing for some kind of transcendence. Despite its upward longing, Frost's poem leads us insistently downward, back to the earth with each apple to be cherished.

There is much darkness in Frost's poetry — darkness of human mood and motivation, darkness of the fear of how individual man may be judged by God should that be the fate that awaits us after death and the darkness of "uncertainty" about what we can know and therefore what we can believe. Yet these troubled emotions combine with Frost's stubborn courage to keep on going to see where the journey of life will lead. Ultimately, we have two pictures of Frost to capture his essence and his genius: the lonely indefatigable walker who is "acquainted with the night" and the contemplative and skeptical observer of nature who, nevertheless, can trust himself to "go by contraries" even in the face of his deepest doubts and uncertainties.

Robert Frost

"Design"

I found a dimpled spider, fat and white,
On a white heal-all, holding up a moth
Like a white piece of rigid satin cloth —
Assorted characters of death and blight
Mixed ready to begin the morning right,
Like the ingredients of a witches' broth —
A snow-drop spider, a flower like a froth,
And dead wings carried like a paper kite.

What had that flower to do with being white,
The wayside blue and innocent heal-all?
What brought the kindred spider to that height,
Then steered the white moth thither in the night?
What but design of darkness to appall? —
If design govern in a thing so small.

····∶····

"After Apple-Picking"

My long two-pointed ladder's sticking through a tree
Toward heaven still,
And there's a barrel that I didn't fill
Beside it, and there may be two or three
Apples I didn't pick upon some bough.
But I am done with apple-picking now.
Essence of winter sleep is on the night,
The scent of apples: I am drowsing off.
I cannot rub the strangeness from my sight
I got from looking through a pane of glass
I skimmed this morning from the drinking trough
And held against the world of hoary grass.
It melted, and I let it fall and break.
But I was well

Upon my way to sleep before it fell,
And I could tell
What form my dreaming was about to take.
Magnified apples appear and disappear,
Stem end and blossom end,
And every fleck of russet showing clear.
My instep arch not only keeps the ache,
It keeps the pressure of a ladder-round.
I feel the ladder sway as the boughs bend.
And I keep hearing from the cellar bin
The rumbling sound
Of load on load of apples coming in.
For I have had too much
Of apple-picking: I am overtired
Of the great harvest I myself desired.
There were ten thousand thousand fruit to touch,
Cherish in hand, lift down, and not let fall.
For all
That struck the earth,
No matter if not bruised or spiked with stubble,
Went surely to the cider-apple heap
As of no worth.
One can see what will trouble
This sleep of mine, whatever sleep it is.
Were he not gone,
The woodchuck could say whether it's like his
Long sleep, as I describe its coming on,
Or just some human sleep.

····∷····

From *"The Death of the Hired Man"*

'Silas is what he is—we wouldn't mind him—
But just the kind that kinsfolk can't abide.
He never did a thing so very bad.

He don't know why he isn't quite as good
As anybody. Worthless though he is,
He won't be made ashamed to please his brother.'

'*I* can't think Si ever hurt anyone.'

'No, but he hurt my heart the way he lay
And rolled his old head on that sharp-edged chair-back.
He wouldn't let me put him on the lounge.
You must go in and see what you can do.
I made the bed up for him there tonight.
You'll be surprised at him—how much he's broken.
His working days are done; I'm sure of it.'

'I'd not be in a hurry to say that.'

'I haven't been. Go, look, see for yourself.
But, Warren, please remember how it is:
He's come to help you ditch the meadow.
He has a plan. You mustn't laugh at him.
He may not speak of it, and then he may.
I'll sit and see if that small sailing cloud
Will hit or miss the moon.'

                              It hit the moon.
Then there were three there, making a dim row,
The moon, the little silver cloud, and she.

Warren returned—too soon, it seemed to her,
Slipped to her side, caught up her hand and waited.

'Warren?' she questioned.

                    'Dead,' was all he answered.

James Joyce

BY JOHN GROSS

One of the questions Napoleon used to ask, when a soldier was recommended for promotion, was "Does he have luck?" Writers need luck, too, and an important aspect of James Joyce's achievement is that he was born at the right time. He was a modernist who was able to get his claim in first.

It was *Ulysses* that brought him fame, and of all that book's qualities the one which struck its earliest readers most forcibly was its originality — many would have said its strangeness. The celebrated "stream of consciousness"; the multiplicity of styles; the mimetic devices and cinematic techniques; the wordplay; the web of allusions and cross-references; the condensed syntax; the splintered motifs — these, and a hundred other innovations, bewildered and excited. It is true that partial precedents could be pointed to in Rabelais, Laurence Sterne, and elsewhere. But the book as a whole was revolutionary. It represented a violent break with the past.

Other writers soon set out to emulate the technical novelties. One could fill a small library with the experimental or avant-garde fiction that has been written since. But for most readers, *Ulysses* still retains an air of boldness. The knowledge that it led the way is something built into the book itself.

The title proclaimed the scale of Joyce's ambition: he aimed to write a modern epic. It also signaled a central principle of the book's construction: the running parallel with the *Odyssey*. Every major episode has its Homeric counterpart ("Circe," "Hades," and so forth). The correspondences are often amusing — between the newspaper office and the Cave of the Winds, for instance, or between Gerty MacDowell and Nausicaa — and when you stand back the mere idea of them can confer a certain comic grandeur. But you aren't particularly aware of them from page to page. Joyce only applied them fitfully, and whatever their value to him as scaffolding they seem less central to one's experience of the book as time goes on.

In principle this is a major structural flaw, and there are lesser ones of a comparable kind. The ground plan of the book also associates each episode with its own color and its own branch of art or science, with a distinctive symbol and a particular organ of the body. In practice, the scheme tends to get lost. Yet such failures are the precondition, or perhaps

Joyce was born on February 2, 1882, in Dublin, Ireland. He died in Zürich, Switzerland, on January 13, 1941.

213

the consequence, of a broader success. For the true greatness of *Ulysses* is that of a novel, and its novelistic qualities triumph over whatever abstract patterns or emblematic designs Joyce sought to impose. The higher meanings may escape us, the hidden meanings may elude us, but the realities of Dublin on June 16, 1904, are always there for us to hold on to.

The city itself is brought to life to an extraordinary degree. As a piece of urban portraiture, there is nothing to compare with it in English, apart from Dickens's London. We are led through a maze of courtyards, lanes and quays, through pub and library, schoolroom and hospital, cemetery and brothel. Voices and faces, hoardings and headlines, birdcries and traffic sounds are all noted. So are Reuben J. Dodd, solicitor, and the one-legged sailor skirting Rabaiotti's ice-cream car, snuffling Nosey Flynn and bald Pat the waiter ("Bald deaf Pat brought quite flat pad ink. Pat set with ink pen quite flat pad"). Shopfronts slip past. We are in a city on the move, a city of criss-crossing routes and chance encounters. And it is rendered in an appropriately dynamic manner. The profusion of detail would pall, if everything were described from the same fixed neutral standpoint. But as it is, every scene has its own tone. Joyce's prose registers the individual sensibility and the distinctive aura.

Ulysses teems with walk-on parts and extras. Beyond that, there are the figures whom we get to know at closer quarters — Buck Mulligan, Blazes Boylan, Mr. Deasy the headmaster, Miss Douce and Miss Kennedy the barmaids, the uncivil "Citizen," fifteen or twenty others. We don't forget them: quite as much as any of the great traditional novelists, Joyce was a master of characterization.

At the heart of the book, supplying the mainspring of such plot as it has, are Leopold Bloom, his wife Molly, and Stephen Dedalus. And memorable though Stephen and Molly are, and even though Molly is given the last word, our assessment of the book finally comes to rest on a single figure, the modern Ulysses himself. The novel's two greatest achievements are the portrait of Dublin and the portrait of Bloom.

When *Ulysses* was first published it was widely assumed that it was above all else a mock-epic and that it was built around a contrast between past nobility — represented by Homer — and present-day tawdriness, in the same spirit as *The Waste Land* (or what it was assumed to be). Seen in this light, Bloom inevitably had to shoulder all the sins of modern mass society. What could be less heroic than a none-too-successful advertising canvasser? What could be more inglorious than Bloom's private life, especially when it was presented in such startling physical close-up, or more banal than the thoughts that course through his brain? Flaubert's *Bouvard and Pécuchet,* with its satire on received ideas, was another parallel that was often cited.

It wasn't long, however, before Bloom's better qualities began to win through. The idea that he was no more than a *petit bourgeois* stooge didn't tally with the experience of actually reading about him. He is a man of good will. (Joyce, who didn't undervalue the fact, called him quite simply "a good man.") He is no fool: indeed, the more we get to know him, the more impressed we are likely to be by his shrewdness and curiosity. He doesn't swallow the values of his society wholesale; he has a humorous awareness of the follies flourishing around him. And while it is impossible not to smile at his own confusions and backslidings, or at his

addiction to cliché, they belong to the world of comedy rather than satire.

We shouldn't take too soft a view of Bloom. There remains an element of scorn in Joyce's approach to him and of the clinical detachment that the young Joyce held up as an artistic ideal. But we finally respect him, even so, for his immersion in life — as a value in itself, and for the contrast it provides with Stephen Dedalus. Stephen the artist is guarded and aloof. He needs Bloom to complement him. Learning to appreciate the older man will rescue him from a narrow aestheticism and release his full creative energy.

At the same time, Bloom is no simple Everyman. As one of the other characters remarks, he has "a touch of the artist." He is an outsider twice over, cut off from his fellow Jews but never quite accepted by the Irish. And there is a good deal of Joyce himself in Bloom. He provides an ironic mask for the writer's sentimentality. He acts out his sexual fears and hang-ups. The book represents a gesture of self-acceptance on Joyce's part no less than on Stephen's.

Joyce's genius was personal in a double sense. He was driven to set down intimate detail; he also assumed that anything that happened to him was grist to the artistic mill. To reconstruct Dublin on paper was to preserve his childhood and youth, while Bloom's experiences and impressions again and again echo his own. His writing abounds in minute detail taken from life, much of it private or arbitrary. No critical study of *Ulysses* offers better guidance on how to read it, in my opinion, than Robert Martin Adams's *Surface and Symbol* (1962), and Adams concludes that the novel is "in part at least, a gambler's act of throwing his whole personality — his accidents, his skills, his weaknesses, his luck — against the world. It does not make a neat allegorical pattern. It does not make a self-contained construct. It never will."

The gambler's throw came off. There are dull patches in the book, but the wonder is how little one resents the "meaningless" detail — how much of it, indeed, is drawn into the main action's field of force. Nor do we ever feel that Bloom is merely a stand-in for Joyce. He exists too firmly in his own right.

He proves equally resilient in the face of the non-naturalistic techniques to which he is subjected in the book's later episodes — the parodies, the expressionist drama that takes place in Nighttown, the pedantic questions and answers in the Ithaca sequence. They are like so many tests of his durability. He is mauled, stretched, flattened, but, like a character in an animated cartoon, he always resumes his own shape. The novel survives the verbal games.

Those games have their fascination. Joyce wouldn't be Joyce without them, any more than he would be without all his other Puzzle-Corner diversions. But the true greatness of *Ulysses* still lies in its human qualities. Sometimes its ingenuities enhance those qualities. Where they don't, they merely add spice.

A key aspect of the book is its popular character. Its roots lie in everyday speech: it is a storehouse of slang, shoptalk, catchphrases, colloquial odds and ends. It is also shot through with borrowings from popular culture — music-hall songs, street lore, advertising slogans, and the like. Joyce's attitude to this material is often ambivalent, especially where music is involved. When he quotes from a musical comedy or a drawing-room ballad, the odds are that he will half burlesque it, half enter into its spirit. At other times he is more obviously satirical. But even then he doesn't necessarily lose sight of the human context. The language of a romantic novelette, however absurd, can still recall "things that other people have desired."

For all its esoteric devices and learned references, *Ulysses* remains constantly open to common concerns. It is one of the most democratic of modern classics (the more so for not being glib or formulaic in its democratic assumptions). It is also — and the two facts are

surely connected — a work of extraordinary vitality. Some readers find it a sad book, and there is certainly a good deal of sadness in it. Others find it sordid, and it has its undeniable share of squalor. But the strongest impression it leaves is one of life and animation. It is forever holding out rich possibilities.

Joyce's earlier works are much more than preludes to *Ulysses*. The clarity and precision of the short stories in *Dubliners* are the product of a distinctive vision. The inwardness and frankness of *A Portrait of the Artist as a Young Man* set it well apart from all but one or two of the young-man-growing-up novels of its period, while what could have been a presumptuous title is fully justified by its originality and the quality of its writing. Both books would still be read and remembered if Joyce had written nothing else. But would we be inclined to talk of "genius"? I think not — though we could hardly help speculating about what the great promise of the *Portrait of the Artist* might have led to.

Finnegans Wake, the book to which Joyce devoted his last sixteen years, is another matter. I have often come back to it; I have never succeeded in reading it, and I am content to think that the fault isn't entirely mine. Yet to talk of it as a work of genius still doesn't seem excessive. Mad genius, perhaps.

In *Ulysses* Joyce tried to fashion an all-inclusive myth, but the realities of the fragmented modern world kept pulling him back. *Finnegans Wake* is a far more determined attempt to go the whole way. Its story is meant to subsume all other stories; it has a hero, H. C. Earwicker, whose initials are made to furnish the slogan, "Here Comes Everybody." Given his ambitions, Joyce was wise to cast the book in the form of a dream. In the daytime world, there would have been a danger of Earwicker acquiring as firm an outline as Bloom (who is Bloom first and *Ulysses* a long way afterwards). In the nocturnal world, he melts easily into new shapes and incarnations.

You don't have to believe in the book's central doctrines to feel their imaginative force. History moves through an endless cycle, the part implies the whole, the same human types keep recurring under different guises — these are stirring notions. But only if it were as simple as that. A brief summary of the principles on which Joyce proceeded can't begin to suggest the crazy complexity of the machinery he rigged up around them — the proliferating subplots, the systems within systems.

All this is compounded, notoriously, by the language in which the book is written — a bubbling stew of verbal compression and distortion, of multi-layered allusions and polyglot wordplay. By virtue of this "mess of mottage," the *Wake* assumes the character of a giant cryptogram. It demands a great deal more devotion than most readers are willing to give.

And yet, in short bursts at least, it can be extraordinarily seductive. There is a happy preposterousness about its humor, a bustling parody of good sense which is unlike anything else in English. The meanings that peep out from its verbal conflations are endlessly suggestive — in the low comedian's sense of the word especially. Nonsense liberates a lyricism that might have remained stuck in sentimentality if it had been expressed in more conventional terms. And the linguistic tricks can produce strange new imaginative effects.

The context, too, even if it is something we have to learn about from Joyce's commentators, often lends a phrase mythic depth. "Only a fadograph of a yestern scene." That is more than a faded photograph: since the "yestern scene" is the Fall of Man, it is a photograph from long ages before actual photography was invented, a snapshot from the Garden of Eden. "Soft morning, city." That would, I think, be a haunting phrase anywhere, but it is doubly so introducing the concluding monologue of Anna Livia Plurabelle (Magna Mater, river goddess, H. C. Earwicker's wife).

In the end, however, *Finnegans Wake* — the full unabridged *Wake* — is strictly for addicts. Joyce believed that "a man of genius makes no mistakes," that his errors were "the portals of discovery"—at least, that is what he has Stephen Dedalus say in the library scene in *Ulysses*. It is all the more ironic that in embarking on the *Wake* he should have committed himself to one of the great aberrations of literature. A mighty aberration, which yielded brilliant "discoveries" along the way, but an aberration nonetheless. If we want to see his genius fully realized, it is to *Ulysses* that we must return.

James Joyce

From A Portrait of the Artist as a Young Man, *chapter 1*

Once upon a time and a very good time it was there was a moocow coming down along the road and this moocow that was down along the road met a nicens little boy named baby tuckoo....

His father told him that story: his father looked at him through a glass: he had a hairy face.

He was baby tuckoo. The moocow came down the road where Betty Byrne lived: she sold lemon platt.

> *O, the wild rose blossoms*
> *On the little green place.*

He sang that song. That was his song.

> *O, the green wothe botheth.*

When you wet the bed, first it is warm then it gets cold. His mother put on the oilsheet. That had the queer smell.

His mother had a nicer smell than his father. She played on the piano the sailor's hornpipe for him to dance. He danced:

> *Tralala lala,*
> *Tralala tralaladdy,*
> *Tralala lala,*
> *Tralala lala.*

Uncle Charles and Dante clapped. They were older than his father and mother but Uncle Charles was older than Dante.

Dante had two brushes in her press. The brush with the maroon velvet back was for Michael Davitt and the brush with the green velvet back was for Parnell. Dante gave him a cachou every time he brought her a piece of tissue paper.

The Vances lived in number seven. They had a different father and mother. They were Eileen's father and mother. When they were grown up he was going to marry Eileen. He hid under the table. His mother said:

—O, Stephen will apologise.

Dante said:

—O, if not, the eagles will come and pull out his eyes.

Pull out his eyes,
Apologise,
Apologise,
Pull out his eyes.

Apologise,
Pull out his eyes,
Pull out his eyes,
Apologise.

····:|:····

From "The Dead," a story in Dubliners

The air of the room chilled his shoulders. He stretched himself cautiously along under the sheets and lay down beside his wife. One by one, they were all becoming shades. Better pass boldly into that other world, in the full glory of some passion, than fade and wither dismally with age. He thought of how she who lay beside him had locked in her heart for so many years that image of her lover's eyes when he had told her that he did not wish to live.

Generous tears filled Gabriel's eyes. He had never felt like that himself towards any woman, but he knew that such a feeling must be love. The tears gathered more thickly in his eyes and in the partial darkness he imagined he saw the form of a young man standing under a dripping tree. Other forms were near. His soul had approached that region where dwell the vast hosts of the dead. He was conscious of, but could not apprehend, their wayward and flickering existence. His own identity was fading out into a grey impalpable world: the solid world itself, which these dead had one time reared and lived in, was dissolving and dwindling.

A few light taps upon the pane made him turn to the window. It had begun to snow again. He watched sleepily the flakes, silver and dark, falling obliquely against the lamplight. The time had come for him to set out on his journey westward. Yes, the newspapers were right: snow was general all over Ireland. It was falling on every part of the dark central plain, on the treeless hills, falling softly upon the Bog of Allen and, farther westward, softly falling into the dark mutinous Shannon waves. It was falling, too, upon every part of the lonely churchyard on the hill where Michael Furey lay buried. It lay thickly drifted on the crooked crosses and headstones, on the spears of the little gate, on the barren thorns. His soul swooned slowly as he heard the snow falling faintly through the universe and faintly falling, like the descent of their last end, upon all the living and the dead.

T. S. Eliot

BY JOHN SIMON

Not many geniuses were pleasant; some quite unpleasant — think Wagner, Rimbaud, Brecht. One may find both Thomas Stearns Eliot's life and work unpleasant, which he ironically acknowledges in the ditty beginning, "How unpleasant to meet Mr. Eliot." But the job of the genius is not to be pleasant but to create works that last down the ages by revealing certain

significant perceptions in a style that sticks in the reader's mind, if not indeed to his ribs. Eliot has done that, at times in complex verse or prose formulations, at others with simple and penetrating phrases giving meaning the added benefit of image, rhythm, and cadence.

Eliot has four separate but related claims on our attention: as a poet, critic, playwright, and thinker. Since we are dealing here with his literary genius, the fourth category need concern us only incidentally. And since his fame rests chiefly on his poetry, this is where we must begin.

Eliot's first publication in book form was *Prufrock and Other Observations* (1917), with the title poem ironically entitled "The Love Song of J. Alfred Prufrock," the first highlight of a poetic career. Appearing against a background of orderly Georgian and Edwardian poetry, "Prufrock," with its rhymed *vers libre,* its free association of ideas and feelings, and daredevil imagery indebted to the French symbolists, made an impact from its very

opening: "Let us go then, you and I, / When the evening is spread out against the sky / Like a patient etherised upon a table. . . ."

Note the fleetness of the first line: swift monosyllables, plain basic words, but also a sense of mystery: who is this *you* being invited? The line is short, with three or four beats and a minimum of unaccented syllables between, making for a quick, propulsive rhythm. But the second line, largely dactylic, is stretched out — indeed spread out like a patient on the operating table. The simile for darkness falling is striking; it extends across the sky, not in comfortable repose, but with the unnatural stupor of sinking into anesthesia. The term, though, is not "anesthetized" but "etherized," with reference to the period's medical practice, which ties it to "ether," a favorite poeticism for the heavens, yet heavenly vastness is reduced and flattened out to a patient on an operating table, with suggestions of sickness and the danger of surgery. In a context of

Eliot was born on September 26, 1888, in St. Louis, Missouri. He died in London, England, on January 4, 1965.

end rhymes, "table" is the only end word that does not rhyme, making it cling disturbingly to the closure-expecting memory.

The entire poem is the interior monologue of middle-aged Prufrock, a timid misfit both in the opening street scene and at the high-toned party that is the poem's main setting. Urban tawdriness and social malaise will be two of Eliot's chief themes, to which can be added unease with women, if not downright misogyny. Thus there is nothing wrong with talking about Michelangelo, but when it is done flitting about at a party and is put into doggerel — "In the room the women come and go / Talking of Michelangelo" — it becomes ludicrous and reprehensible. Prufrock and companion must disingenuously "prepare a face to meet the faces that you meet," and audacity must be summoned up not to run away — not to "disturb the universe" or even just to "eat a peach." So it would be easier to be "a pair of ragged claws / Scuttling across the floors of silent seas," but even there the mermaids are not singing to Prufrock, though his insecurity would make him linger "in the chambers of the sea." Alas, "human voices wake us, and we drown." Paradoxically, human intercourse on *terra firma* and not a sea fantasy is where you and I, Prufrock and the reader, drown.

That the poem has achieved lasting relevance is borne out by Robert Pinsky's finding in the Favorite Poem Project that "one of the most widely admired poems named by participants . . . of very different ages and levels of sophistication" is "'Prufrock.'" Eliot was in his early twenties when he presented himself as Prufrock, but as the critic Richard Ellmann noted, "Eliot was addicted to the portrayal of characters who had missed their chances,

become old before they had really been young." In his next major poetic achievement, "Gerontion" (1920), he is already the little old man of the title. The motto he appends, "Thou hast nor youth nor age / But as it were an after dinner sleep / Dreaming on both," is from *Measure for Measure,* but, as usual, Eliot doesn't give the source. Truly, he was a man precociously old, as seen in many of his works, but he also retained a childlike playfulness, as in *Old Possum's Book of Practical Cats,* where he chases after the youth he missed out on when young. As the poet-critic John Crowe Ransom observed, "Gerontion" is where Eliot "first worked out . . . the brisk prosody which was to be his staple thereafter." Here is the celebrated passage about the deceptions of history, which misleads and frustrates when it should teach, prefaced by the simple yet devastating formulation, "After such knowledge, what forgiveness?" Gerontion has known too much and so lost his innocence. History — experience — "gives with such supple confusions / That the giving famishes the craving." The needed appetite for enlightenment is starved by knowledge from "the wrath-bearing tree," whose forbidden fruit had been better left untasted. Note how, especially in the poem's last section, the "brisk prosody" leaps from image to image, until the protagonist's memories — tenants of the house of his recollection — are no more than "Thoughts of a dry brain in a dry season," the wintry waiting for death.

"Gerontion" points the way to one of Eliot's surefire masterpieces, *The Waste Land* (1922). In five parts and 434 lines, it became the anthem of doomed youth — not those who died in the Great War but those who survived into its perplexing, anticlimactic aftermath. It is impossible here to analyze in detail this epochal poem; I direct the reader to what may still be its best explication, an essay by Cleanth Brooks in his *Modern Poetry and the Tradition*. Eliot rejected the usual (not unwarrantable) interpretation of it as expressing "the disillusionment of a generation," resenting equally the notion of a generation and the idea of endorsing anyone's "illusion of disillusion." He stated that "Various critics [interpreted it] in terms of criticism of the contemporary world . . . as an important bit of social criticism. To me it was only the relief of a personal and wholly insignificant grouse against life; it is just a piece of rhythmical grumbling." This may be taken as one of Eliot's frequent expressions of Christian humility or, conversely, as his habitual mock modesty cloaking a deep-seated arrogance.

Consider merely the superscription of *The Waste Land*, combining Latin, Greek, and Italian without indication of the sources: Petronius and Dante. This may be viewed as intellectual snobbery (uncultivated readers, stay away!) or as a curiosity-inducing signpost to the poem's conclusion, whose original-language quotations are drawn from the Upanishads, Dante, the Pervigilium Veneris, Gérard de Nerval, and Thomas Kyd, this time acknowledged in the not-all-that-helpful notes to the poem. These quotations are "fragments I have shored against my ruins," against the falling down of London

The job of the genius is not to be pleasant but to create works that last down the ages by revealing certain significant perceptions in a style that sticks in the reader's mind, if not indeed to his ribs. Eliot has done that, at times in complex verse or prose formulations, at others with simple and penetrating phrases giving meaning the added benefit of image, rhythm, and cadence.

Bridge. The poet-protagonist may be proceeding from an insignificant personal grouse, but the quotation-rich destination is a universal call for tradition and culture as shorers up against annihilation. From insignificant grumbling to the rumbling of Sanskrit thunder, from the irritation of the grain of sand to the pearls of wisdom, this is a polyglot plea for the survival of European, indeed global, civilization. Let me say merely that *The Waste Land* adroitly combines the themes of the pursuit of the Holy Grail, scenes of the megalopolis as a wasteland inhabited by spiritually aimless multitudes, and tiny dialogues of upper-class anomie and lower-class frustration, along with a symbolic vision of a drowned and sea-cleansed sailor and of a thunderstorm that finally comes to quench the desiccated wastes. And much more, as glimpses of joyless fornication and abortion are superseded by salvation in the guise of a Buddhist slogan for "give, sympathize, control," which leads to *shantih*, the peace that passeth understanding.

In her indispensable critical biography *T. S. Eliot: An Imperfect Life*, Lyndall Gordon quotes the poet's response to the critic I. A. Richards's assertion that the poem was "devoid of belief": "I cannot for the life of me see the 'complete separation' from all belief. . . . A 'sense of desolation,' etc. (if it is there) is not a separation from belief; it is nothing so pleasant. In fact, doubt, uncertainty, futility, etc. would seem to prove anything except this agreeable partition; for doubt and uncertainty are merely a variety of belief."

With "The Hollow Men" (1925) — another, but much shorter, five-part poem — the personal problem becomes more explicit: "This is the way the world ends / Not with a bang but a whimper" — unless hollow, sightless men allow eyes to reappear "As the perpetual star / Multifoliate rose . . . / The hope only/ Of empty men." The imagery is Dantesque; Eliot, through much of his life, carried *The Divine Comedy* in his pocket and Dante in his mind and soul.

"The Hollow Men" was his pre-conversion poem. In 1927, Eliot joined the Anglican church and, in 1928, became a British citizen. His post-conversion poem is "Ash Wednesday" (1930), a much longer, six-part work. It chronicles the slow and arduous religious progress from the wasteland, partly as a climb up a winding stair, and partly as the need to find one's way out of the desert — from "The desert in the garden" to, with typical Eliotian inversion, a chiastic "garden in the desert / Of drouth." That Eliot advocated "impersonality" in poetry does not preclude the veiled autobiographical element. So the Lady behind "Ash Wednesday" and the Hyacinth Girl in other poems is based on Emily Hale, a young woman Eliot met during his Harvard days and to whom he may or may not have proposed. He was, or imagined he

> *"I cannot for the life of me see the 'complete separation' from all belief. . . . A 'sense of desolation,' etc. (if it is there) is not a separation from belief; it is nothing so pleasant. In fact, doubt, uncertainty, futility, etc. would seem to prove anything except this agreeable partition; for doubt and uncertainty are merely a variety of belief."*

was, rejected by her; in fact, she developed a lifelong love for him. When his flighty, neurasthenic first wife, Vivienne, who was eventually committed to an institution, died, Emily was sure Tom would marry her. He didn't, in the end ditching her, as he did another longtime female companion with similar hopes. Was this some sort of perversity or simple fear of commitment? Emily long remained on Eliot's back burner, a simmering symbol of what might have been, almost up to the time when, already aging, he married the much younger Valerie Fletcher, surely in part as secretary, nurse, and executrix. With her he seemed to find surcease from the sense of guilt he associated, first, with the sexual act, and, second, with his abandonment of Vivienne. Emily, at any rate, is in "Ash Wednesday" the "Lady of silences / Calm and distressed / Torn and most whole / Rose of memory / Rose of forgetfulness. . . ."

Long and discontinuous in gestation and made to accommodate disparate layers of inspiration, *Four Quartets* (1942) is, in my view, not so much great poetry as great technique. That technique is what Eliot was evolving all along—collage. Around a central concept, a variety of elements is accreted: private experiences, abstruse allusions, historical divagations, free association. All this with total formal freedom, ranging from traditional verse to what is simply prose laid out as *vers libre*. As he stated,

"No poet can write a long poem unless he is a master of the prosaic." Take one example from "East Coker," the second of the four quartets: "The only wisdom we can hope to acquire / Is the wisdom of humility: humility is endless." There follows a line of blank space, then "The houses are all gone under the sea." Another blank line, then "The dancers are all gone under the hill." What could be more prosaic? The houses, presumably, are those vanishing from the sight of Andrew Eliot, a Puritan ancestor sailing for the New World from the village of East Coker. The dancers hark back to an earlier passage of the poem, beginning "In daunsynge, signifying matrimonie." That passage, here representing the dance of life, comes from *The Governour* (1531), by the austere Sir Thomas Elyot, another putative forebear. There, dancers "Leaping through the flames" · evoke the "everlasting fire" of Heraclitus, from whom the motto of "Burnt Norton," the first quartet, comes. It contains — in untranslated Greek — the paradox, "The way upward and downward are one and the same," which to Eliot means heavenward salvation through delving

down into the inner darkness of sin and guilt. Hence the downward motion of the houses (under the sea) and the dancers vanishing under the hill. Those two verses suggest Robert Louis Stevenson's "Home is the sailor, home from the sea, / And home the hunter from the hill." Yet what in Stevenson is plain as can be, becomes in Eliot obscure, and provocatively surrounded by suggestive white space. This is the technique that conquered modern poetry, with such eminent disciples as George Seferis in Greece, Eugenio Montale in Italy, and Pierre Jean Jouve in France. The American scholar Elizabeth A. Drew aptly summarized *Four Quartets* as Eliot's complete "expression of the 'experience of believing in dogma'; of the moments of intuitive apprehension of its truth; and of the relation of these to a view of history and to the general living of life."

After that, Eliot gave up on serious poetry but continued writing influential criticism. His criticism comprises several volumes, with much still unpublished, and became a cornerstone of the New Criticism, which gave us much of America's best critical writing. Impossible to summarize, it consists of close reading of a text and situating it within the author's total output, that of his contemporaries, and also of the tradition behind it. Entailed is evaluating both its aesthetic and moral elements, and referring them to a higher criterion, which for Eliot is Anglican dogma, though his own religion is more Calvinist, deriving from his New England Puritan ancestry.

For Eliot, the major criticism of poetry, his chief concern, comes from critics who were poets themselves, and some of his best essays and lectures, or passages in them, are about poet-critics — Dante, Dryden, Johnson, Coleridge, Arnold, and Baudelaire — and about the Elizabethan and Jacobean dramatists and, of course, Shakespeare. His approach is to proceed from rigorous assessment of detail and razor-sharp discriminations to cautious generalization. To be sure, his preference is for Christians or *animae naturaliter Christianae,* such as Virgil. He either underestimates or ignores those whose beliefs or politics offend him, such as Shelley, Goethe, Shaw, and D. H. Lawrence. But there are, among others, important essays on Donne and the Metaphysical School, "Tradition and the Individual Talent," "What Is Minor Poetry?," "The Music of Poetry," and those for and against Milton.

Eliot's dramas are of secondary quality, partly because of an outmoded insistence on verse, but of (however disguised) autobiographical interest. *Murder in the Cathedral* remains in favor with colleges, especially religious ones; *The Family Reunion* matters as an expression of guilt about Vivien, even as *The Cocktail Party,* Eliot's only commercial success, besides containing a harrowing tale of martyrdom, is a left-handed tribute to Emily. The two last plays are best ignored. Of real interest is the ribald fragment *Sweeney Agonistes* (1926–7), which reverts amusingly to his early licentious poems included in the posthumously published *Inventions of the March Hare* (1996).

Unfortunate blemishes on the man and his work are snobbery, anti-Semitism, and a misogyny variously attributed to latent homosexuality, sado-masochism, or some form of impotence. As the physician-poet-essayist Gottfried Benn, who was admired and quoted by Eliot, once asked, "Is there such a thing as a healthy genius?" As for the religious fanaticism, even nonbelievers who lament with the poet Stevie Smith Eliot's retreat "from largeness into smallness, a flight in fear to a religion of fear, from freedom to captivity" cannot discount so much of Eliot's verse and prose as to deny the rest as ample evidence of genius.

T. S. Eliot

...indeed there will be time
To wonder, "Do I dare?" and, "Do I dare?"
Time to turn back and descend the stair,
With a bald spot in the middle of my hair —
(They will say: "How his hair is growing thin!")
My morning coat, my collar mounting firmly to the chin,
My necktie rich and modest, but asserted by a simple pin —
(They will say: "But how his arms and legs are thin!")
Do I dare
Disturb the universe?
In a minute there is time
For decisions and revisions which a minute will reverse.

For I have known them all already, known them all: —
Have known the evenings, mornings, afternoons,
I have measured out my life with coffee spoons;
I know the voices dying with a dying fall
Beneath the music from a farther room.
　　So how should I presume?

　·　·　·　·　·　·　·　·　·　·　·　·　·

　　And I have known the arms already, known them all —
Arms that are braceleted and white and bare
(But in the lamplight, downed with light brown hair!)
Is it perfume from a dress
That makes me so digress?
Arms that lie along a table, or wrap about a shawl.
　　And should I then presume?
　　And how should I begin?

From "The Love Song of J. Alfred Prufrock"

William Faulkner

BY JOSEPH BLOTNER

He began as a poet in adolescent efforts to advance youthful romances. He would later deprecate them, but his affinity for poetry would remain the keystone to his style and power. In maturity he would define poetry as "some moving, passionate moment of the human condition distilled to its absolute essence." He said he thought the writer wanted to render the poignancy of

human experience in fourteen lines, and if he could not do that, he would try with two thousand words in a short story, the next most demanding medium. And failing that, he would take a hundred thousand and write a novel. Faulkner would continue to write verse, though, adding, "I think of myself now as a failed poet, not as a novelist at all but a failed poet who had to take up what he could do." In every form he tried, he adapted much that he had learned as a poet for the purposes of prose. In its compression and allusiveness, its irony and paradox, and many other devices, his prose tends toward the condition of poetry. His early efforts in this transition reveal lengthy imitations of modernists such as T. S. Eliot.

At the same time, Faulkner was learning from masters of American prose. One of the earliest was Sherwood Anderson. For Faulkner, Anderson had not "the power and rush of Melville, who was his grandfather, nor the lusty humor for living of Twain, who was his father;

he had nothing of the heavy-handed disregard for nuances of his elder brother, Dreiser." But Anderson provided example and instruction for his young protégé with wide-ranging gifts. "You've got too much talent," he once told him. "You can do it too easy, in too many different ways. If you're not careful you'll never write anything." He gave him crucial advice he would never forget. "You're a country boy; all you know is that little patch up there in Mississippi where you started from. But that's all right too." Faulkner listened and "discovered that my own little postage stamp of native soil was worth writing about and that I would never live long enough to exhaust it, and that by sublimating the actual into the apocryphal I would have complete liberty to use whatever talent I might have to its absolute top."

With this crucial discovery, Faulkner was free to spend the rest of his life exploiting it. Conceiving it as "a cosmos of my own," he could draw not only upon his wide reading

Faulkner was born on September 25, 1897, in New Albany, Mississippi. He died in Byhalia, Mississippi, on July 7, 1962.

but also upon familial memories going back six generations with a pervading sense of the country where the Faulkners had lived out their lives. He transmuted much of Faulkner history into that of another family in his novel *Sartoris* (1929). These families also appear in other works. As he explained, "they are horses in my stable and I can run them whenever I want to." He adapted a local Chickasaw place-name for his cosmos, and it became Yoknapatawpha County. Younger writers would follow this example of interconnectedness. In an astonishingly short time he had made the transition from conventional fiction to the experimental. For his prose he borrowed again, not only from Eliot but also from James Joyce, whose *Finnegans Wake* he called a case of "a genius who was electrocuted by the divine fire."

In *The Sound and the Fury* (1929) Faulkner employed devices that would become hallmarks of his art. In the four different sections of the novel, the Compson family narrators used time as a fluid medium without concessions to the reader, who would gradually learn to differentiate and identify on the basis of speech and incident. Interior monologue and stream-of-consciousness narration — whether from Quentin, a neurotic Harvard freshman, or Benjy, a thirty-three-year-old idiot, or Dilsey, an old black servant — conveyed not only the sense of individuality but also of the dysfunctional Compson family, often reflecting qualities of society and region.

Vying with this novel for the critics' designation as his best work is *Absalom, Absalom!* (1936). Steeped in the history of Yoknapatawpha, Quentin engages with Shreve, his Canadian roommate, in an attempt to understand events in the emblematic life of the parvenu Colonel Thomas Sutpen before, during, and after the Civil War and ending with his murder. The use of dialogue, recollection, and letters provides the effect of multiple narration. Drawing upon the Old Testament, the novel seemed to André Malraux to constitute the intrusion of Greek tragedy into the detective story. From another perspective, it posed a problem in ways of knowing, with Sutpen appearing differently to each of those around him.

Intervening between these novels were two others whose dramatic events showed Faulkner's continuing efforts to devise narrative means to explore widely varied situations and dilemmas. In *As I Lay Dying* (1930), fifteen characters set forth in fifty-nine interior monologues the life and death of the mother, Addie Bundren, and the tortuous, fire-and-flood-plagued funeral journey from Yoknapatawpha's hill country down to Jefferson to bury her putrefying corpse. Mixing the tragic and the grotesque, Faulkner showed both the bizarre and heroic actions of which these hill people were capable in their hard lives of subsistence farming.

In *Light in August* (1932) Faulkner explored the problem of identity in the life of one man who, he said, didn't know who he was. Raised first in an orphanage, Joe Christmas has been led to believe that his father probably had Negro blood, but he is never sure, and he is unable to achieve a sense of kinship among either whites or blacks. Brutalized, he becomes brutal in turn and murders his white mistress, goading a proto-fascist white man into projecting upon Christmas the stereotypes that feed his hatred and provoke his castration and murder of Christmas. As Greek imagery reinforces other novels, so Christian parallels here deepen ironic tragic aspects of life in Yoknapatawpha County. As a foil, Faulkner used Christmas's opposite in Lena Grove, a pregnant country girl, as she sets out to find the lover who betrayed her and so achieves salvation through a good man who rewards her innate faith in people.

Short stories had been among Faulkner's earliest efforts to increase his slender income, and by now, coincidentally with *Sanctuary* (1931), his most notorious novel, he had produced several stories that would remain models of the genre. In them, economy in the depiction of complex characters and violent events produced power that gained him increased attention. Within a few brief years, four of his stories in prominent magazines explored the human capacity for tragedy and evil in individual lives and in society. "A Rose for Emily" gradually revealed the effects of parental dominance and frustrated love culminating in murder and something like necrophilia. In "Dry September" a neurotic spinster's frustrated love fueled rumors that produced a lynching by another Yoknapatawpha apostle of hatred and violence. "That Evening Sun" was a psychological study of the terror of the Compson children's black nurse awaiting the murder she is sure will come at the hands of her vengeful lover. "Red Leaves" drew on another Yoknapatawpha subgroup: this gradual relation of the ritual killing of a dead Chickasaw chief's Negro servant produced another psychological study in terror.

Sanctuary led to notoriety, brief affluence, and Hollywood employment — which proved a mixed blessing. Faulkner would say that it was "basely conceived" and written in haste to make money. This story of a vain and shallow Mississippi coed follows Temple Drake through her grotesque rape by an impotent gangster and her sequestration in a Memphis brothel. Apart from the murders in the sordid milieu there is the concomitant horror of the discovery that she has an affinity for evil. On another level, the novel shows the corruption in several levels of society from criminal classes to politicians and the affluent. Faulkner's mother defended her son against outraged responses. "Billy looks around him," she told her bridge group, "and he is heartsick at what he sees." Not only the

brilliantly successful exploitation of trends in popular fiction, but also the Hogarthian depictions were the work of a moralist who could even interpolate scenes of high comedy. Congratulated by a friend who said he would be remembered for his accurate predictions in a football game, he replied saturninely, "No, I'll always be the corncob man."

For Shelby Foote, one of Faulkner's great gifts was his vivid sensory rendering of the natural world. In *Go Down, Moses* (1942) he interwove the novella-length "The Bear" and six other stories into an account of interrelated black and white families. The book was at the same time a meditation on slavery as well as man's relationship to the land. Contrasted with the exploitive plantation system was the mystique of the hunt, combining the literal and the symbolic. Old Ben, the enormous bear, represented for Faulkner "the obsolete primitive" in the vanishing wilderness. In the part-Chickasaw Sam Fathers he showed old values but imperfectly transmitted by him to young Ike McCaslin, who makes an unsuccessful attempt to redress some of the wrongs perpetrated by whites such as his own ancestors upon blacks and other victimized classes. Though he tries to renounce his inheritance, Ike is a victim of the curse of slavery and its attitudes. From "the old lift of the heart" that exhilarates the hunters to the grief felt by those few such as Ike at the destruction of the Big Woods, Faulkner depicted the emotions of men in both their social and personal interactions. His dense, polysyllabic prose bodied forth both the gloom of the deep woods and the anguish of "the human heart in conflict with itself," one of his avowed perennial subjects.

In every form he tried, he adapted much that he had learned as a poet for the purposes of prose. In its compression and allusiveness, its irony and paradox, and many other devices, his prose tends toward the condition of poetry.

Over the years he meditated the history of Yoknapatawpha and its families, and with *The Hamlet* (1940) he began a trilogy whose events would extend through much of the twentieth century. The Snopes family was a tribe of amoral avaricious poor whites who gradually made their way from Frenchman's Bend in the county's southeast corner to its seat in Jefferson. As General Compson, Colonel Sutpen, and Ike McCaslin had been emblematic of another time and class, so Flem Snopes represented more than just himself. Father Abraham to the acquisitive tribe Faulkner called "the Peasants," he cared only for gain and progressively surrendered the claims of humanity to its pursuit. Members of the older classes are no match for him, and the quixotic Gavin Stevens, who had struggled unsuccessfully in *Sanctuary* to cope with evil, is left to observe Flem's passionless acquisition of Eula Varner, a rural embodiment of divine life force inexplicably manifested in rural Yoknapatawpha. Always adroit with contrasts, Faulkner juxtaposed their bloodless union with the passion of the idiot Ike for a cow, described in a richly poetic *tour de force* of romantic imagery.

In *The Town* (1957) and *The Mansion* (1959) Faulkner followed Flem's triumphal progress into Jefferson culminating in his murder by Linda, Eula's beautiful love child fathered by

Stevens's successful rival. As historical background for these principal narrative lines, there were changes undergone by Jefferson as symbolized by the advent of the automobile presaging changes marked by the disappearance of old homes and the appearance of Veterans' Village at the end of World War II.

Whereas earlier novels had encompassed matters as various as postwar disillusionment, as in *Soldiers' Pay* (1926), doomed fliers in *Pylon* (1935), Civil War ravages as in *The Unvanquished* (1938), tragic love in *The Wild Palms* (1939), rural murder mystery in *Intruder in the Dust* (1948), and domestic tragedy in *Requiem for a Nun* (1951), two other novels in the closing decade of his career turned backward in a further demonstration of the range and fertility of his imagination. Numerous short stories had shown the continuing fascination World War I held for him, but it finally fueled a massive effort costing years of labor over *A Fable* (1954), which he mistakenly called his magnum opus. As different from it as imaginable was his last effort in *The Reivers*

(1962), a grandfather's hearkening back to boyhood modeled on Faulkner's own, a mellow valedictory story of initiation and growth that made some people think of Prospero breaking his wand.

It was not only Faulkner's genius displayed in literary techniques both classic and experimental — stream of consciousness and dramatic narration, shifting chronology and altering point of view, symbolism and mythic constructs — that made him one of the masters of twentieth century literature and a key figure in the American canon. It was also his range, from pastoral poetry to drama and detective story thrillers. He evoked nature in Yoknapatawpha County with an immediacy that suggested Melville and Twain and had an obsession with moral questions reminiscent of Hawthorne and Dreiser. This gave his work sweep and originality of a kind that evoked Hardy's Wessex and Balzac's *Human Comedy*. Before he completed his lifetime's labor William Faulkner achieved the creation he had envisioned of "a cosmos of my own."

William Faulkner

From As I
Lay Dying
(Darl Bundren)

Before us the thick dark current runs. It talks up to us in a murmur become ceaseless and myriad, the yellow surface dimpled monstrously into fading swirls travelling along the surface for an instant, silent, impermanent and profoundly significant, as though just beneath the surface something huge and alive waked for a moment of lazy alertness out of and into light slumber again.

It clucks and murmurs among the spokes and about the mules' knees, yellow, skummed with flotsam and with thick soiled gouts of foam as though it had sweat, lathering, like a driven horse. Through the undergrowth it goes with a plaintive sound, a musing sound; in it the unwinded cane and saplings lean as before a little gale, swaying without reflections as though suspended on invisible wires from the branches overhead. Above the ceaseless surface they stand — trees, cane, vines — rootless, severed from the earth, spectral above a scene of immense yet circumscribed desolation filled with the voice of the waste and mournful water.

····:¦:····

From The Sound
and the Fury,
*(Quentin
Compson)*

When the shadow of the sash appeared on the curtains it was between seven and eight oclock and then I was in time again, hearing the watch. It was Grandfather's and when Father gave it to me he said I give you the mausoleum of all hope and desire; it's rather excruciatingly apt that you will use it to gain the reducto absurdum of all human experience which can fit your individual needs no better than it fitted his or his father's. I give it to you not that you may remember time, but that you might forget it now and then for a moment and not spend all your breath trying to conquer it. Because no battle is ever won he said. They are not even fought. The field only reveals to man his own folly and despair, and victory is an illusion of philosophers and fools.

····:¦:····

From Absalom,
Absalom!
(Thomas Sutpen)

You see, I had a design in my mind. Whether it was a good or a bad design is beside the point; the question is, Where did I make the mistake in it, what did I do or misdo in it, whom or what injure by it to the

236

extent which this would indicate. I had a design. To accomplish it I should require money, a house, a plantation, slaves, a family — incidentally, of course, a wife. I set out to acquire these, asking no favor of any man. I even risked my life at one time, as I told you, though as I also told you I did not undertake this risk purely and simply to gain a wife, though it did have that result. But that is beside the point also.

····:····

Bought nothing. Because He told in the Book how He created the earth, made it and looked at it and said it was all right, and then He made man. He made the earth first and peopled it with dumb creatures, and then He created man to be His overseer on the earth and to hold suzerainty over the earth and the animals on it in His name, not to hold for himself and his descendants inviolable title forever, generation after generation, to the oblongs and squares of the earth, but to hold the earth mutual and intact in the communal anonymity of brotherhood, and all the fee He asked was pity and humility and sufferance and endurance and the sweat of his face for bread.

····:····

It seemed to him he could feel the Mink Snopes that had had to spend so much of his life just having unnecessary bother and trouble, beginning to creep, seep, flow easy as sleeping; he could almost watch it, following all the little grass blades and tiny roots, the little holes the worms made, down and down into the ground already full of the folks that had the trouble but were free now, so that it was just the ground and the dirt that had to bother and worry and anguish with the passions and hopes and skeers, the justice and the injustice and the griefs, leaving the folks themselves easy now, all mixed and jumbled up comfortable and easy so wouldn't nobody even know or even care who was which any more, himself among them, equal to any, good as any, brave as any, being inextricable from, anonymous with all of them: the beautiful, the splendid, the proud and the brave, right on up to the very top itself among the shining phantoms and dreams which are the milestones of the long human recording — Helen and the bishops, the kings and the unhomed angels, the scornful and graceless seraphim.

From Go Down, Moses, *"The Bear" (Isaac McCaslin)*

From The Mansion

Ernest Hemingway

BY JAMES L. W. WEST III

One sees Hemingway's style best in his early short stories. In these experimental works, most of them composed in Paris in the 1920s, one finds the basic elements of his approach to writing. Hemingway did not exactly invent his style: he had been learning about close observation and economy of expression from Chekhov and Turgenev, and he had also learned,

probably from Chekhov, how to write without using a plot. This method of composition seems to have come naturally to him. In his reminiscences in *A Moveable Feast,* he recalls composing his early stories (on his best days) in an almost trance-like state, as if the words flowed smoothly from his subconscious mind through his pencil and onto the paper. All young writers should be so lucky.

To see how unusual Hemingway's short stories must have seemed to their first readers, one should look at the formula fiction that was routinely appearing in mass-circulation magazines during the 1920s. Short stories in the *Saturday Evening Post, Liberty, Redbook,* and other high-paying outlets occupied a place in American life that has since been taken over by television sitcoms and crime shows. The typical formula story of the time began with action or dialogue to catch the attention of the reader paging through the magazine. The narrative then advanced through an artificial plot toward

a climax, usually involving an unanticipated twist or the unmasking of a character as a hero or villain. These stories always concluded with what the critic Henry Seidel Canby called a "final suspiration." This kind of ending, frequently moralistic or saccharine, was designed to leave the reader instructed, amused, and soothed. Willa Cather called the writing of such stories "a business as safe and commendable as making soap or breakfast foods."

Some very good authors learned to write within the formula. Edith Wharton, in "Roman Fever" and "The Lady's Maid's Bell," and F. Scott Fitzgerald, in "The Offshore Pirate" and "Bernice Bobs Her Hair," made skillful use of the conventions of formula fiction. For them the formula was a framework within which they could portray their characters or examine the manners of American social classes. In "The Offshore Pirate," for example, Fitzgerald gives us Ardita Farnam, a spoiled and petulant child of wealth who wants to marry for

Hemingway was born on July 21, 1899, in Oak Park, Illinois. He died in Ketchum, Idaho, on July 2, 1961.

239

romance, not money. When we first see Ardita she is in the tropics, sitting on the deck of her uncle's steam yacht and pouting. A handsome fellow named Curtis Carlyle pops over the railing and hijacks the yacht, taking Ardita along as his hostage. Curtis looks exactly as he should: "He was a young man with a scornful mouth and the bright blue eyes of a healthy baby set in a dark sensitive face," Fitzgerald tells us. "He was trimly built, trimly dressed, and graceful as an agile quarter-back." Curtis wins Ardita's heart in the pages that follow, then reveals himself at the end to be a rich boy named Toby Moreland, matrimonially suitable even to Ardita's snooty family. The tale ends with Ardita "reaching up on her tiptoes" and kissing Toby softly. One is almost obliged to sigh and smile.

Fitzgerald recognized that Hemingway's stories had nothing in common with the formula fiction that other American writers had been producing. "There is not a single recourse to exposition," he noted. "A picture — sharp, nostalgic, tense — develops before your eyes."

Fitzgerald could spin out this kind of confection with ease, but he often complained about the limitations of formula fiction. His dissatisfaction prompted him to publish an essay in the May 1926 *Bookman* called "How to Waste Material, A Note on My Generation." This discursive piece is primarily a review of Hemingway's first full-length collection of stories, *In Our Time*, which had been published in October 1925 by Boni & Liveright. Fitzgerald, after some preliminary throat-clearing, declared himself to be entirely captured by Hemingway's stories. He had read them, he said, "with the most breathless unwilling interest I have experienced since Conrad first bent my reluctant eyes upon the sea." Fitzgerald could not say precisely why Hemingway's prose so fascinated him, only that it was "temperamentally new." He recognized that Hemingway's stories had nothing in common with the formula fiction that other American writers had been producing. "There is not a single recourse to exposition," Fitzgerald noted. "A picture — sharp, nostalgic, tense — develops before your eyes." Nor was there a final suspiration: "When the picture is complete a light seems to snap out, the story is over."

Fitzgerald singled out "Soldier's Home" for special praise. The narrative concerns a young man named Harold Krebs who is attempting to re-enter life in his Kansas home town after returning from the war in Europe. Krebs finds the readjustment difficult. His parents and friends do not understand what he has seen and lived through. The local girls cannot help him; they demand elaborate rituals of courtship that are too complicated for Krebs to follow. It had been easier for him with the French and German girls during the war. "There was not all this talking," he remembers. "You couldn't talk much and you did not need to talk." The only person with whom he feels comfortable is his kid sister, Helen, but they limit their conversation to simple things like indoor baseball, a game she plays with her friends. Krebs's mother, worried by his taciturnity, tries to persuade him to talk. When she fails, she makes him kneel and pray with her.

He kneels because it is easier to do so than to resist, but he cannot bring himself to pray. Krebs decides, near the end of the story, that he will have to leave home and live elsewhere. Hemingway now brings the story to its conclusion: "He wanted his life to go smoothly. It had just gotten going that way. Well, that was all over now, anyway. He would go over to the schoolyard and watch Helen play indoor baseball." There the story ends — with no final suspiration, only an uneasy feeling of suspension.

One detects a sense of detachment in Hemingway's best stories. This quality is apparent in the first paragraph of "In Another Country," first published in *Scribner's Magazine* in April 1927.

In the fall the war was always there, but we did not go to it any more. It was cold in the fall in Milan and the dark came very early. Then the electric lights came on, and it was pleasant along the streets looking in the windows. There was much game hanging outside the shops, and the snow powdered in the fur of the foxes and the wind blew their tails. The deer hung stiff and heavy and empty, and small birds blew in the wind and the wind turned their feathers. It was a cold fall and the wind came down from the mountains.

The narrative voice in this paragraph is almost entirely detached, and the effect is unnerving. The man telling this story has lived through a great deal: he will tell us some of it by and by, but he will not reveal everything. He will only describe; he will not attempt to explain. We learn in the next few paragraphs that he is a young American, a volunteer in the Italian army who is recuperating from a leg wound in a hospital in Milan. He and his fellow convalescents are serving as test cases; every day they are attached to exercise machines that are supposed to rehabilitate their damaged legs, hands, and arms. The machines are a joke, but no one seems to mind being harnessed to them. For now these soldiers are behind the lines, safe from harm.

"In Another Country" is about loss — of movement, freedom, beliefs, and illusions. The central figure is an Italian major, a former fencing champion whose damaged right hand is now shrivelled "like a baby's." He is bitter, but not over his withered hand. He is angry, rather, because after he knew that he was safely excused from the war he reinvested himself in life. He married a young woman whom he loved, but soon thereafter she died from pneumonia. The major attempts to describe his mistake to the narrator. A man, he explains with great vehemence, "should not place himself in a position to lose. He should find things he cannot lose." But of course there is nothing in life that cannot be lost. The answer? Do not invest yourself deeply in anything — in political or religious beliefs, in patriotism or love. Try to remain detached.

Fitzgerald reached a similar conclusion a few years later. In his 1934 novel *Tender Is the Night,* he wrote about "emotional bankruptcy," a condition that came upon men in their middle years if they had invested themselves unwisely. Fitzgerald borrowed his metaphor from the world of finance. One had limited emotional resources for investment, he believed, and these resources did not renew themselves. If a man invested his emotional capital shrewdly, then he enjoyed the returns later on — satisfaction with accomplishments, for example, or loyalty and love from others. But if he invested impulsively and then continued to throw good emotion after bad, he became emotionally bankrupt. Fitzgerald's solution, which he was never able to manage in his own life, was to invest sparingly and carefully, or not to invest at all.

Hemingway would have agreed, but he might have added that it is difficult to withdraw entirely from life, to withhold oneself from the risks that one must take. The protagonists of his stories, especially his alter ego Nick Adams, seem always to be relearning this lesson. They avoid commitment to causes and reject the love of others for a time, but eventually they re-enter life and invest themselves again. Human beings are almost obliged to do so. The price for complete withdrawal is emotional sterility and a loss of the capacity to love.

Hemingway's style reflects this idea because its very parts are detached (that word again) from one another. This detachment is revealed most clearly in the diction and grammar and in the absence of connective words — of conjunctions such as "therefore" or "nevertheless" or "moreover" or "consequently." Nothing is a consequence of any other thing; in Hemingway there is no causality. A statement does not flow logically from an earlier one any more than an action in life is related to an earlier action. Thus the conjunctions that signify causality are inappropriate. Almost the only connectives used by Hemingway are "and" and "but." No one event explains another; things simply happen and are described. Sometimes even "and" and "but" are dispensed with, as in the following passage from "Big Two-Hearted River" in which Nick Adams is setting up his camp in the woods:

Across the open mouth of the tent Nick fixed cheese-cloth to keep out mosquitoes. He crawled inside under the mosquito bar with various things from the pack to put at the head of the bed under the slant of the canvas. Inside the tent the light came through the brown canvas. It smelled pleasantly of canvas. Already there was something mysterious and homelike. Nick was happy as he crawled inside the tent. He had not been unhappy all day. This was different though. Now things were done. There had been this to do. Now it was done. It had been a hard trip. He was very tired. That was done. He had made his camp. He was settled. Nothing could touch him. It was a good place to camp. He was there, in the good place. He was in his home where he had made it.

This is Hemingway at his elliptical best. There is no explanation, only description, and yet the reader senses Nick's safety and satisfaction. Nick is trying to avoid something: this has been clear since the earliest paragraphs of the story. It turns out that he wants to flee from thinking itself, from memories and fears that he does not wish just now to bring out and examine. He has deliberately tired himself with a long hike, and he has carefully set up his camp. Now his brain is slowing down, a process suggested by the short sentences from the middle of the paragraph on. By concentrating on simple tasks, Nick can allow weariness to numb his thoughts. Then perhaps he can sleep. For one night at least he will be fully detached, safe in the good place.

Hemingway could also write scenes of action. The passage below is from "The Undefeated," a bullfighting story that he completed in November 1924, just after finishing "Big Two-Hearted River." Hemingway is describing the work of Zurito, a veteran picador who knows his trade. Zurito is preparing a bull for Hernandez, a young matador with promise; we are watching the action from the perspective of a bullfight critic from the local paper, *El Heraldo:*

The critic looked up to see Zurito, directly below him, leaning far out over his horse, the length of the pic rising in a sharp angle under his armpit, holding the pic almost by the point, bearing down with all his weight, holding the bull off, the bull pushing and driving to get at the horse, and Zurito, far out, on top of him, holding him, holding him, and slowly pivoting the horse against the pressure, so that at last he was clear. Zurito felt the moment when the horse was clear and the bull could come past, and relaxed the absolute steel lock of his resistance, and the triangular steel point of the pic ripped in the bull's hump of shoulder muscle as he tore loose to find Hernandez's cape before his muzzle. He charged blindly into the cape and the boy took him out into the open arena.

The bullfight critic does not recognize Zurito's skill, but Hemingway does. This passage, with its rhythms and pacing, depicts the violence of the scene in a kind of tableau. Zurito is bringing the bull under control, frustrating him and ripping the hump of muscle on his shoulders in order to bring his head down. Then the matador will be able to go in over the bull's horns and kill him with his sword. The passage is given to us in slow motion; Hemingway captures Zurito's coolness and strength as he wears the bull down and delivers him, wounded and confused, to the matador.

Hemingway's style can be described and analyzed. It can also be imitated and parodied, but it cannot be duplicated. His style is more than a patterning of words. It is a method of writing that grows from his convictions, his way of looking at life. That is why his prose retains its freshness and stands up well to rereading. The Hemingway style, though mannered, is so nearly flawless that one is scarcely aware of its artifice. The illusion is of simplicity and control — difficult things to achieve in life, but possible for Hemingway on the printed page. Hemingway was far from a powerful thinker, yet within his style resided a genius that made him, as genius always is, utterly distinctive.

Notes on the Contributors

Joseph Epstein is the author of nineteen books, the most recent of which are *Friendship: An Exposé, Alexis de Tocqueville: Democracy's Guide,* and *In a Cardboard Box: Essays Personal, Literary, and Savage.* For more than twenty years he was editor of *The American Scholar.* A contributor to *The New Yorker, Commentary, The Atlantic,* the London *Times Literary Supplement,* and other magazines, he also taught for many years in the English Department at Northwestern University.

Barry Moser is an illustrator, author, and designer whose work appears in museums and libraries around the world. He has published over three hundred titles, including Lewis Carroll's *Alice's Adventures in Wonderland,* which won the American Book Award in 1983. His 1999 edition of the King James Bible received international acclaim. A member of the National Academy of Design, he has served on the faculty of Rhode Island School of Design and is currently on the faculty of Smith College, where he is Printer to the College and has taught in both the art and religion departments.

Joseph Blotner's work includes biographies of William Faulkner and Robert Penn Warren. He is a member of the Fellowship of Southern Writers and the French Legion of Honor. He has taught at the Universities of Idaho, Virginia, North Carolina, and Arizona. He is Professor Emeritus at the University of Michigan.

Eavan Boland is a Professor of English and the Director of the Creative Writing Program at Stanford University. Her most recent book of poetry is *Domestic Violence.* Her previous book, *Against Love Poetry,* was a *New York Times* notable book of 2001. She is also the author of *Object Lessons: The Life of the Woman and the Poet in Our Time,* a volume of prose, and the co-editor of *The Making of a Sonnet: A Norton Anthology of the Sonnet* (with Edward Hirsch), to be published in 2008.

David Bromwich is Sterling Professor of English at Yale University. He is the author of *Hazlitt: The Mind of a Critic* and *Skeptical Music: Essays on Modern Poetry* and has edited a selection of Edmund Burke's writings, *On Empire, Liberty, and Reform.*

David Carkeet has written the novels *Double Negative, The Full Catastrophe,* and *The Error of Our Ways* and a memoir titled *Campus Sexpot,* which won the creative nonfiction prize given by the Association of Writers and Writing Programs. His

essays have appeared in *The New York Times Magazine, Poets & Writers,* and *The Oxford American.* He teaches in the University of Nebraska low-residency MFA program and lives in Middlesex, Vermont.

Paula Marantz Cohen is Distinguished Professor of English at Drexel University and the author of five nonfiction books, among them *The Daughter as Reader: Encounters between Literature and Life, Alfred Hitchcock: The Legacy of Victorianism,* and *Silent Film and the Triumph of the American Myth.* Her essays and reviews have appeared in *The Hudson Review, The Yale Review, Raritan, The American Scholar, The Times Literary Supplement, Boulevard,* and many other publications. She has also written three novels, including most recently *Jane Austen in Scarsdale or Love, Death, and the SATs.*

Stephen Cox is Professor of Literature and Director of the Humanities Program at the University of California, San Diego. He is the author of *Love and Logic: The Evolution of Blake's Thought, The Titanic Story,* and *The Woman and the Dynamo: Isabel Paterson and the Idea of America.* His most recent book is *The New Testament and Literature: A Guide to Literary Patterns.*

Daniel Mark Epstein is a poet, playwright, and biographer, whose books include seven books of poetry, biographies of Nat King Cole and Edna Saint Vincent Millay, and most recently a double biography of Abraham Lincoln and Walt Whitman. His work has appeared in *The New Yorker, The Atlantic, The Paris Review, The New Republic,* and in many anthologies. His honors include a Guggenheim Fellowship as well as the Rome Prize and an Academy Award from the American Academy of Arts and Letters.

Bruce Floyd recently retired from teaching English for more than two decades. He was educated at the University of South Carolina, where he took both undergraduate and graduate degrees in English literature. An avid diarist, he lives in Florence, South Carolina, with his wife.

John Gross was the editor of the London *Times Literary Supplement* from 1973 to 1981 and on the staff of the *New York Times* from 1983 to 1988. Since 1989 he has been theater critic of the London *Sunday Telegraph.* His books include *The Rise and Fall of the Man of Letters, Joyce* (in the Modern Masters series), *Shylock: A Legend and Its Legacy,* and a memoir,

A Double Thread. He has edited a number of anthologies, including *The Oxford Book of Aphorisms* and *The New Oxford Book of Literary Anecdotes.*

Anthony Hecht was the author of, among other works, *Collected Later Poems* and *Melodies Unheard,* a collection of critical essays. He was the winner of the Pulitzer Prize, the Wallace Stevens Award, the Eugenio Montale Award, and the Robert Frost Medal.

Dan Jacobson was born in Johannesburg, South Africa, but has spent most of his adult life in England. He is the author of many novels and short stories, critical essays, and memoirs. Professor Emeritus in English at University College London, Jacobson has also taught and lectured at several American universities, among them Stanford, Harvard, and Syracuse. His most recent book is *All for Love,* a sardonic account of a once-famous love affair within the court of Emperor Franz Joseph of Austria.

Justin Kaplan is the author of *Walt Whitman: A Life,* which won the National Book Award and was reissued in 2003. His earlier biography, *Mr. Clemens and Mark Twain,* won a Pulitzer Prize and National Book Award. He is a member of the American Academy of Arts and Letters and General Editor of *Bartlett's Familiar Quotations.* His most recent book is *When the Astors Owned New York.* Kaplan is married to the novelist Anne Bernays. Together they've written two books of nonfiction, *The Language of Names* and *Back Then: Two Lives in 1950s New York.*

Elizabeth Lowry is a novelist and Research Fellow in English at Greyfriars Hall, Oxford University. She is also a regular writer for the *Times Literary Supplement, The London Review of Books, The Spectator,* and other journals.

Hilary Mantel's latest novel is *Beyond Black.* She is the author of eight previous novels, a short story collection, and a memoir called *Giving Up the Ghost.* She writes for the *New York Review of Books* and a range of other papers. She lives in Surrey, England, a few miles from "Jane Austen country."

Robert Pack is the author of eighteen books of poetry, most recently *Elk in Winter, Rounding It Out, Minding the Sun,* and *Fathering the Map: New and Selected Later Poems.* His most recent book of criticism is *Belief and Uncertainty in the Poetry of Robert Frost.* He currently teaches in the Honors College of the University of Montana and is completing a book about Shakespeare's major plays.

Lois Potter is the Ned B. Allen Professor of English at the University of Delaware. Her publications include *Secret Rites and Secret Writing: Royalist Literature 1641–60,* the Arden edition of *The Two Noble Kinsmen* by Fletcher and Shakespeare, and the volume on *Othello* in the Shakespeare in Performance series of the University of Manchester Press. She is also a frequent reviewer of plays. She is at work on a biography of Shakespeare for the Blackwell Critical Biographies series.

Reynolds Price has published thirty-six volumes of fiction, poetry, plays, essays, and translations. He is James B. Duke Professor of English at Duke University and has taught the poetry of John Milton since 1968. He is at work on a third volume of autobiography.

William H. Pritchard is the Henry Clay Folger Professor of English at Amherst College. His books include studies of Wyndham Lewis, Robert Frost, Randall Jarrell, and John Updike. He has also published three collections of essays and reviews, the most recent of which is *Shelf Life.*

Frederic Raphael is the author of more than twenty novels, including *The Limits of Love, The Glittering Prizes, Coast to Coast,* and *A Double Life.* He has written many stories, essays, and screenplays, including *Darling* and *Two for the Road,* as well as biographies of Lord Byron and Somerset Maugham. The new volume of his notebooks, *Cuts and Bruises, Personal Terms III,* was published last year, as was *Some Talk of Alexander,* a journey in time and space through ancient Greece. He contributed an essay on Karl Popper to *The Great Philosophers,* which he co-edited with Ray Monk. He has published a number of translations from Greek and Latin, most recently the *Satyrica* of Petronius. *Eyes Wide Open,* a memoir of working on *Eyes Wide Shut* with Stanley Kubrick, won the Prix Simonnet.

Tom Shippey is the Walter J. Ong Chair of Humanities at Saint Louis University. He previously taught at St. John's College, Oxford, and the Universities of Birmingham and Leeds in England. He has published several books on Old English, two monographs and a collection of essays on his Leeds predecessor J. R. R. Tolkien, as well as many articles on Middle English, Old Norse, and related topics.

Notes on the Contributors

John Simon is the New York theater critic for Bloomberg News and a theatrical columnist for Broadway.com. He is a freelance literary critic for the *Weekly Standard,* the *New Criterion,* and the *New York Times Book Review* among others, and has won a George Jean Nathan Award in drama criticism, a George Polk Memorial Award in film criticism, and an American Academy of Arts & Sciences Award in literary criticism. His most recent books are *John Simon on Theater, John Simon on Film, John Simon on Music, Dreamers of Dreams: Essays on Poets and Poetry,* and *The Sheep from the Goats: Selected Literary Essays.*

James L. W. West III is the Edwin Erle Sparks Professor of English at Pennsylvania State University. His most recent books are *William Styron: A Life* and *The Perfect Hour: The Romance of F. Scott Fitzgerald and Ginevra King.* West is general editor of the Cambridge Edition of the works of F. Scott Fitzgerald.

A. N. Wilson is the author of many novels, among which are *The Sweets of Pimlico, The Healing Art, Wise Virgin,* and *The Lampitt Papers,* a five-volume sequence. A member of the American Academy of Arts and Letters, he has written a biography of Tolstoy and his studies of the nineteenth century include *God's Funeral,* an account of the Victorian crisis of faith, and *The Victorians.* His latest book is *Iris Murdoch as I Knew Her.* His novel *My Name Is Legion* was published in Spring 2004.

David Womersley is the Thomas Warton Professor of English Literature at the University of Oxford and a Fellow of St. Catherine's College. He has edited various works of Gibbon, Johnson, and Burke for Penguin Books and has published monographs on Gibbon with Cambridge University Press and Oxford University Press. His current projects include an edition of Boswell's *Life of Johnson* for Penguin, an edition of *Gulliver's Travels* for the forthcoming Cambridge University Press complete edition of Swift (of which he is also one of the general editors), and a monograph on historical writing and historical drama in the sixteenth century.

Also from Paul Dry Books

www.pauldrybooks.com

SO MANY BOOKS
Reading and Publishing in an
Age of Abundance
by Gabriel Zaid　978-1-58988-003-0

So Many Books is not so much a book as a conversation: about books, about reading, about the mad business of how a book is born every thirty seconds. It is a book of proposals and arguments and debate about books, from the age of Socrates to our own. Join the conversation!

"Genuinely exhilarating." —Leon Wieseltier

WRITERS ON THE AIR
Conversations about Books
by Donna Seaman　978-1-58988-021-4

"Highly recommended." *—Library Journal*

"Seaman's interviews yield tidbit after tidbit about the authors' work habits and their thought patterns, until readers understand not only what a book means but also how it means. Insightful collections of interviews with authors abound, but none I have read is superior to Seaman's collection."

—San Francisco Chronicle

THE 64 SONNETS
by John Keats　978-1-58988-014-6

"In the sonnets, Keats conveys the range of his interests, his concerns, his attachments, his obsessions.... Some are polemics, or romantic period pieces; others are brooding testaments or compulsive outpourings, which seem to expand on the page. These sonnets are replete with a sensuous feeling for nature–'The poetry of earth is never dead'–that looks back to Wordsworth and forward to Frost. They also luxuriate in the spaces of imagination–'Much have I travell'd in the realms of gold'—and trigger the daydreaming capacities of the mind."

—from the Introduction by Edward Hirsch

MY BUSINESS IS CIRCUMFERENCE
Poets on Influence and Mastery
Edited by Stephen Berg　978-0-9664913-9-5

Contemporary American poets provide a multifaceted view of the creative process. Contributors include A. R. Ammons, Gillian Conoley, Hayden Carruth, Judith Hall, Jane Hirshfield, Yusef Komunyakaa, Dana Levin, Thomas Lux, Jane Mead, Jack Myers, and Gerald Stern.

"An intimate and diverse look at the interactive processes of reading and writing." *—Rain Taxi*

"The collection's abundance should last you several seasons at the very least." *—Jewish Exponent*

STYLE: AN ANTI-TEXTBOOK
Second Edition, Revised
by Richard A. Lanham　978-1-58988-032-0

Why do so many writing courses, with their earnest handbooks and narrow focus on "clarity," bore students and fail to teach them how to write well? Richard Lanham provides answers, and an antidote, in the seven witty and provocative chapters of *Style: An Anti-Textbook*.

"Imperative reading for all teachers and students of writing." *—Choice*

"Lanham's own style is notable for its audacity, liveliness, and grace." *—Times Literary Supplement*

THE FICTION EDITOR, THE NOVEL, AND THE NOVELIST
Second Edition, Revised
by Thomas McCormack　978-1-58988-030-6

Drawing upon twenty-eight years of experience as the CEO and Editorial Director of St. Martin's Press, Thomas McCormack gives practical guidance about how to plan, write, and revise a novel.

"Required reading for all those who care about good fiction." *—Kirkus Reviews*

"Writers will actually learn things here."

—Los Angeles Times

THE TRIVIUM
The Liberal Arts of Logic, Grammar, and Rhetoric
by Sister Miriam Joseph　978-0-9679675-0-9

A thorough presentation of general grammar, propositions, syllogisms, enthymemes, fallacies, poetics, figurative language, and metrical discourse—accompanied by lucid graphics and enlivened by examples from Shakespeare, Milton, Plato, and others —makes *The Trivium* an essential book for teachers, students, writers, lawyers, and all serious users of language.

SHAKESPEARE'S USE OF THE ARTS OF LANGUAGE
by Sister Miriam Joseph　978-1-58988-025-2

In Shakespeare's time, every grammar school student would have recognized the two hundred figures of speech that Renaissance scholars had derived from Latin and Greek sources (from *amphibologia* through *onomatopoeia* to *zeugma*). Sister Miriam Joseph organizes these figures into simple, understandable patterns and illustrates each one with examples from Shakespeare.